Golf on the Rocks

Golf on the Rocks

A Journey Round Scotland's Island Courses

Gary Sutherland

First published in 2011 by
HACHETTE SCOTLAND, an imprint of
Hachette UK

2

Cataloguing in Publication Data is available from the British Library

ISBN: 978 0 7553 1978 7

Typeset in Perpetua by Ellipsis Digital Limited, Glasgow
Printed and bound in Great Britain by CPI Mackays, Chatham ME5 8TD

Hachette Scotland's policy is to use papers that are natural, renewable
and recyclable products and made from wood grown in sustainable forests.
The logging and manufacturing processes are expected to conform to the
environmental regulations of the country of origin.

HACHETTE SCOTLAND
An Hachette UK Company
338 Euston Road
London NW1 3BH

www.hachettescotland.co.uk
www.hachette.co.uk

For Mam, Stewart and Julieann.
He was great, wasn't he?

Golden is the Day

Golden is the day
When summer sounds echo
Around my brain

Fortune in the sound
Of golf crack on white roller
As wave crashes by

Ghosts of other greens
Lie around the hole
Lie around the bay

Peter Noble

Acknowledgements

Golf on the Rocks was fuelled largely by CalMac break-fasts. I'd like to thank Caledonian MacBrayne for those breakfasts and their ferry timetables. Hats off also to NorthLink Ferries - that open deck proved a challenging putting surface. Cheers to all the island buses and post-buses, and those who drove them. And thanks to all the hotel and B&B owners and hostel wardens who put up with us. Big up to the golf clubs that welcomed us and a special shout out ('Fore!') to all those we golfed with. Plus a nod to all the other characters we encountered on our travels. There was never a dull moment; there was many a daft moment.

Love and smiles to my mam, my brother Stewart and my sister Julieann for their encouragement and for playing such a big part in this. Love and gratitude to my dad who was with me at all times. Love and kisses to my wife Clare and my daughter Isabella who witnessed the unthinkable conclusion. And hello to baby Alexander who arrived safely in the aftermath.

A toast to my friend Riley Mcferrin who was up for that first island round and very nearly became a shepherd. I also raise a glass to my friend Fraser Walsh for his compan-ionship during the closing rounds (and for that keg of Colonsay IPA). Multiple toasts and thanks to my friend Brian Noble for his quality banter, his superb drawings, his superior knowledge and undoubted love of golf. I know you enjoyed this as much as I did and reckon we'll be laughing about it for years to come. And one more toast to my friend Peter Noble for that magical poem. You said it all in a few lines.

Thanks to my agent Stan, my publisher Bob McDevitt and everyone else at Hachette Scotland, my editor Julian Flanders and Chris Hannah for the cover design.

Cheers to Laura Gillespie for her generosity and thanks to Eunice Willox for the tip-off on Moncreiffe Island.

Finally, I'd like to thank Mrs Maciver, one of my biggest influences, and Liz McGillivray, one of my greatest supporters - two amazing and inspiring women to whom this book is also dedicated.

Contents

Golf on the Rocks

Location of 18 Scottish island golf courses

Key:

Location of Golf Course

The Courses:

1. Port Bannatyne Golf Club, Isle of Bute
2. Isle of Skye Golf Club, Sconser, Isle of Skye
3. Isle of Harris Golf Club, Scarista, Isle of Harris, Outer Hebrides
4. Sollas Golf Course, Sollas, North Uist, Outer Hebrides
5. Benbecula Golf Course, Isle of Benbecula, Outer Hebrides
6. Askernish Golf Club, South Uist, Outer Hebrides
7. Isle of Barra Golf Club, Isle of Barra, Outer Hebrides
8. Shiskine Golf Club, Isle of Arran
9. Vaul Golf Club, Isle of Tiree
10. Iona Golf Course, Isle of Iona
11. Craignure Golf Club, Scallastle, Isle of Mull
12. Isle of Seil Golf Club, Isle of Seil
13. King James VI Golf Club, Moncreiffe Island, Perth
14. Whalsay Golf Club, Skaw, Whalsay, Shetland Isles
15. Asta Golf Club, Asta, Scalloway, Shetland Isles
16. Stromness Golf Club, Stromness, Orkney
17. Colonsay Golf Course, Isle of Colonsay
18. The Machrie, Isle of Islay

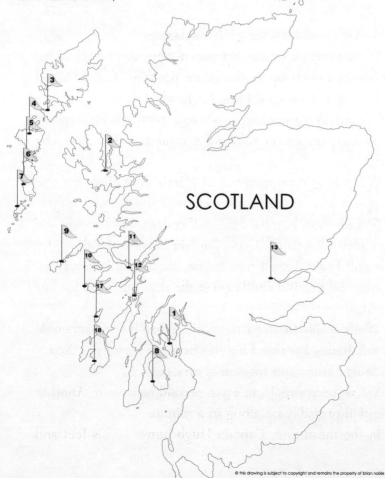

SCOTLAND

Charting a Course

'Take cover under your golf baaaaaaaags!'

Captain Hugh shouts his instruction, dives behind his trolley and curls up in the brace position: knees tucked to his chest, hands shielding his head.

Donald the greenkeeper shrugs, pulls on his cagoule hood and carries on rolling his cigarette. 'It'll pass,' he says.

Bill, a long-time member of Harris Golf Club and the Happiest Man in the World, points at the sky and laughs.

As hailstones bombard the golf course, Noble Brian and I wonder what to do. Copy Captain Hugh and hide under our golf bags? Act all nonchalant like Donald the green-keeper? Be like Bill and laugh at the sky? Or reach for our brollies?

While Noble Brian battles with his brolly and I scramble to join him – I realise I haven't brought a brolly – the icy onslaught stops and the sun comes out.

We've been caught in a ten-second hailstorm. Another one will probably be along in a minute.

In the meantime, Captain Hugh jumps to his feet and

plays his next shot. Donald the greenkeeper takes down his cagoule hood and lights his cigarette. And Bill carries on laughing.

Noble Brian watches with amusement as I reach for my five iron and nearly get knocked over by a gust of wind.

Golf in the Outer Hebrides. It's out there.

That I ended up in the Outer Hebrides, trying to play golf but struggling to stand up, can be put down to my dad's putter. If it hadn't been for my dad's putter, I wouldn't have been there. Had my dad still been here, I wouldn't have had his putter. But he's not, so there I was, trying to play golf but struggling to stand up.

In an ideal world, I wouldn't have gone gallivanting around the islands of Scotland with a bag of golf clubs, but you never know how things are going to turn out, and you make what you can of life. You lose someone you love and you're lost for a bit. An idea emerges, becomes important. You wonder why you can't – then decide that you can.

I followed my heart and charted a course round the far corners of my country. I fell in love with golf again and had the time of my life.

One rainy morning in September, the Sutherland clan – my mam, my brother, my sister and myself – gathered in the Highlands. We couldn't see the hills for the clouds, but we were glad to see each other.

We'd come together to play a round of golf on dad's birthday, the first since he'd passed away. It was our tribute to a wonderful man who'd loved his family and loved his golf. Our way of dealing with the significance of the date. A game of golf would enable us to cope better, make a difficult day that bit easier. Hitting a ball seemed a more appealing prospect than moping about the house or having a really bad day at the office. The plan was to make it an annual outing and play a different golf course each year.

It was me who'd suggested Boat-of-Garten for this first family golf game. I'd heard only good things about the course, that it was incredibly beautiful. And this surely was a day for being surrounded by beauty, even though much of that beauty looked like being masked by bad weather.

I'd caught the first train north from Glasgow and the rest of my family had driven down from the Moray coast. We met and hugged on the platform at Aviemore station. There were no tears. We were intent on being strong for one another.

As my mam drove the few miles to Boat-of-Garten, it occurred to me how apt the choice of golf course was, at least in name. My dad had spent much of his life on boats, leaving school and going straight to sea on board my Granda Sutherland's boat, the *Onward*. Dad went on to skipper the *Ocean Star* and the *Adonis*. And later, after he left the fishing, he became the captain of the *Grampian Pride*, a standby boat for the oil rigs. And when he wasn't on a boat, dad was on the golf course. So Boat-of-Garten golf course, though in the middle of the Highlands and nowhere near the sea, made some sort of weird sense.

Before teeing off, we had coffee and bacon rolls in the clubhouse, watching the rain stream down the windows,

obscuring the course from view. Not that the foul weather
mattered, for the date was all-important. We'd have golfed
in a hurricane as long as it was 16 September and the
course was open.

Between sips of coffee, my brother put forward the suggestion that we have a competition. Nothing too serious, just
a bit of fun. We wondered what form such a contest should
take and all agreed that simply rewarding the best score of
the day didn't seem right. Too predictable, too golfy.

We were here because of dad and, as much as he loved
his golf, he was never hell-bent on winning. Sure he wanted
to win all of his ties and do well in the monthly medals,
but ultimately he played for the sake of playing, because
he enjoyed the game. It was in this sense that dad was a
great golfer. He looked forward to each round like he
looked forward to each and every day of his life, a life that
should have been longer.

St Andrews might be the Home of Golf, but to my mind
our house in Hopeman was the Home of Golf when dad
was there. Mam would head off to work and dad would
complete his morning errands before walking over to the
golf course to join the One o'Clock Gang for a round and
afterwards a couple of rounds in the bar. And he always
made it home in time to have mam's supper on the table
for her coming in the door.

When I think of my dad on the golf course, I hear his
laugh and his reactions to his shots. 'Ooh-ya!' when he hit
a good one. 'Ooh-ya beauty!' when he really surprised
himself. And 'Ach!' when he made a hash of it. I can hear
him now. 'Ooh-ya!' 'Ach!'

Everyone's swing is unique, but dad's was more unique than most. Short like the man himself (he was only five foot eight) and quick like his wit (he was very sharp), dad's swing probably broke every rule in the book and it wouldn't have looked right on anyone but him. But it worked for him. He rarely hit the ball high. Invariably they were low trundlers – handy for a windy coastal course. On and on his ball would run, over the humps and through the hollows.

The one club dad could never get to grips with was his pitching wedge, but then he'd no cause to use it. His ball could be lying 30 feet off the green and he'd pull out his putter. Often he'd get down in two. I was forever on at him to at least have a try with his pitching wedge, otherwise what was the point in him carrying one about in his bag? But he just laughed. He couldn't chip for toffee, so he didn't. I'd play a neat pitch and he'd putt ugly and always end up nearer the hole. It was exasperating. He thought it was hilarious.

Sitting in the Boat-of-Garten clubhouse, hoping that the rain would let up for at least some of our round, I suggested that whoever holed the best putt should be declared the winner. Best being the longest, unlikeliest, most dad-like putt. And we'd get a trophy sorted out later. No, not a trophy. Dad's putter. Whoever holed the most ridiculous putt got to keep dad's putter for a year, until our next get-together. Everybody was in agreement. Rewarding the best putt felt appropriate, plus it sounded like fun.

A few hours later, I was all made up. The rain had stopped, the sun had popped out and I'd holed the longest putt, a 20-footer I'd had no right to hole. The rest of my family declared it the winning putt, following a vote on the final green. Dad's putter was mine for the next 12 months.

We headed off to the Cairngorm Hotel in Aviemore for a few drinks. We talked about the golf and we talked about dad. We laughed, remembered, sighed and coped with the backdrop to it all. My mam, brother and sister waved me off at the station and I spent the journey to Glasgow reflecting on the day, recalling good times with my dad and thinking about his putter. I'd have to pick it up the next time I was up in Hopeman. I wondered if it would improve my putting any.

Autumn turned to winter turned to spring. Seven months had passed since our round at Boat-of-Garten. My clubs had gone back up to Hopeman that day in the boot of my mam's car (at my request) and had remained there ever since. You could say I wasn't hitting the golf course that often, not with my clubs 200 miles north.

I'd been back to Hopeman a couple of times with my wife and our baby daughter in those seven months and had planned to fit in some golf while I was up there, but I'd not quite managed it. Even though the reason behind me having my clubs at my mam's house was that I was more likely to play golf in Hopeman than in Glasgow.

In Glasgow, I had found that my clubs just languished in the shed. It wasn't that Glasgow lacked golf courses. Goodness knows, there were enough of them. It's just that in a decade or so of living in the city, I had never felt like playing any of them.

To my mind, none of them could possibly be a patch on my old course at Hopeman, with its views of the Moray Firth, all that fresh sea air, the bright yellow broom in the summer months and the wonder that is the Prieshach, Hopeman's signature hole. A stunning par three by the shore with a drop of 100 feet from tee to green. Landscape and challenge combined beautifully at Hopeman's wonderful 12th hole. The Prieshach was golfing perfection as far as I was concerned. And even better enjoyed with a beer in summertime and a dram in wintertime. That's what me and my dad and my brother always did after teeing off.

But, as long as I was in Glasgow and my clubs were in Hopeman, I wasn't playing golf anywhere. That round at Boat-of-Garten had been the exception rather than the norm. And I'd done nothing but neglect my dad's putter since winning it. I'd have to give it back in five months' time and I hadn't even laid my hands on it yet.

As I sat in my kitchen, I calculated that I hadn't had a handicap in 20 years. Not since school, when I'd last been a member of Hopeman Golf Club. For someone who said he was into golf, I didn't play the game much. Truth was, I was a lapsed golfer.

In the Hopeman of my youth, you couldn't drag me off the golf course. I would run home from school, ditch my bag and get changed and run across the field, which was then all that separated our house from the golf club, that field being full of houses now. But when it was only a field, I'd sometimes look out of the living room window with my dad's binoculars to see if any of my friends were standing on the first tee. If they were, I'd phone the club-house to tell them to wait for me.

During the perfect summers of my childhood, we'd be out on the golf course until 10 or 11 o'clock at night. Once we'd played enough holes, and there was no one else out on the course, we'd play crazy golf. This involved targeting the wrong greens from the wrong tees. We'd try to pull off the most impossible shots and our laughter would ring round the course as another ball plunged into the broom. And when we were bored of crazy golf, we'd head back across the field, stopping to climb about on the bales of hay, before returning to our homes, worn out but happy.

I promised myself that the next time I was in Hopeman – and I'd make it soon – I'd play 18 holes with my dad's putter in my bag. Then I'd bring it all back to Glasgow and actually make an effort to get out on a golf course near my home. That way, I'd be in shape for the next family get-together. Yes, I was going to get back into golf in a big way.

As I stuck on the kettle, I remembered that I had a golf map of Scotland that I'd got free once with a Sunday newspaper. I looked around and found it in a drawer. It was crumpled, but not torn. I unfolded the map on the kitchen table. Before me was Scotland and all of its golf courses, hundreds of them, each course represented by a coloured and numbered dot. The Glasgow area was covered in dots. There looked to be at least a dozen courses within a few miles of my house. Maybe it was time that I tried one or two of them.

I looked up at the Moray coast to check that Hopeman was on my golf map of Scotland. Of course it was, next to Lossiemouth. I studied the map in more detail. That the Kingdom of Fife was full of dots was hardly surprising, and there seemed to be plenty of courses in Perthshire too. One thing that struck me though was the number of islands that had dots. There were more island golf courses than I had imagined.

I knew that Islay had a golf course. I'd played the Machrie course as a teenager, while visiting my Granny Sutherland on the island. My granny, in the later years of her life, had lived on Islay with my auntie and my uncle who was then the manager of Bunnahabhain distillery. And I'd tackled the Machrie with my cousin Lawrence. I remember it being a tough gig among the dunes with countless blind shots and the wind to contend with. It had been a struggle to complete the 18 and I don't think I broke 100. I wondered what it would be like to go back there now, 20 years later, and take on the Machrie again.

Studying the islands, I saw that Arran had no fewer than seven golf courses. I knew of one of them. Shiskine. I hadn't played it, but had heard plenty about it from my friend Johnny, whose family holidayed on Arran every summer and golfed Shiskine. It was that rarest of things, a 12-hole golf course. But besides that, it had a mind-boggling par three called the Crow's Nest. Johnny made Shiskine sound magical and had urged me to go and play it. I hadn't got round to it. Perhaps it was time I did.

I poured myself a coffee and sat down with the map again. There were golf courses in Orkney and in Shetland.

There were several in the Outer Hebrides. I was aware that Barra had a golf course. I'd recently sat in Franco's cafe at Central Station, looking at the many postcards that cover the walls. One in particular had caught my eye. A picture of a green with the most beautiful beach of white sand beyond it. And I'd thought, 'I'd like to go and play there one day.'

I started counting up the islands that had golf courses. Islay ... Colonsay ... Arran ... Barra ... Harris ... Benbecula ... Mull ... and stopped once I got to 18.

That was it. That's what I was going to do. I was going to go and play golf on 18 Scottish islands. That would get me back into the swing of things. And I'd take my dad's putter along for the ride. It was a sufficiently daft idea for my dad to have appreciated it. After all, daftness is something to aspire to. It can really take you places. Skye ... Tiree ... Iona ...

In bringing my dad's putter to these islands, I would be leaving traces of him on distant greens. That's how I viewed it anyway. A golfing voyage across the seas with a nod to Captain James. Here was a journey worth undertaking. It was time to well and truly blow the cobwebs off my golf clubs.

A summer of island hopping. Island hacking! No, not island hacking. I was out of practice, but I wasn't that much of a nightmare on the golf course. I'm not the best golfer in the world, but I'm by no means the worst either.

My last handicap was 19, I think when I was 19. I've had one lesson in my life and that was when I first took up the game. I'd have been around ten. My dad arranged for me to have an hour with the local pro who set to work on my grip and by the end of the hour my fingers were in agony. I never took another golf lesson. I developed my own swing. My family say it's a nice swing, and perhaps it is. It's just that the results aren't always great.

The only golf prize I've ever won – besides my dad's putter – was a little trophy at my cousin Marco's stag-do, when I shot the best round at Hopeman, partly because I knew the course and partly because I was the least drunk. I made up for my lack of drunkeness later that night in Aviemore when, high on the success of my golfing exploits, I caught up in the drinking stakes and surged ahead, getting spectacularly inebriated and becoming something of a liability, slumped on the steps outside a nightclub and having to be carried back to our accommodation. Not something to be proud of and it sort of took the shine off my golfing triumph.

So I'm not the best golfer in the world and I'm not the best drinker in the world. But as far as the golf was concerned, I wanted to be pitching up on these Scottish islands with my A-game (the A standing for Acceptable). I didn't want my islands adventure turning into a golfing disaster. I was out of practice, that much was certain. I hadn't so much as lifted a club in seven months. No matter how beautiful the island was, if I was going to shank my way round the golf course, I wasn't going to enjoy it very much. I needed to be reunited with my clubs as quickly as possible.

My mind now focused firmly on golf and this ambitious challenge that I'd set myself, I went and scanned my bookcase for golf books. I plucked *100 Golfing Tips* from the shelf, not remembering owning such a book. I opened it up and read the message on the first page. 'Merry Christmas to the Sutherlands. Love from Santa xxx, 2003.'

It was mam's handwriting. Dad must not have been home that Christmas. It was the biggest drawback of him being at sea. We were used to him being away for weeks at a time, missing birthdays and other special occasions, but not to have him home for Christmas, well that was always hard. It must have been hard on him too.

My fondest Christmas memory is of a year that dad was home. My brother and I had got up on Christmas morning at our usual ridiculous hour and ran through to the kitchen. The night before we'd left a plate of shortbread and a glass of whisky on the table, for Santa, and a carrot for Rudolf. What we found was a plate of crumbs, an empty glass and a carrot stalk. Plus a note! Except that neither of us could make head nor tail of it. The letters looked all funny.

We went through to mam and dad's bedroom and woke them up and showed them the note. Dad suggested that we hold it up to the wardrobe mirror. We held it up to the mirror and read the words THANKS, SANTA. My brother and I were stunned. Dad explained that in Lapland they wrote backwards.

I had a flick through *100 Golfing Tips* – the Sutherland family Christmas gift from Santa that had somehow ended up in my bookcase – to see if I might find some tips that could turn me into an accomplished golfer overnight.

'Golf can be frustrating,' were the introductory words. Well, I knew that.

Some of the first tips included 'loosen your muscles' (what muscles?) and 'warm up'. Now there was something I rarely did. Usually I just teed up and hit the ball. I once played golf with an Ayrshireman who commented on my lack of practice swing and wondered if it had to do with the fact that I was from the north-east and didn't want to waste anything. The cheek of the man.

100 Golfing Tips was full of tips, at least a hundred of them. There was advice on how to address the ball ('ball, you shall fly where I intend it!') and the observation that your right shoulder should be slightly lower than your left shoulder and your head slightly behind the ball. I tried to visualize this, but ended up thinking it was maybe time to get some shopping in.

There were tips regarding stance, backswing, downswing, but none on swearing. I guessed Santa wouldn't have brought *100 Golfing Tips* down our chimney had the book included tips on swearing.

This clean-cut bible of advice also dealt with golf in testing weather conditions. Now this was surely useful. I wasn't banking on golfing 18 Scottish islands in bright sunshine. I imagined it might get a wee bit blustery at times.

Talking of which, 'Wind was invented to make the golfer's life a misery.' I had to agree completely with the author of *100 Golfing Tips* on that one. 'You can't beat the wind.' Oh. I began to worry that strong winds on the islands might render my golf unspeakably bad. I enjoyed the tip on golfing in thunder and lightning. 'The best tip in such conditions is to get off the course.' I decided that I would bear this in mind.

Having digested *100 Golfing Tips* (or at least some of them)
I turned my attention to the only other golf book on my
shelves, a dog-eared copy of a book I'd once picked up in a
charity shop, purely on the strength of its title. *Golf My Own
Damn Way: Playin' the Game and Lovin' Life* by John Daly.

I once saw John Daly play in the Scottish Open at Loch
Lomond. He launched a tee shot into outer space and by
the time his ball had re-entered the earth's atmosphere
and landed, Daly had scoffed a chocolate bar and smoked
a cigarette. He's some man, Daly. I wondered what wisdom
I could pick up from the Wild Thing of golf that might
stand me in good stead for the islands. So I started readin'
Golf My Own Damn Way: Playin' the Game and Lovin' Life and,
like, learnin' stuff.

'Don't walk onto the first tee cold,' advised Daly.

But what if it's freezing, John? We're talking Scotland
here and not even the mainland either. The islands, John.
Scotland in extremis. What else have you got?

'Bring enough stick to the dance.'

Pick the right club, I've got you.

'See your shot before you hit it.'

It's in the bushes! (Sorry John, a bit of the old Scottish
fatalism creeping in there, I'm afraid.)

'Check your shoulders.'

Aye, still there. Not that I have any control over them.

'Leave the big dog in the trunk.'

Leave the whit? Oh, you mean leave the driver in the
boot! All this American talk can get pretty confusing.

'No club can bite you in the ass harder if you hit it
wrong.'

That's fine John, but what about the midges?

Wise Thing had one last piece of advice.

'Hey.'

Yes, John.

'Remember that golf spelt backwards is flog.'

You want me to sell my clubs?

Between *100 Golfing Tips* and *Golf My Own Damn Way: Playin' the Game and Lovin' Life* I felt ready to take on Scotland's island golf courses. What I required now, of course, was a plan of attack.

Which island should I visit first? And should I draw up a list of islands and tick them off in that order? Or would it be better if I just made it up as I went along? I figured that a combination of the two would work best. Some semblance of order, with room for improvisation.

What about transport? Obviously there would be a fair number of ferries involved, but how was I going to get to the courses once I was on the islands? I wasn't planning on taking a car, mainly because I can't drive. Hopefully there would be buses on the islands. Yes, buses that dropped you off right next to the golf courses. If not, I would walk. Perhaps some friendly islander would stop and give me a lift.

At least it was summertime, which meant better weather. Better weather by Scottish standards. As in the occasional hint of sun and the certainty of rain, but summer nonetheless. The Scottish summer isn't actually very long. In fact, some years it's barely there at all. And even when it is around, it's often interrupted by winter. I had to be prepared. Not usually my strong point. I needed to pack wisely for the islands. I wondered if my golf bag could double as my suitcase.

And what would the actual courses be like? The Machrie was a proper golf course, but they wouldn't all be like that. I imagined stripped back golf in its rawest state. Fields in some cases, with cows and sheep and other creatures. None of these courses were on the Open rota. I doubted they had dress codes. Good. I could turn up in my jeans. Dad used to play golf in his jeans, although he'd smarten up for competitions by putting on a pair of proper trousers.

Right. Time to break out of this city existence and let my spirits – and hopefully my golf balls – soar on these islands. But which one first?

Within days I was bound for Bute with the Man Who Beat Tiger Woods.

kames bay

port bannatyne

TO ROTHESAY
& FERRY

Port Bannatyne Golf Club, Isle of Bute

Route Plan of the 13 hole golf course

Clubhouse

BUTE
Port Bannatyne Golf Club
Rothesay

SCORE CARD

HOLE NO.	PAR	WHITE YARDS	YELLOW YARDS	RED YARDS	PAR
1 (&13th)	4	362	256	232	4
2 (&14th)	4	304	289	285	4
3 (&15th)	4	330	316	309	4
4 (&16th)	3	187	177	165	3
5 (&17th)	4	320	302	295	4
6	4	289	383	273	4
7	4	297	350	224	4
8	4	287	377	269	4
9	4	253	239	223	4
10	3	164	121	118	3
11	4	274	369	266	4
12	4	296	329	179	4
13 (&18th)	3	219	178	169	3
TOTAL	49	3582	3166	3007	49

Chapter 1

A Round with Riley – Bute

I was debating which island to tee off with when my friend Riley called to say he fancied a game of golf. Riley lived in San Francisco, but he and his wife and son had flown over to Scotland to attend the wedding of mutual friends of ours in Glasgow. We were all going to the wedding and Riley figured that since he was in Scotland he might as well fit in a round of golf. I was more than happy to make arrangements.

The only problem was that my clubs were in Hopeman and I'd no time to get hold of them. But then Riley's clubs were in California so we were going to have to borrow clubs anyway. I thought about us playing a course in Glasgow, but my mind was on the islands and I thought it seemed like a nice idea to get Riley involved. It would mean playing my first round of island golf without my clubs, or my dad's putter.

After considering my dilemma for about ten seconds, I decided that I could live with playing my first island round with borrowed golf clubs. I'd collect my clubs and my dad's putter ahead of my second island, wherever that might be, making that trip extra special. The point of life was to have fun while you could and taking Riley for a round of island golf fitted into the fun category.

Now all I had to do was rustle up two sets of golf clubs and find an island course within reasonable range of Glasgow. The only day we had to play with was the day after the wedding, so I couldn't make this complicated. Beautiful simplicity, that's what I was aiming for. I consulted my golf map of Scotland, checked the ferry times and settled on Bute.

Riley was happy to play any island. 'I just wanna play 18 holes.'

I explained to him that we'd only be playing 13 holes. 'I just wanna play 13 holes, then.'

Riley was up for whatever, which was just as well really.

Port Bannatyne on the Isle of Bute is the only 13-hole golf course in Britain. I'm not sure how surprising a statistic that is really. I mean, who in their right mind builds a 13-hole golf course? Of course, it was perfect for my purposes. If I was insisting on golfing 18 islands, I might as well start with a 13-hole golf course.

Riley and I met at Central Station the morning after the wedding. Already we were off to an impressive start. In truth, we were more bleary-eyed than bloodshot-eyed. It hadn't been a late night for either of us. The wedding was wonderful. It had been great sharing Laura and Dave's big day. But Riley and I, young dads now, had eventually taken our little ones home to let our wives enjoy the rest of the evening.

As the train travelled to Wemyss Bay, I warned Riley

not to expect lush fairways and smooth greens. He wasn't
fussed. He just wanted to 'get out there and hit some golf
balls'. He even shrugged off the forecast of rain. Nothing
was going to dampen Riley's day. It was a good way to be.

I was delighted to be kicking off my islands adventure
with Riley, though I was no match for him as a golfer. The
man once beat Tiger Woods. Besides Riley being an accomplished wielder of a club, he was as laid-back as California
gets, and terrifically upbeat, all of the time as far as I could
see. Riley could never have been Scottish. I was glad that
he had brought his particular brand of sunshine from the
west coast of America to the west of Scotland.

We'd played golf together once before, a few years back,
when I'd had the pleasure of introducing Riley to Hopeman
on one of those beautiful clear days that the Moray coast
has a habit of serving up. That round with Riley was one
of the most enjoyable I'd ever experienced. It had everything. Perfect weather, course in great condition, good
conversation and a beer at the Prieshach. I believe Riley
had enjoyed it too.

It would have been great had my dad been home, but
he was away at sea at the time. He would have loved
showing Riley round his home course. I reckon the pair
of them would have got on great, although I doubt Riley
would have understood a word my dad said. Between my
dad's strong dialect — Hopeman is quite different to English
— and the speed at which he spoke, Riley would have been
fairly flummoxed.

Less than an hour after leaving Glasgow, we arrived at
Wemyss Bay station, with its elegant curves and glass ceiling.

In its heyday, it would have been busy with Glasgow families, alighting to catch the boat to Rothesay, as we were doing now. There weren't many making a beeline for Bute this morning. Just Riley and me, one or two other tourists, and some men in blue blazers, all members of a bowling club.

The ferry across the Firth of Clyde to Bute only takes half-an-hour. Rothesay was a thriving seaside resort for many decades until cheap foreign holidays came along and tastes changed. With its promenade and Victorian villas, the town retains some of its charm. Step off the ferry and right away you feel like you are on holiday. That feeling would have been stronger still had the sun been out, but at least those clouds weren't dumping the predicted rain on us yet.

Riley and I crossed the pier and boarded the next bus to Port Bannatyne, a couple of miles up the coast. Port Bannatyne is a lovely little village, beautifully situated in Kames Bay. It's a popular spot for yachters, and on this particular day golfers. Dropping us off, the bus driver gave us directions to the golf course which seemed to be on the big hill behind the village.

Strolling along a quiet country road towards the golf club, Riley and I bumped into Sandy the shepherd and his sheepdog Meg. Riley was excited to find himself in the company of a shepherd. There weren't too many of them on the streets of San Francisco, what with there not being many sheep on the streets of San Francisco.

Riley asked Sandy how hard it was to train a sheepdog. 'Some dogs are impossible, others are quite easy,' said

Sandy, pointing to his van. 'I've got one in there that's quite hard to train. The son of a good bitch, and he's not the least bit like her. The wee pup just goes straight for the sheep.'

Sandy enjoyed teaching sheepdogs new tricks, even though it was often a wrench to have to hand them back to their owners once his work was done. 'I trained one for a farmer. Had it for two years from when it was a pup. I could do anything with it. It was a sore yin having to give it back, but it was his dog.'

Riley, as well as being an excellent golfer, was an artist and carpenter and he couldn't help but admire Sandy's crook. 'It's hazelwood,' said Sandy, running his hands over it. 'You're supposed to cut it in February when the sap's out, and leave it for two years to mature. You can heat it for a wee twist and bend it straight. The top's buffalo horn, though most are sheep horn.'

I imagined that once he got back home Riley was going to set to work on a crook.

Sandy looked a great deal younger than his professed 85 years. He was a fantastic advert for shepherding. 'If I stopped this, I would die,' he smiled, looking at the fields which he still took to daily. 'I go to different farms and give them a hand.'

With all this shepherding talk, Riley and I had quite forgotten about our game of golf. The conversation took a natural turn to weather, as conversation often does in Scotland. According to Sandy, summer was late to Bute this year. 'I've only heard the cuckoo once,' he said. I hadn't heard any cuckoos in Glasgow.

A man out for a walk stopped and said hello.

'No' so cold today,' said Sandy, 'though it's supposed to rain.'

'Aye, later on,' said the man, climbing over a stile. He wished us a good day and set off across the field for a traipse in the hills.

Sandy turned and nodded at Riley. 'This man here looks like he could walk.'

'Yeah, I've done a bit of walking,' smiled Riley, six foot plus and the picture of Californian health.

Sandy and Meg had sheep to round up and Riley and I had a round of golf to play. We said cheerio to Sandy and continued our walk to the golf club. Riley wondered why Sandy had singled him out as the walking type. I figured it had something to do with his lankiness and aura of well-being.

'Made me feel good anyway,' said Riley.

'There's no hope for me.' I smiled. 'I think Sandy was looking to train you up as a shepherd.'

Riley found this idea most appealing. 'Hey, if you could just make up a story about how I stayed here and took root.'

I could see I was going to have to keep a watchful eye on him and make sure I got him off the island. Otherwise I'd be going back to Glasgow alone, faced with the prospect of explaining to Riley's wife Sara that her husband had found a new calling and that perhaps they wouldn't be getting on that plane back to San Francisco. 'Sara, Riley's become a shepherd and he'd like you all to move to Bute.'

We came to the golf club. The modern designed clubhouse had a veranda and a palm tree in front of it. I'm always surprised to see palm trees in Scotland. Bute's mild climate, a benefit of the Gulf Stream, suits palm trees. Rothesay's promenade is lined with them. I just hoped it would remain mild for the next couple of hours.

The only person in the clubhouse was Jack who took our green fees (£12 each) and produced the two sets of clubs that I'd called ahead and organised. Jack explained to us that if we wanted to play 18 holes we should do what the members did in competition – that is, play 12 holes, repeat the first five, then finish off on the 13th. Riley and I liked the novelty of 13 holes and decided to stick with that odd number. Jack wished us a good round and out we went for a game of island golf.

'This is great,' said Riley, standing on the first tee, looking out across Kames Bay with its yachts to the Cowal Peninsula. My American friend settled into his stance and with one graceful swing smacked his ball for miles. Riley still had the hang of this golf thing. My turn. I looked down the fairway and steadied myself and all I can say is that I did nothing too embarrassing, which is always my aim on the first tee.

I ran a quick inventory on my bag: driver (with chicken head cover), three wood (which I'd just hit), five iron, seven iron, pitching wedge, sand wedge, putter. And plenty of golf balls, though I'm not one for losing golf balls. Well I do sometimes, of course, but what I lack in distance, I tend to make up for in accuracy. I'm not the biggest hitter around, but I'm far from being the wildest.

We crossed a burn. Riley called it a creek. But apart

from that, it was apparent from the outset that playing golf at Port Bannatyne was like playing golf on a ski slope, minus the snow. We could have done with a chairlift. Depending on the direction of the hole, you were faced with either an uphill scramble, a downhill slalom or a series of awkward stances hitting across the hill. Before long I was feeling dizzy. What we were dealing with here was a new kind of golf. Vertigolf.

With the course essentially being the side of a hill, the greens jutted out. They had to, or else you'd have been putting down a hill. 'Unbelievable!' cried Riley, as we approached a typical Port Bannatyne green. 'They built a shelf and put a green on it!' It was pretty much the case.

I crouched to line up a putt. Beyond the surface of the green, all I could see was the sea. It reminded me of those infinity pools you see in travel magazines. I felt that if I overhit my putt, my ball would end up in the water.

Riley had vanished. Having missed the infinity green with his approach shot, he was either down below the green or swimming in the bay. I walked round the side of the green and had a peek over the edge. There he was, contemplating his next shot. In all honesty, he faced an awkward chip. But being Riley, he got it to within a few feet of the pin. If you can get the better of Tiger Woods, you can conquer a lopsided 13-hole golf course on a Scottish island.

We moved on to the next hole, a downhill dogleg, downwind. This idiosyncratic island golf course was growing on me. The Highland Boundary Fault runs through Bute, accounting for the bottom half of the island being reasonably flat and the top half more hilly. We were definitely in the top half of the island.

Riley picked a relic of a five iron from his bag and scrutinised it. '"Made in Scotland, 1950." Nobody plays with blades any more. It's nice, like stepping back in time. Let's see what kind of damage this can do to my hands!'

He survived impact, his ball shooting off into the distance. I produced my best shot yet, a solid seven iron to the heart of the green. 'Good effort,' said Riley who, as well as being a useful golfer, was a considerate golfing partner. Relaxed in his own ability and far from being an intimidating figure on the course, his was a reassuring presence. Riley was full of encouragement and goodwill. And besides, this was a round between friends. I was having fun, even if I felt that at any moment I might topple down the hill and fall into the bay.

We tackled a hole that involved a near vertical climb, or so it seemed at the time. In between finding footholds, Riley and I spoke about, appropriately enough, the ups and downs of a round of golf. About how, as much as suffering a bad hole can leave you low in confidence, a good hole can transform your outlook. All I ever really wanted from a round of golf was a good run of shots and to keep the run going.

'Yeah,' said Riley. 'You play a great hole and think if you can just play the next hole well and keep getting better, one day you'll have the perfect round. Even if you hit a successful shot once in a blue moon, you still think you can be successful. As long as you feel capable of hitting a good shot, you're happy.'

It was partly because my last couple of shots had been good that I was happy. But I still worried about what I might do next.

Riley stood on the tee, full of confidence. 'I'm going to hit the green ... I can feel it ... this is it!' He drove the green all right. The wrong green. Not that Riley minded. He was getting a kick out of playing this bizarre golf course. Port Bannatyne, instead of being the stuff of nightmares, was, in a way, a dream come true for him.

Riley explained that as a child he loved drawing imaginary golf courses, and some of them even looked like Port Bannatyne. 'For fun, I drew two kinds of courses. Ones with rolling hills, old stone walls and creeks ... rugged, picturesque courses like this. And then I drew exotic islands where you would tee off through palm trees towards a green floating out in the ocean.'

I wondered if it might be possible that Port Bannatyne was based on one of Riley's childhood sketches and that this topsy turvy golf course was in fact his brainchild.

'You got honour!' said Riley. Somehow I'd bettered him on the last hole. Now it was my turn to take the lead and tee off first. How long would that last? This next hole was most unusual, even by Port Bannatyne standards. In front of the tee was a drystane dyke – a dry stone wall to Riley – and that might have been it. Clear the dyke and find the fairway. But no. Instead, the dyke turned 90 degrees and ran up the hill to the right of the green. The line for the green was basically the dyke. Everything to the left was fairway, everything else was field.

This head scratcher of a golf hole was called the Hill,

something Riley took issue with. 'This hole shouldn't be called the Hill! It should be called the Wall! What's up with this wall?' Riley was waving his club at the dyke. And then he became the dyke. 'Hey, I'm just gonna jut out right in front of you and see if you can deal with me!'

Both of us managed to block out the dyke and remain in bounds. The end of the Hill – or the Wall, as Riley would have it – was the high point of the round. We had gone as far up the hill as it was possible to go while keeping to the course, the dyke now running behind the green. It was all downhill from here. I felt like having a lie down, regaining some energy before we began our descent. There was no real hurry. We were the only people on the course.

Riley soaked up the superb view from the summit and delivered his verdict on the golfing side of things. 'It's a ridiculous concept putting a golf course on a steep slope like this.' It was sort of intended as a compliment, because you had to have some kind of grudging admiration for the mad genius who'd dreamt up this course.

The next hole, the Kyles, played across the hill and Riley and I judged it to be the best hole at Port Bannatyne. I sent a solid tee shot along the line of the dyke (it was still keeping us company), my ball settling in the middle of the fairway. I was loving this loaned three wood and wanted to take it home with me.

Trees framed either side of the green. Behind the green, the bright yellow broom reminded me of Hopeman. I chipped to ten feet and very nearly made my birdie putt. 'An epic hole,' said Riley, picking up the soapstone he'd found earlier and was using as a marker.

I asked him about the time he beat Tiger Woods. I'd heard the story before, but wanted to hear it again. Not every golfer had such a tale to tell.

'We had a good golf team at my school,' said Riley. 'We had a good reputation and all the other schools wanted to play against us. So, with the Tiger Woods thing, he went to a school with shitty golfers. Most of the guys on his team sucked, but they played at an amazing country club and we wanted to play them because they played a pretty nice golf course. Our coach was always trying to play these places.

'We played Tiger before he was famous, but everybody knew he was a good golfer. It wasn't really like a big deal. It was kind of like going to play this guy who, rumour had it, was a really good golfer.

'Tiger, and maybe one other guy, were the only good golfers on their team. The real competition would be between Tiger and our number one guy, Dave, who went on to college and became a good golfer in his own right. Dave beat Tiger and the next time Tiger beat Dave pretty badly. But we'd beat the team.'

Riley the Tiger tamer, or at least part of the team that tamed Team Tiger. Still, as golf anecdotes go, it was a good one.

I was long overdue a bad drive and managed it at the hole called the Bay, skying it something terrible. The view of the bay put me off. (That's my story and I'm sticking to it.) Riley was having problems of his own. 'What the … ?!' he yelled as his massive tee shot flew past the next tee. Riley was making this crazy golf course even more bizarre.

He then nearly managed something totally outlandish – a hole-in-one. I actually thought it was going to go in. It was certainly very close. I asked if I could borrow his nine iron, partly because I didn't have a nine iron in my bag, but partly because I secretly hoped that some of Riley's golfing magic might rub off on me. Except that I forgot that I couldn't hit the ball as far as him, and though my tee shot was well hit, the ball fell short of the green. I should have stuck with my seven iron. I remembered the words of John Daly. 'Bring enough stick to the dance.' Riley tapped in to claim his birdie. Though arriving on the green to pick his ball out of the hole would have been sweeter. 'Closest I've ever been,' he sighed. Golf is full of regrets.

Port Bannatyne saves its most exhilarating holes for last. The 12th was a thrilling prospect. Standing on the tee I felt like a ski jumper about to take off. Riley's drive was spectacular, his ball hanging in the sky for ever. We never found his ball either, even though he had hit it straight down the fairway. 'I've never been so happy with a shot,' said Riley. 'Like a million dollars and then it just vanishes … gone.' It was a genuine golfing mystery. Port Bannatyne was bloody bamboozling.

Since we weren't repeating the first five holes to make it the full 18, we had to trek back up the hill a bit to reach the 13th tee. Once there, we were confronted with more of the same. Downhill all the way, but this time all the way to the clubhouse. Desperate for my ball to soar, I fired it into the bushes. I had another go, this time connecting, my ball taking an eternity to come back down to earth, the severity of the slope exaggerating the trajectory of my drive, making it look far more glorious than it ever was. But it was fun to watch, all the same.

Heading down that final fairway with the brakes on, Riley and I reflected on parenthood and how much our lives had changed since we'd last met a few years ago. Changed for the better. Riley had a beautiful son and I had a beautiful baby daughter and was just waiting for her first words. 'She's thinking these thoughts now,' said Riley, 'and pretty soon they'll all come flooding out!'

We shook hands as dads on the final green. It occurred to me that at no point during the round had I asked Riley for any little golfing tips that might stand me in good stead for the summer, as had been my intention. I'd simply got on with my own game and tried to keep up with the Man Who Beat Tiger Woods.

The extent to which you've enjoyed a round of golf sometimes doesn't sink in until it's over. Golf lends itself to reflection. Port Bannatyne with Riley had been a real pleasure. I was glad to have shared my first round of island golf with my American friend. He was unlikely to experience another 13-hole golf course like it.

We handed the clubs back to Jack and he asked how we'd got on. We said we'd enjoyed it, which we had, and that we'd especially liked the eighth hole, the Kyles. Jack said it was the favourite hole among the members. The tee at the top of the course made for a natural break in the round. 'Not for the view,' said Jack, 'but the drink.' Something like the Prieshach then. I hadn't thought to bring a beer with me. Well, there was always next time.

Bute had a couple of other golf courses besides Port Bannatyne and I asked Jack about them. He assured me that we'd just played the island's best golf course. 'Nothing to do with the fact I'm the assistant greenkeeper,' he smiled. Jack offered us a lift down to the village – he was about to lock up – but Riley and I were happy to walk. The sun had come out. It was turning out to be a beautiful day in Scotland.

We walked back along the quiet country lane and saw Sandy in a field with Meg, rounding up the sheep. We gave Sandy a wave and Riley leaned on the fence and watched him work. 'I could watch this for ever,' he said. Riley was mesmerised. He had definitely been bitten by the shepherding bug. Maybe I was going to have a bit of bother getting him back to the mainland.

A passing car stopped. It was Jack. He leaned out of the window and handed Riley and I Port Bannatyne Golf Club pin badges. We thanked him and he drove off. Riley and I ate a late lunch at the Russian Tavern on Port Bannatyne's seafront. Only a village with a 13-hole golf course would have a pub themed on Imperial Russia. I had the smoked trout sandwich and Riley went for the Russian sausage. We washed down our meals with pints of Peter's Well, straight from the cask.

As we got off the bus in Rothesay, the ferry was leaving. No matter, we'd catch the next one. We had a wander about the town, discovering a putting green next to the Rothesay Winter Garden. 'Misbehaving on the putting green will lead to an automatic ban,' said a sign. Riley and I couldn't have misbehaved if we'd tried. And anyway,

we had little appetite for putting after our round of
vertigolf.

Instead we went and checked out Rothesay Castle,
admiring the moat, a serious water hazard. And just before
boarding the ferry we paid a visit to Rothesay's other key
tourist attraction: the Victorian toilets on the pier. An ornate
lavatory where one can urinate in splendour and flush with
a flourish. On the wall by the entrance was an article from
an American newspaper extolling the virtues of a visit to
Rothesay's Victorian toilets, under the headline 'Ten Places
to Go When You Really Wanna Go'.

As the ferry sailed for Wemyss Bay, Rothesay's Victorian
villas receded into the distance. Back in the bustle of
Glasgow, Riley and I popped into the Horseshoe for a pint
to round off our day. We said goodbye to each other on
busy St Vincent Street. Riley was flying home the following
day. 'Always a pleasure,' he said as he shook my hand. In
all likelihood, I wouldn't see Riley for another few years,
but when we did hook up again, we'd probably play another
round of golf.

Isle of Skye Golf Club, Sconser, Isle of Skye

Route Plan of the 9 hole golf course

TO PORTREE

TO BROADFORD

A87

Clubhouse

Portree

SKYE

Broadford

Isle of Skye Golf Club

sound of raasay

rough
burn
copse
moor / marsh
rock shore / shingle beach
rock shore
moor
quarry
ditch

SCORE CARD

HOLE NO.	PAR	WHITE YARDS	LADIES YARDS	PAR
1	4	307	250	4
2	4	447	347	4
3	3	153	153	3
4	4	280	280	4
5	3	162	162	3
6	4	349	301	4
7	3	146	146	3
8	4	294	294	3
9	4	268	268	4
TOTAL	33	2406	2201	33

Chapter 2

Wedges and Midges – Skye

The departed leave behind memories and belongings. One day, when they felt up to the task, my brother and sister went over to the Hopeman clubhouse and emptied dad's locker. They cleared out his bag, his trolley, his golf shoes and other traces of his golfing life. A scrunched up cagoule, an empty Lucozade bottle, a few crumpled scorecards, some loose tees. My brother took over dad's locker and dad's clubs ended up in the garage.

A week after playing Port Bannatyne with Riley, I was back in Hopeman. I'd my cousin's wedding to go to and a rare round of golf with my brother to look forward to the following morning. Clearly this was the new combo, weddings and golf, in the wrong order. After playing Hopeman with my brother I was heading off to Skye and the Outer Hebrides, with the prospect of a further six island courses. By the time I left Barra on the ferry, I'd have achieved more than a third of my target number of islands. There were rich pickings to be had on my impending trip.

The morning after Amy's wedding – the best kind of wedding, a Highland wedding – my brother and I stumbled onto the first tee at Hopeman. Neither of us had slept much. It's fair to say it had been a late one. But, given the amount of celebration involved in a Highland wedding, especially one where the bride's dad is a distillery manager, her brother is a cooper and half the guests work in the whisky industry, well, considering all that, we weren't in too bad shape. Hungover, yes, but not so much that we couldn't swing a club.

I gazed up the first fairway, something I had done countless times, though not enough in recent years. Bushes to the left, rough to the right and, at the top of the hill, two bunkers, one to either side. And right beneath the tee, the ditch. I could probably play Hopeman with my eyes closed, but then I would lose a lot of golf balls.

The ultimate shame at the first was in not clearing the ditch. The other big worry was hooking the ball into the bushes. Aim between the bunkers and everything will work out fine. It was good to be back.

Our golf course, thou art in Hopeman, hallowed be thy greens ...

I wondered how I would fare this fine morning with my head still half full of whisky. I tucked my scorecard into my back pocket. I always carried a scorecard and I never filled it in. It would end up in the bin or in my bag, unmarked, or I'd use it as a bookmark. If I got off to a good start, I would keep the score in my head. Until disaster struck, as it usually did. Then I'd forget about my score and enjoy the rest of my round.

Give us this day our daily birdie, and lead us not into deep bunkers ...

I didn't top my tee shot into the ditch and I didn't hook it into the bushes. Despite my grogginess in the wake of the previous night's excesses, I drove straight down the middle between the bunkers. It didn't go far, but it didn't go wrong either. My second shot, played with my trusty five iron, was most unusual in that I made the green. I hardly ever reached the first green in two. This required consecutive good shots, some measure of consistency. Most of the time this proved beyond me. I was capable of pulling one rabbit out of the hat, but two? Now I faced a birdie putt on the first green and I felt giddy just thinking about it, unless my giddiness was down to the pints and drams I'd consumed at the wedding.

I took out my dad's putter. Half-an-hour earlier, half-asleep and dehydrated, I'd gone into the garage and, among the old bikes and gardening tools, found my dad's golf bag. I'd touched it and thought about my brother and I going to play a round of golf and dad not being there to join us. I reflected on the family wedding and dad not being there to enjoy it.

In the gloom of the garage, I'd wondered if I was doing the right thing. And then I reached for the trophy I'd won at Boat-of-Garten, and wished it wasn't so.

My dad's putter was one of those mallet putters with the half-moon head and with it being silver it reminded me of a spaceship. It was certainly a far fancier looking putter than my own. Dad had had several different putters over the years and this had just been the latest one. But it would have been one of the last things held by those hands that held me as a child. I stepped from the garage into the morning light. I put my dad's putter in my bag and promised to look after it in the coming months. It was certainly going places.

Half-an-hour later, I three-putted the first green at Hopeman, turning a possible birdie into a definite bogey. I looked at my dad's putter and looked at my brother.

'Aye, not so good,' said Stewart.

For some reason I'd expected to knock the ball into the hole with my first putt. And now I was surprised and disappointed that I hadn't. Yet I had no right to feel that surprise or disappointment. Yes, I held my dad's putter in my hands, but if I was going to perform miracles with it, I needed to putt well. On the second green, I lipped out from 30 feet and my brother raised an eyebrow. That was much better.

The course was in great condition. I'd rarely seen it look so good. The same could not be said of the Sutherland brothers who were beginning to wilt in the sun. The wedding revelry was taking its toll. 'I can't feel my arms,' said Stewart. Not being able to feel your arms can be a problem when you're trying to swing a club. It was fast becoming apparent that golf and weddings don't mix, at least not in the order we'd insisted upon. Perhaps we'd overdone it, but it was our cousin's wedding. What were we supposed to do? Stay sober?

I played a shot from the sand, my ball catching the lip of the bunker and shooting off at an angle and striking my brother on the leg. He'd seen it coming, but was too sluggish to jump out of the way. At least it didn't hurt. Stewart couldn't feel his legs either. Numbness through whisky.

The round unravelled, shanks followed by laughter. I left a head cover on the tee and had to run back and get it. I tried to put dad's putter in my brother's bag, mistaking it for my own. We were all over the shop. Though not in as muddled a state as a certain friend of mine who, partial to the odd joint during a round of golf, once walked to the next tee without realising he'd left his clubs on the green. No, we weren't that frazzled.

The Prieshach soon woke us up. That idyllic par three by the sea, the golfing amphitheatre offering no shortage of drama. It must be something, I thought, to see the Prieshach for the first time. I never grew tired of arriving there, especially on a warm summer's day with the wall of yellow broom behind the green and the Moray Firth sparkling in the sunshine. The Prieshach is Paul Lawrie's favourite par three. The 1999 Open champion played Hopeman a lot in his youth. I remember him turning up with his massive golf bag and hitting the ball like I'd never seen anyone hit a ball before.

Naturally my dad loved the Prieshach. Some of my fondest memories are of being there with him, sitting on the bench with a beer or a dram after teeing off, a key part of the Prieshach experience. Chatting about something or other or perhaps just sitting there, taking in the view of the green and the sea and enjoying the moment. Not any more. Robbed of all those rounds we might have played together. Regret that I hadn't joined him more often on the golf course.

Every time I played the Prieshach I wanted to make it count. You selected the club to suit the day, however strong

the wind was blowing and in which direction. You struck
that ball into the sky and it would take a long time to
land. When it did, if you'd done everything right, that ball
would be lying on that giant bowl of a green, giving you
a birdie chance on one of the most beautiful short holes
in Scotland. And you'd march down that path to the green
with just a putter in your hand.

Lifted by the splendour of the setting and the pure challenge of the hole – no beer or dram this morning – I
parred the Prieshach. It's all I ever asked of a round at
Hopeman. A birdie was always welcome, though in my
experience rare. Whereas a hole-in-one was the hope of
all hopes. No, a par was absolutely fine. I'd hit a seven
iron into the wind, my ball landing at the back of the
sloping green. I got the line and the weight of my long
putt just about right and tapped in for a three. I looked
out to the sea, as I always did, and smiled. Basically, I could
endure 17 bad holes at Hopeman, as long as I measured
up at the Prieshach.

My good fortune at the peerless 12th seemed to spur
me on. Now I had a spring in my step and was swinging
with confidence. On the next hole, we met Donnie and
Linda who run the village shop. They were out for a Sunday
morning walk. 'You don't mind us watching, do you?'
joked Linda as I got ready to play my approach to the
green. I didn't mind at all. I'm often a better golfer with
an audience. It seems to help me focus, want to do well
and not make a fool of myself. I played a decent five iron,
my ball stopping just short of the green, and crucially
avoiding the bunker. Donnie and Linda walked the rest of

the hole with us as they headed back to the village. I pitched to three feet and holed my putt for par, playing to the gallery. 'You can watch for the rest of the round!' I said to Linda.

My brother and I enjoyed the remaining holes in the sunshine then had a pint in the clubhouse. It wasn't often we got to do this, with me living in Glasgow. I get on extremely well with my brother. He's my best friend. We didn't mention dad, but sitting with our pints, looking out on the course, we were both thinking about him. I couldn't be in this clubhouse and not think about dad. The next table was where he sat with the One o'Clock Gang. The day after dad died, a pint of John Smith's sat untouched on the bar counter. 'That's for James,' said one of dad's golfing buddies.

It was time for me to leave Hopeman again. I had a train to catch. My brother was planning to join me and play one or two of the island courses at some point, but for now, it was back to work for him the next day. Meanwhile I had to get to Inverness, where I was spending the night before leaving for Skye in the morning. I wasn't going alone though. In the past few days, I had acquired a travelling companion. Waiting for me in Inverness was Noble Brian.

When I'd mentioned to Noble Brian what I was up to – this notion of 18 island golf courses – he'd got very excited. And I'd said he was welcome to join me on any islands that appealed to him. And he'd said he'd like to do all of them.

'All of them?'

'Aye, laddie.'

Noble Brian talks like this. By the way, his name's Brian
Noble. I've turned his name around for dramatic purposes.

I was a little taken aback by his enthusiasm for my project,
but I really shouldn't have been. You see, Noble Brian hails
from Aberdeenshire where the minute they're born they're
handed a set of golf clubs and told to get on with it. Let
me be clear that Noble Brian loves his golf. Not only that,
he makes his living from the game. He's a golf architect.
The man knows where to put a bunker. But besides loving
the game and making a living from it, Noble Brian is as
daft as I am. This island golf caper was right up his street.
In fact, it was a dream come true.

'This is a dream come true this,' said Noble Brian on
the phone.

'What, spending the summer with me?'

'No! Golfing the islands. Golf as it used to be. Golf in
the raw!'

'Yes, you'll probably need a thick jumper.'

'Old Tom Morris!'

'He's coming too, is he?'

'Askernish!'

'Bless you.'

I had to break it to the poor guy that I'd already been
to Bute, so he'd only be playing 17 islands. For Noble
Brian, this was not a problem. He'd go and play Bute
himself, maybe take his girlfriend with him. This island
golf bonanza was a once-in-a-lifetime opportunity, something not to be missed. As far as the golf architect was
concerned, it was the ultimate field project. It would add

to his knowledge of course design and golf history. He would chart all the courses too.

'Besides,' said Noble Brian, 'there's the banter.'

Yes, there was always that. The Banter Potential would be greatly enhanced with Noble Brian on the scene. Otherwise I'd just be talking to myself.

Having got used to the idea that I'd be visiting most of these islands on my own, I now had to get used to the idea that I wouldn't be. And I liked the idea of exploring Scotland's islands with Noble Brian. He liked golf, I liked golf. He liked a laugh, I liked a laugh. He liked a beer, I liked a beer. He liked Celtic, I liked Rangers.

Not that football came into it. No, we were far too sensible for all that nonsense. This was about golf. We were friends. Still, it was a little bit awkward that here was me on my way to Inverness to meet Noble Brian a couple of hours after Rangers had clinched the title. Naturally I was delighted with the outcome. Noble Brian though would be gutted.

He didn't look too glum when I stepped off the train in Inverness station. His face wasn't tripping him. And he wasn't short with me. Although he is short. It would not be stretching the truth if I said that Noble Brian is no giant. How tall is he? Well, I'll tell you. He's half the height of Ian Woosnam.

Speaking of the Welsh, Noble Brian's girlfriend Abbi was with him. They'd been enjoying a break in the Highlands and now Abbi was driving back to Edinburgh, where they lived, leaving her man with me for the week.

I had deliberately not said anything about Rangers being

the champions, leaving it for Noble Brian to bring it up. 'Aye, well done,' he mumbled. I allowed myself the opportunity to look pleased for a moment, then let it go, putting the football to one side. We were on a golfing mission.

Rather than compare the fortunes of our football clubs, we compared golf clubs. Noble Brian and I had discussed at length on the phone the logistics of our trip to Skye and the Outer Hebrides and had agreed that, as we would be reliant on public transport and might end up lugging our bags about a fair bit, the sensible approach would be to cut down on clubs and bring only a half set. A lot of these island courses were short 9-hole affairs anyway.

We hadn't talked about which clubs to take. But as it turned out, I'd gone for the selection of driver, five iron, seven iron, nine iron and pitching wedge (and my dad's putter, of course), while Noble Brian had plumped for driver, four iron, six iron, eight iron, pitching wedge and sand wedge (and putter). Between the two of us, we pretty much had a full set of clubs. Noble Brian and I seemed to find this infinitely more interesting than Abbi did, as she listened to us blether about club choice on the station concourse.

Noble Brian wanted to know why I hadn't brought a sand wedge. I replied that I wasn't planning on finding any bunkers. (The truth was it had slipped my mind to bring a sand wedge. Och well, I could always borrow his when I got into trouble.)

I had actually succeeded in turning my golf bag into a suitcase, stuffing clothing and toiletries into different pockets. Anything I hadn't been able to shove in my golf bag had gone in the small backpack I was also carrying.

Having a golf bag slung over one shoulder and a small backpack over the other lent me equilibrium. Well, that's what I told myself anyway.

Noble Brian was sporting a similar set up, except that instead of a small backpack he had a satchel and rather than a regular golf bag he had a pencil bag. It had to be said he was travelling impressively light, but then he is several inches shorter than me. He'd even managed to pack a pair of golf shoes. I had the shoes I was standing in and that was it.

Abbi gave her man a send-off kiss and asked me to look after him. I promised I would, even though I have trouble looking after myself. I guessed that I was doing her a favour by taking him off her hands for a bit. Abbi headed to her car and Noble Brian and I walked out of the station towards the hostel in which we were spending the night before leaving for Skye in the morning. I had booked a hostel instead of a hotel because we would be using hostels on some of the islands so I thought we might as well get used to hostel life right away.

Hostels tend to cater more for backpackers than golfers so I felt slightly self-conscious parking my clubs at the front desk. The woman behind reception was Australian, which didn't surprise me one bit. I'd once been checked into a hostel in Melbourne by a bloke from Glasgow. The woman was very friendly and showed no sign of prejudice towards golfers at all. We were handed our room key along with a card that carried the following piece of advice, 'PLEASE, you must go to the correct bed. If it is occupied, please return to reception.'

The room was interesting. Not endlessly interesting, since it wasn't that big. You couldn't swing a club in it, not without injuring Noble Brian anyway. I'd expected the room to be a bit more spacious. Why I'd had expectations for a room at a hostel I don't know. Three sets of bunk beds filled up most of the room. It was clear that we had four room-mates as two sets of bunks were taken up with bags and clothes on crumpled sheets. Noble Brian grabbed the remaining bottom bunk, leaving me with the modest climb up a ladder. A T-shirt that wasn't one of mine was hanging on my bedknob. I reluctantly picked it up and placed it on the radiator. On the window sill above the radiator was a pair of climbing boots stuffed with thick socks. Fortunately the window was open.

What we'd failed to notice was the room's theme. That is, the theme beyond two golfers sharing a cramped space with four climbers. Each bunk was named after a loch. Mine was Loch Lochy, while Noble Brian would be sleeping in Loch Linnhe.

Reluctant to hang about our loch-themed room a minute longer, Noble Brian and I made a beeline for the nearest pub, the Castle Tavern opposite Inverness Castle. We tried some unpronounceable but very drinkable ales and Noble Brian filled me in on his latest design project, which involved adding bunkers to an existing course.

'So how do you build a bunker, then?' I asked.

'Och, you just need dynamite.'

'Eh?'

'I'm joking.'

And I'd just like to make it clear that Noble Brian was

joking, before he gets blacklisted by the institute of golf architects or whatever. My knowledgeable and responsible friend constructs bunkers in the traditional manner. By rolling up his sleeves, picking up a shovel and digging a great big hole before tipping in several wheelbarrows of sand. Yes, there's no substitute for hard work.

After the intense labour of polishing off a few pints, Noble Brian and I toddled back up the road to the hostel and crept to our beds, considerate of the fact we were sharing a glorified broom cupboard with four strangers. I was awoken in the early hours of the morning by the sound of singing Rangers fans and breaking glass. There are an awful lot of Rangers fans in the Highlands. I'm one of them, I suppose.

In the morning, Noble Brian and I met our room-mates. They turned out to be a cracking bunch of lads from Orkney. We actually only met three of them, the fourth still fast asleep beneath his blanket. I noted his bed was Loch Ness. We'd seen it all in this modest hostel room. Six lochs, three Orcadians and the Loch Ness Monster.

Noble Brian and I checked out of the hostel and roamed the streets of Inverness with our golf clubs, searching for a cafe that would do us a nice bacon roll and a cup of coffee. We eventually found one and I bought a newspaper featuring a special souvenir pullout of Rangers' title cele-brations. I showed it to Noble Brian but he wasn't inter-ested and returned to his bacon roll.

After breakfast, we caught the train to Kyle of Lochalsh. It's a stunning journey to the west coast and not one I'd experienced before, which made me feel silly, given that

I'd grown up in these parts. The train rolled past mountains, lochs and forests, Noble Brian describing the scenery
as 'biscuit-tinny'. You could have taken any of the views
we were treated to and stuck them on a tin of shortbread.
Once upon a time, I worked in a shortbread factory. Mostly
I remember having to wear a blue hairnet and trying not
to scald myself with the lava-hot butter. I also recall family
and friends being unwilling to come anywhere near me
after my shift, due to the stale stench I gave off. It's a
smelly business, shortbread.

Two-and-a-half hours after leaving Inverness, we came
to the end of the line. Kyle of Lochalsh is not as lovely as
it sounds, but then we weren't planning on hanging around.
We were jumping on the next bus to Skye. Crossing the
Skye Bridge on a bus isn't the most romantic way of reaching
Skye (a boat across the water would be) but it's not like
Noble Brian and I were on honeymoon.

It was raining in Kyle of Lochalsh, as we walked past
something that made me stop dead in my tracks. I hadn't
imagined anywhere besides Rothesay having toilets that
were considered to be a tourist attraction, but I had reck-
oned without Kyle of Lochalsh, which boasts the Loo of
the Year. After paying my 20p to get through the turnstile,
I was confronted by a blizzard of Scottishness, the walls
covered in tartan and antlers and pictures of Robert Burns
and William Wallace. I took a couple of quick pictures,
then put my camera away. I was in a public toilet.

'Well! That was something!' I said to Noble Brian,
emerging from the Loo of the Year. I began describing the
experience to him and showing him my pictures, but he

was less than impressed. I urged him to go and check out the Loo of the Year for himself, but Noble Brian said he didn't need to go and didn't want to go. The Loo of the Year meant nothing to him. He wasn't such a lover of art and culture as myself.

We picked up pre-packed sandwiches from a super-market and ate them in the bus shelter, while watching the rain. Drizzle is the wallpaper of Scotland. It suits the place. You could give the country a makeover of bright sunshine, but it just wouldn't look right.

Just then a red-faced man joined us in the bus shelter and asked where we were going.

'Sconser,' I told him.

'Sconser? There's fuck all in Sconser.'

'We're going to play the golf course,' I said, indicating my clubs.

'There's a quarry,' said the red-faced man.

'Sorry?'

'There's a quarry.'

'Is there?'

'Have you seen the quarry?'

'No, I haven't.' It was true. I hadn't seen the quarry. I'd never been to Sconser before.

The red-faced man grinned. 'Oh, you'll see the quarry!'

The bus pulled up, putting an end to the conversation about the quarry. Noble Brian and I let the red-faced man board the bus first, so that we could choose our seats strategically.

'Speed bonnie bus, like a bird on the wing, over the bridge to Skye ... '

Well I had to sing something to mark the occasion of us crossing the Skye Bridge. I sang quietly so as not to annoy our fellow passengers or attract the attention of the red-faced man. Only Noble Brian heard me sing and he winced. Or grimaced. One of the two.

We got off the bus at Broadford where we had to switch to another bus that would get us to the golf course. I'd been in Broadford once before, on my only previous visit to Skye for the wedding of friends of mine. During the course of the evening, I'd popped outside for some fresh air and within seconds my knees were ravaged by midges. The dangers of wearing a kilt on Skye. And the menace of Scotland's least loved beasties.

At least I wasn't wearing a kilt today. That would never have worked on a golf course. But if the midges can't get at your knees they'll go for your face and neck. I hadn't thought about midges until now and I hadn't brought any insect repellent. Not that insect repellent was of much use against the dreaded midge which is renowned for being repelled by nothing. They just tuck in as they please. Perhaps it wasn't yet midge season on Skye. I'd hold on to that hope for the moment.

A brand new bus turned up and I asked the driver if he was going to Sconser.

'Aye,' he said.

'Do you go by the golf course?'

'No.'

Now I could have taken the driver's 'no' as a no, but I can tell when one of my countrymen is being sarcastic. He *was* going by the golf course. I could tell by the tone of his voice. He just didn't want to say. Scotland must get awfully confusing for tourists sometimes. Taking the driver's 'no' as a yes, we jumped on the bus with our golf clubs.

The bus followed a winding road past hills that looked like crumpled paper in the pale morning light. We were skirting the edge of the Red Hills, or Red Cuillin. The larger Black Cuillin, the most spectacular and challenging mountains in Britain, attract mountaineers from all over the world. Skye is astonishing in its ruggedness and, for many, Skye is the Cuillin. The only thing is you can't play golf in them. It's no secret though, Skye. Routinely swamped by tourists, afflicted by wet weather and midges and blessed with unbeatable scenery.

We passed a group of bikers who'd got off their bikes to take pictures of Highland cows in a field. Hairy men in black leather photographing hairy cattle. Not long after that, the bus driver stopped by the golf course. 'Any closer and you'd be on the green,' he said.

Noble Brian and I walked into the modest clubhouse and met Murdo, the club steward. He was the only person around. It had been a quiet summer so far for the Isle of Skye Golf Club.

'It usually picks up well,' said Murdo, 'but the weather's been that bad. The last week's been horrendous with the rain. We had to cancel a competition. And the midges have just started this morning. They're early. Damp and no wind, you see. They're a menace, so they are.'

The midges were here. Damn. I said to Murdo that neither of us had brought any insect repellent but that nothing much worked against the midges anyway. Murdo recommended an Avon product called Skin So Soft. 'Great stuff, amazing,' he said. 'People swear by it. We sell a lot of it here. Walkers and climbers come here because they know we have it.'

'So you've got it then?'

'We're waiting on it.'

Of course, the midges were early. Noble Brian and I paid Murdo our green fees (£14 each) and I tied my ticket to my bag.

'There's an honesty box in winter,' said Murdo, 'for those that are honest.' I'd read that honesty boxes were pretty common on island courses. When there was no one around to take your money, you simply dropped it in the honesty box and teed off. That anyone would be so dishonest and cheap to play without paying, well, you'd want to catch them at it. It seemed such a mean thing to do, to deny income to a small golf club where probably every penny was a prisoner.

Murdo offered us a coffee and pointed to the board of club champions. His grandson's name was up there. Twice. He had a two handicap. My sister's name is on the board of ladies' champions at Hopeman. Dad was always telling Julieann that it was about time she got her name up there. And she'd come close a couple of times, before finally winning it a few months after he passed away. He didn't get to see his daughter's name up on that board. He would have been so proud of her. He was proud of her.

I asked Murdo if he played much golf himself. He said that his playing days were pretty much behind him. 'I'm getting too old for it, but I do miss it. I stand here watching people, thinking I could do better myself.'

I hoped Murdo wasn't going to watch me tee off.

Noble Brian and I started getting ready for our first round of island golf together. Murdo explained that the head greenkeeper was on holiday, but that his part-time colleague had been out on the course earlier. The greens were cut two or three times a week. Murdo pointed us in the direction of the first tee, which was beyond a little bridge over a burn.

We stood on the tee, taking in our surroundings. Behind us was a mountain that seemed to tower over the entire course. It was Glamaig, one of the Red Cuillin. Before us lay the fairway, a dry stone dyke down the left, the green in the distance. Beyond the green was the sea and the little island of Raasay, with its distinctive flat-topped hill called Dun Caan. 'Looks like it's been sanded off,' said Noble Brian. He took a couple of practice swings. 'I love this. A lumpy tee by the main road. Can you get any better, laddie?'

Noble Brian insisted I go first. I had to admit I felt pressure. We had enjoyed lots of rounds in the pub in the past, but had never played golf together. This had more to do with my lack of golfing action in recent years than anything else. I've known Noble Brian since my university days, having met him through my wife Clare who studied architecture with him in Aberdeen.

I was aware that he was a good golfer and I didn't want to be a bad golfer in front of him. I hadn't thought of it like this until now. I managed to get off a decent drive and felt better right away. Noble Brian stepped up and with a smooth and effortless swing which spoke of growing up in the golf country of Aberdeenshire smashed his ball miles past my own. It didn't take much to beat me for length on a golf course, but the wee man was evidently a big hitter.

What a mess I made of my second shot, trying to reach the green but lifting my head to Raasay. Meanwhile my playing partner was busy bemoaning a perceived design flaw in this opening hole. 'Why the hell would you build a bunker at the back of the green?' But Hopeman had bunkers behind greens. What exactly was wrong with a bunker at the back of the green? Obviously it was a no-no in Noble Brian's eyes. He calmed down to take his putt but fell short with his effort. 'Nae enough porridge,' he sighed.

I took out my dad's putter for the first time on the islands. I had a ten-foot putt from the edge of the green and there seemed to be a sizeable break on it. I chose my line and rolled the ball into the hole for my par. 'Ye cannae script that,' said Noble Brian. 'That putter obviously travels well.'

It did feel good in my hands. I'd played awkwardly with it at Hopeman, perhaps due to my hungover state or maybe because I hadn't yet got used to the idea of playing with my dad's putter. How was I supposed to feel? The putter was a big part of this adventure, but when I'd holed that putt there it had felt just like any other putter.

The second hole was a long par four along the shore, but I only had eyes for the quarry beyond the green. The red-faced man at the bus shelter in Kyle of Lochalsh had really built up this quarry. It did kind of spoil the view of the green. Nevertheless it was an impressive quarry, as quarries go.

After three shots, I was still 15 feet short of the green. I tend to struggle with long holes. Instead of chipping, I decided to putt in the spirit of my dad. It was an uphill struggle but I judged it well and tapped in for a bogey that felt like a par on such a long hole. If I was being honest, I was a touch disappointed that my long putt from off the green hadn't dropped. I was beginning to believe too much in the power of my dad's putter. As if, somehow, I could channel golfing magic from it. Which, of course, was a load of nonsense.

The third was a gorgeous par three, Glamaig providing a gobsmacking backdrop. 'A stunning wee hole,' said Noble Brian. I did it justice with a promising tee shot. 'Shot sir!' said Noble Brian as my ball flew suspiciously towards the pin. 'I hope there's whisky in the clubhouse!' cried my optimistic colleague. There was to be no outrageous hole-in-one, but I had given myself an excellent chance of a birdie. Noble Brian was also in the hunt. 'Let's get a pair of twos,' he suggested. We ended up looking like a pair of idiots with a pair of threes.

The round was going pretty good. It wasn't raining and there was no sign yet of the midges. This wasn't Skye at all. The course was fun, the views were fantastic and I was enjoying playing with Noble Brian. I'd very much expected it to be the case, his relaxed nature replicated on the golf course. Noble Brian was really a Scottish version of Riley. Both of them very good golfers but cheerful with it and full of encouragement. And I wasn't doing too badly. In fact, I was holding up quite well.

Mind you, I didn't take it very well when I landed in a bunker and, remembering I didn't have a sand wedge, asked Noble Brian if I could borrow his, and he said no. I asked him again.

'Brian, can I borrow your sand wedge?'

'I'm afraid not.'

'Why?'

'Because it's not within the spirit of the rules.'

'What rules?'

'You've got your clubs and I've got mine.'

'But I'm in the bunker.'

'Aye, I see that. You should have brought your sand wedge.'

'But you've got a sand wedge.'

'Aye, I know.'

This wasn't going anywhere. He was actually sticking to his guns on this. So my playing partner was relaxed and cheerful on the course and full of encouragement and he wouldn't let me use his sand wedge because it wasn't within the spirit of the rules. I grabbed my pitching wedge and got myself out of the bunker with that. Was he really not going to let me borrow his sand wedge at all over the coming days? You think you know a person. Then you invite them on an islands golf adventure and find out what they're really like. Unbelievable. After Skye and the Outer Hebrides, I'd be making sure I had a sand wedge in my bag.

What with it being only a 9-hole course, we were halfway

round before we knew it. As we approached one of the greens we saw what looked to be a dead cat, but on closer inspection turned out to be a fluffy black head cover someone had dropped. A little later, we caught up with its owner, the only other golfer out on the course. Noble Brian handed the man his head cover and the man thanked him and asked how we were getting on. 'Struggling,' said Noble Brian. 'Same here,' said the man.

I hadn't thought we were struggling. Maybe in Noble Brian's eyes it had been a struggle. I wondered if the man was struggling. It was quite possible he was faring OK. It's not the done thing to tell a stranger you're in blistering form. 'Me, mate? I'm on fire!' Or even that you're playing well. I'm not sure if it's a Scottish thing or a golf thing, but it seems far more natural to suggest that you're having a hard time and that the golfing gods are conspiring against you. It gives your fellow golfer the opportunity to show that they too are battling with the complexities of this infernal game and that we're all in it together.

We struggled on. Arriving at the seventh hole, an uphill par three, Noble Brian shook his head. 'What not to do in golf,' he said, gesturing towards the green. I didn't quite follow him. I was thinking about which club to select. 'What's this?' I asked, meaning yardage. 'The silliest hole in golf,' said Noble Brian. He really did have a problem with it. To my untrained eye, it looked fine. There was a tee, a green, it was a golf hole. Noble Brian pointed out that he couldn't see the surface of the green. 'Is that a problem?' I asked. Of course it was a problem. A raised green on an uphill par three broke one of the cardinal

rules of golf architecture. Noble Brian had taken a dim
view of this hole, before he'd even played it. With a heavy
heart, he teed up and dealt masterfully with the silliest
hole in golf by landing his ball on the heart of the green
and holing his birdie putt. Noble Brian, the Master of
Silliness.

The final hole ran parallel to the opening hole, hitting
back towards the clubhouse. On the other side of the dyke,
a group was walking down the first. One man had hooked
his shot over the dyke and his ball had come to a stop next
to the final tee, where Noble Brian and I were standing
now. We delayed our drives to let him play his shot.

The man nodded and got down to business, taking about
eight practice swings. He was wearing some expensive
looking golf gear and seemed to be taking this shot very
seriously indeed. We waited for him to pop the ball back
over the dyke, but he was too cute with it. The ball hit the
top of the dyke and bounced back. The man had another
go at it – after another eight practice swings – but this time
succeeded only in topping his ball a couple of feet. Getting
increasingly flustered, he had a third stab at it and thinned
the ball hard up against the dyke. Now he'd left himself with
an impossible shot. Noble Brian and I didn't know where
to look. The man looked like he was about to explode with
anger. He slammed his club back in his bag, grabbed his ball
and stomped off to join his playing partners.

Once Noble Brian had stopped laughing, he skied his
final drive into some savage looking rough. I asked what
he thought his chances were of finding his ball. 'Slim to
bugger all,' came the reply. Bugger all it proved to be.

One final outrage awaited Noble Brian, and that was the pot bunker in front of the final green. It's not that he put his ball in it. He didn't. No, it was the scale of the pot bunker that offended him. The golf architect paced its length to get the measure of it. One step (one Noble Brian step) and he'd reached the other end. The bunker, more a child's sandpit really, was about one yard wide and two yards deep. 'Possibly the world's smallest bunker,' said Noble Brian. Well, at least we'd both avoided it, even if my friend was standing in it, wondering what it was all about.

As soon as he was over it – and out of it – we putted out and shook hands. The Isle of Skye golf course, my second island golf course and Noble Brian's first, our debut round of golf together, done and dusted in an hour-and-a-half.

Back in the clubhouse, Murdo showed us the club's plans to extend the course to 18 holes. Noble Brian studied the drawings on the wall and I could tell by the look on his face that he didn't much like the look of them. 'I think it's a very ambitious project, I have to say,' he said. The proposed extension of the existing golf course involved having to cross the road and also appeared to require getting rid of the third hole, the pretty par three towards Glamaig that Noble Brian and I had enjoyed most of all. We wondered what was wrong with nine holes between the mountains and the sea.

Murdo offered us a lift into Portree, where Noble Brian and I needed to get to next. It would save us having to wait for the next bus and Murdo was shutting the clubhouse anyway. He had to go and meet his wife to take her shopping. 'She'll be chomping at the bit,' said Murdo.

Noble Brian and I waited in the car while Murdo locked up the clubhouse. Noble Brian had taken the front passenger seat and I noticed from the back that the front seatbelts were personalised. They said 'Murdo' and 'Margaret'. 'I'll be Margaret,' said Noble Brian, strapping on his seatbelt.

As Murdo drove to Portree he talked about life on Skye. He was originally from the Central Belt, but had lived on the island now for nearly three decades. He had worked in Portree, but had been retired ten years now, not counting his days at the golf course. 'Can't seem to get away from it,' said Murdo. 'I always say I will. It's good though. You meet a lot of people.'

We passed a busy looking campsite at the head of a loch. Murdo said the campsite was popular with climbers. He told us that he had once cycled round the island. Given that Skye is one of Scotland's largest and most varied islands, that must have been some bike run.

Murdo dropped us off in the main square in Portree. 'You're a gentleman,' said Noble Brian. Murdo waved and drove off to meet his wife for the shopping. With an hour until our bus, Noble Brian and I walked down to the harbour and had a fish supper. The best kind, fried-to-order. We scoffed our fish suppers by the water, then went and found a store in order to get some supplies in for the evening. Beer, crisps, the essentials basically.

With our golf bags, secondary bags and bags of shopping, we boarded the last bus of the day to the top of the island. The road north of Portree up the east side of the island is astonishing. Noble Brian and I sat back and enjoyed the journey as the bus travelled through a peculiar and incredible landscape. The weird pinnacle of the Old Man of Storr is a striking introduction to the geological bonanza of the Trotternish Ridge, a succession of fantastical rock formations that are the result of ancient landslips. I had never seen anything like it. So this was Skye.

The driver made his final stop, dropping us, his only remaining passengers, off by the side of the road, next to the most outlandish rock shapes of them all, the eerie Quiraing. Noble Brian and I stood with our bags, looking up at this dramatic and almost frightening phenomenon, then turned and walked across a cattle grid and down a lane towards the sea and the Dun Flodigarry Hostel, our base for the night.

As we walked, I sensed that something was not right. My bags. I wasn't carrying all of them. I had my golf clubs. I had my small backpack. What I didn't have was the bag of beer. I'd left it on the bus. What an idiot. So an early night was on the cards then. It wasn't as bad as the time I had gone camping in the mountains of Washington state, leaving the tent at a Seattle bus stop, but it was still careless.

The wonderful location of the hostel, looking out across the sea to the mainland, cheered me up a bit. The friendly warden at reception handed over our bed linen and informed us we'd be sharing our room with four French girls. Hmm, I thought, maybe they had beer. I said to the warden that I'd managed to leave a bag of beer on the bus and he pointed out that the hotel next door had a bar if we fancied a pint.

Ten minutes later (no sign of the French girls in our room) Noble Brian and I were in the hotel bar drinking the local beer at city prices. It wasn't much of a bar, more a bit of a bar in the corner of a room of mostly empty tables with one or two couples eating their dinner in silence. It seemed a joyless place for such an idyllic location, the hotel enjoying the same stunning views as the hostel. It didn't take us long to decide that our better option was being back at the hostel.

On the walk back, we stopped at the gate of a cottage and learned that it had once been the home of Flora MacDonald who featured in one of the most romantic episodes of Scottish history. It was Flora who brought the fugitive Bonnie Prince Charlie over the sea to Skye on a boat from Benbecula, the Prince disguised as Flora's Irish maid Betty Burke. The Prince, on the run from government troops after the defeat of the Jacobites at Culloden, parted with Flora in Portree and was ferried over to Raasay before escaping safely back to France.

When Flora's role in the Prince's escape became known, she was arrested and put in the Tower of London. After she was set free, Flora returned to Skye and married Allan MacDonald, a captain in the British Army. They lived together in this very cottage at Flodigarry, where five of their seven children were born. You can stay in the cottage, as it's now part of the hotel.

By the time Noble Brian and I got back to the room,

our French room-mates were asleep. We crept to our beds, not wishing to disturb them, and tried to show the same consideration early in the morning. But we failed miserably, tiptoeing out of the room with our golf clubs clanking.

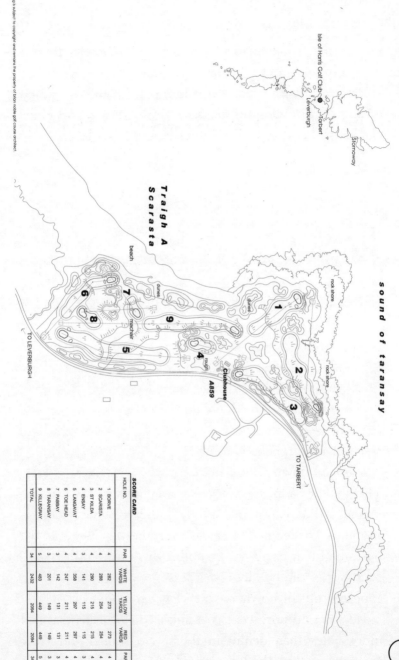

Isle of Harris Golf Club

Leverburgh

Tarbert

Stornoway

s o u n d   o f   t a r a n s a y

rock shore

rock shore

Traigh A
Scarasta

beach

dunes

dunes

machair

rough

Clubhouse

A859

1

2

3

4

5

6

7

8

9

TO LEVERBURGH←

TO TARBERT

SCORE CARD					
HOLE NO.	PAR	WHITE YARDS	YELLOW YARDS	RED YARDS	PAR
1 BORVE	4	282	273	273	4
2 SCARISTA	4	288	254	254	4
3 ST KILDA	4	290	215	215	4
4 ENSAY	3	141	115	115	3
5 LANGAVAT	4	358	297	297	4
6 TOE HEAD	4	247	211	211	4
7 PABBAY	3	142	131	131	3
8 TARANSAY	3	201	149	149	3
9 KILLEGRAY	5	483	449	449	5
TOTAL	34	2432	2094	2094	34

Chapter 3

A Mighty Wind – Harris

Noble Brian and I stood by the side of the road, squinting at the Quiraing in the rain. Those rocks looked even more ridiculous with a rainbow on top of them. Bleary-eyed and surrounded by bleating sheep, we waited for the first bus to Uig. Either it was late or it was running according to island time. What a miserable morning. Skye in all its glory, dreich beyond belief. Noble Brian looked like a water-logged haddock, though I didn't want to say. It was too early in the day for conversation. And besides, I may have resembled a drenched halibut.

I looked down to see my backpack lying in a puddle. That puddle hadn't been there a moment ago. My camera, phone, MP3 player and all the other electrical accoutrements I'd deemed necessary for the trip were at the bottom of that bag. Ach, they'd be fine. I moved the backpack out of the puddle just in case, as a wild-haired man appeared out of nowhere, carrying a toolbox.

He wore a fluorescent coat and a pair of jeans that had more holes than denim in them. No sooner did Holy Joe turn up than the bus arrived. He'd timed his walk to perfection. He must have known when the bus would get here. The benefit of local knowledge, as opposed to the cluelessness of two visiting golfers. Noble Brian and I squelched onto the bus behind Holy Joe who was as dry as a bone.

The bus driver looked familiar. It was the same bus driver who had dropped us off last night. The bag of beer! Was this why the bus was late? Had the driver drunk all our beer and slept in? He looked a bit red in the face, right enough. Unless he always looked red in the face. Had he looked red in the face last night? I couldn't remember. I examined his eyes for some sign of guilt, but could detect none. Deciding not to quiz him about the beer, I sat down like a good passenger. We were relying on this bus driver, whether he'd drunk our beer or not, to get us to the ferry on time.

The bus journeyed along the road, stopping regularly to pick up children going to school in Portree. A group of long-haired boys in blazers and heavy metal T-shirts sat across from me and continued their conversation. The topic was music and there seemed to be a lot of love on the bus for AC/DC and Black Sabbath (had these children been at school since the 1980s?) as well as a healthy hatred of lesser bands.

'That is the gayest of that particular genre,' said one boy, delivering a damning verdict on a band his friend had just mentioned. The subject switched from music to hair-styles as one boy's barnet was held up to ridicule.

'How can you look in the mirror in the morning and say "that's nice hair?"'

It seemed a cruel thing to say, but then teenagers say cruel things. At least the retort was good.

'How can you look in the mirror in the morning and say "that's a nice face?"'

Teenagers. They have all the answers – and there's always another one.

'Who'd look in the mirror in the morning and say "that's a nice face?"'

The mirror insults were interrupted by a boy with something else on his mind.

'Imagine if your hair had nerves and you got a haircut? Ouch.'

The boys were silent as they contemplated the far-out concept of having to deal with sensitive hair.

Noble Brian and I got up. It was our stop.

'Why would anyone want to get off at Uig?' wondered one of the boys aloud, snapping out of his hair reverie. It was a fair enough question.

The bus didn't actually drop us off in Uig. Instead we were deposited at the top of a hill looking down on Uig. We could see the ferry terminal – Uig doesn't amount to much more than a ferry terminal – but how the heck did we get down there?

'Are you looking for the pier?' shouted a woman, standing at her front door in her dressing gown. She must have looked out of her window and seen two forlorn figures with golf clubs. We cried back that we were looking for the pier and she shouted over directions.

Noble Brian and I followed a long and winding road

down the hill in the rain. After some time, we reached the bottom.

'Look how far we've walked!' said Noble Brian pointing back up to where the bus had dropped us off.

'At least it killed some time.'

'It's killing my feet,' moaned my hard done by colleague.

Noble Brian turned down my offer of a foot massage and we continued towards the ferry terminal. Passing a work yard, I was surprised to see, standing in front of a shed, the red-faced man from the bus shelter in Kyle of Lochalsh. I thought about giving him a wave and calling over to him that we had witnessed the quarry, but he looked annoyed to be standing in front of a shed in the rain, so I didn't.

Once in the Caledonian MacBrayne ferry office, after waiting our turn behind two German motorcyclists, we bought two tickets to Harris. 'You be dad,' said Noble Brian, suggesting I hold on to them.

I was in dire need of a coffee and went off in search of one. I found three cafes in Uig but all of them were closed. One was advertising GENUINE HOME BAKING AND REAL CHIPS. I'd have to try those real chips another time.

Noble Brian and I were first on the ferry, apart from the crew. And when those canteen shutters came up, we were first in line with our trays, asking for the full works of sausage, bacon, black pudding, egg, beans and tattie scone. Plus two slices of toast and coffee. The CalMac breakfast is the breakfast of champions. No morning ferry journey is complete without it. As I tucked into my fried concoction, saving the black pudding until last, I dreamt of all the other CalMac breakfasts I'd enjoy in the coming weeks. I'd be lucky to be able to swing a club by the end of it all.

Across the table, Noble Brian mopped up the last of his beans with his toast, then stretched out in his seat, letting it all sink in. The CalMac breakfast. It's worth catching the ferry just to experience it.

I must admit I'd been worried about the ferry to Harris, anxious that we might be in for a rough crossing, despite Uig to Tarbert being the shortest crossing there is to the Outer Hebrides. The thing was, I hadn't so much forgotten to bring my sea legs, I'd just never owned a pair. I might be the son of a fisherman, but I consider myself to be useless at dealing with waves. The one time I went on my dad's boat, as a youngster, I spent the entire trip clutching a bucket. Never again, I thought. Not that my dad ever wanted me to go to sea. He always preferred I did something else.

But I needn't have fretted about the journey to Harris. The sailing turned out to be remarkably smooth, the sea flat calm. Not only that but the rain had remained in Skye. Ahead of us was only blue sky and the clear outline of the Outer Hebrides.

Noble Brian and I stood on deck trying to work out which island was which. It was like being on a geography field trip without the teacher. The small island to the south, we figured, must be Barra. The next one up, smaller still, would be Eriskay. Then South Uist, Benbecula and North Uist (although it was difficult to tell where one ended and the next one began). Then Harris, where the ferry was heading for, with Lewis stretched out and eventually disappearing to the north.

I was excited at the prospect of golfing in the Outer Hebrides, excited about being in the Outer Hebrides. Any picture I'd ever seen of these islands, like the postcard of Barra at Franco's cafe at Central Station, showed them to be incredibly beautiful. Then there were the words Outer Hebrides themselves, suggestive of somewhere far away, requiring an effort to get to. These islands, also known as the Western Isles, existed on the edge of Europe, next stop America. They got their fair share of wind and rain, bearing the brunt of the Atlantic weather systems, but when the sun came out, so I'd heard, it was glorious and there was nowhere better and we were heading there right now.

It looked promising, but if you're Scottish you know to treat a bright outlook with a degree of caution, because you know all too well that everything could take a turn for the worse in a matter of minutes. You learn to take the rough with the smooth, and spend more time moaning about the former than celebrating the latter. For once though, I was going to relish the stunning moments and try not to grumble too much about the rest. We were going to the Outer Hebrides to play golf.

This ferry business was a breeze. It was as if the waves had been ironed out with the sea free of creases. But if the still water had a calming effect, the first proper sight of Harris was terrifying, a grim yet utterly memorable welcome to the Outer Hebrides. No sandy beaches here because the east face of Harris is barren beyond belief. A bleak rocky landscape that doesn't look like it belongs to this world. In fact, Stanley Kubrick had it filmed for *2001: A Space Odyssey*. For Harris, read Jupiter.

We were still getting over our surprise introduction to the Outer Hebrides when the ferry docked in Tarbert. We had an hour to spend in Harris' main village before catching the bus to the west side of the island where the golf course was. Because there was no way on earth you could have a golf course on the east coast of Harris. Your clubs would get mangled in no time.

Noble Brian and I bought coffees from a cafe next to the bus station and sat and drank them at a picnic bench. A cat sidled up to my golf clubs and then a man ran over and asked us where we were golfing. Harris, we told him. Plus a few other courses. The man looked flustered. Once he'd got his breath back, he explained his predicament.

He was in charge of a group of tourists, driving them round the Outer Hebrides in a minibus. He hadn't lost any of them. It was worse than that. Some of the group were keen golfers, but the golf aspect of their holiday was in jeopardy because one of them had lost the key to the roof box. The roof box containing the golf clubs. And now everyone, including the culprit, was hunting high and low for the missing key. What was otherwise a beautiful morning on Harris wasn't going according to plan.

'Don't leave your clubs lying about,' said the man. 'They might get half-inched if we can't get into this thing!'

I pictured Noble Brian and I being targeted by desperate tourists and having to fend them off with our clubs.

The man, clearly at the end of his tether, wished us a

good day's golf and ran off. As much as I sympathised with his situation, the sun was shining and I for one was looking forward to our first round of golf in the Outer Hebrides.

Noble Brian stood up.

'How tall are you?' I asked.

He sighed. 'Five foot four. On an extremely good day. With the right kind of wind.'

We left Tarbert behind, the bus climbing through a strange otherworld. There appeared to be no respite from the rockiness of Harris. But, after several miles of unremitting bleakness, the bus reached the top of a hill and an astonishing scene unfolded before our eyes. Our first glimpse of the west coast of Harris and one of the most fantastic beaches I'd ever seen. Luskentyre beach, a vast stretch of white sand met by turquoise waters. This was the Harris of my imagination and of magazine pictures and now I saw that it was true. Noble Brian and I looked at each other and understood this: that Harris is breathtakingly beautiful.

Several bends in the road later, we stepped off the bus and into a gale. Waiting for us by a gate was a bearded man in a cagoule, smiling and rolling a cigarette. 'You must be the architect and the writer!' he shouted over the wind. 'I'm Donald the greenkeeper!' The rest was lost as he led us through the gate onto the golf course.

I tried to take it all in. I'd never seen such a dramatic setting for a golf course. If the wind didn't take your breath away, the views did. Another striking white sand beach to the south, and dark mountains to the north. Fairways of rich machair tumbling down to the sea, machair being the

Gaelic word for that windsculpted terrain of seaside grass and dunes that's just so perfect for golf. This was some golf course and I hadn't even played it yet.

Donald led us towards the clubhouse, a long green shed tucked into the hill, not visible from the road. If hobbits played golf, they'd have such a clubhouse. Standing in front of it, tall and unhobbitlike, was Captain Hugh, his hand outstretched for a warm welcome. As with Donald, I warmed to him immediately. Captain Hugh pointed at the clubhouse, or the Bunker as he called it. 'We're going to extend it!' he yelled in the blustery conditions. 'We're going to have a wing coming out, you know! It's going to be changing quite a bit! Come in!'

We stepped inside, out of the wind. Sitting on a bench was Bill, one of the members. Bill smiled and we shook hands. He reminded me of my dad. Not so much a physical resemblance, though he was short, stocky and had a beard, all very much like my dad. More his nature. Bill looked delighted to be on a golf course and happy with life in general.

Captain Hugh suggested he and Bill make up a foursome with Noble Brian and myself. Donald would walk round with us. It sounded like a plan. I sensed this was going to be a heap of fun. They'd known we were coming and we'd tried to contact all the courses in advance, especially given the distances we were travelling. Here we had a fantastic welcome party and what looked to be an amazing golf course.

The only thing that worried me was the wind whistling outside the Bunker. The words in that golf book from Santa to the Sutherlands, *100 Golfing Tips*, came to my mind. 'Wind was invented to make the golfer's life a misery.'

We remained inside for a bit longer, sheltering from the elements and blethering about golf. Captain Hugh asked if we were planning on playing Askernish. Indeed we were. Askernish was the course on South Uist. It had been a nine-hole golf course of no real note until recently when it had emerged that Old Tom Morris, the legendary golfer and pioneering course designer, the founding father of the game, had laid out a golf course among the dunes at Askernish at the tail end of the 19th century. The original course had been abandoned decades ago, but now it had been brought back to life, a rediscovered masterpiece. Askernish had been getting some publicity and was said to be one of the most amazing and pure golf experiences you could possibly have. Noble Brian, the golf architect, was very excited about playing there.

'It's come out of nothing,' he said.

'A bit of a story,' grinned Donald, leaning against the wall.

'A bit fictional?' I asked.

'Well, let's just say they're making great progress. They'd cattle and tractors on the course, but they've found a resolution, come to an understanding. Just waiting for the land court to clarify. The course is still under crofting tenure.'

'We had the same problem here for a long time,' said Captain Hugh. 'The land belonged to the crofters and we had a golf course on it. This time of year, May, was common grazing. May was lambing and September was out as well because that's when they were fattening the lambs for the sales, so there was no play in those months. Of course, when you did play there was no rough or nothing. You didn't have to cut it. The best greenkeepers you could have, the sheep.'

'The course is owned now by the golf club. A deal was done 15 odd years ago. Up the hill behind the church was not in crofting, it belonged to the church. So the golf course bought that land and then the crofters moved from here. Did a swap. The church agreed to it. So that's how we managed to get this ground and there's no sheep or cattle.'

That was some of the history of the Isle of Harris Golf Club, but they were very much focused on the future.

'We've got this development money,' continued Captain Hugh, 'for equipment, sheds, clubhouse upgrade, fencing, just general.'

'I need to get new toys,' grinned Donald the green-keeper.

Captain Hugh nodded. 'We need the money to move the club on. We've reached a certain level and the course has got quite a high profile through various things. One being the location.'

'And another thing,' said Donald, 'being the committee's foresight. We've a lot of life members, and that basically paid for the place, didn't it?'

'Well, it helps,' said Captain Hugh. 'We have 700 life members. Life membership started off at £50 a head and everybody jumped on that as a Christmas present. Now it's up to £250, which is still ridiculously cheap. And the result of it is, we have life members all over the shop. And they've

been very kind to us. A cheque comes in now and then.
They know they've got a good deal! Life membership has
given us a high profile and given people a connection with
the club and we have a tournament for them every year.
They come over and play the day before our Open.'

'They're in for a shock this year,' laughed Donald who'd
been busy working on the course since his recent arrival
from Stornoway Golf Club in Lewis. 'I did 15 years in
Stornoway and came back here because I think this club
is going places. In 20 years' time, it's going to be totally
different.'

'I hope I'm here in 20 years' time,' smiled Captain
Hugh, 'but I don't think I'll be playing golf.'

'I'll be in the old folks' home or something,' chuckled
Bill. 'Zimmer frame!'

'Golf cart!' laughed Donald.

'Yes,' said Captain Hugh, getting back to the golf course.
'You'll start to see the definition on the fairways now.
Donald's had a cutting on the rough.'

'Knee deep,' said Donald.

'That's all the greenkeepers love,' said Bill, shaking his
head.

'I hate 300-yard drives,' said Donald, warming to a
theme. 'It's taking away. It's totally changed now because
of the golf balls and the drivers. Now they're all whacking
it.'

Noble Brian agreed with Donald. 'Club and ball technology have changed golf. When's the last time you actually saw the top guys shaping shots? All away up in the sky
and you just think ...'

'I remember watching golf in the 1980s,' said Donald, 'and you could see the flight of the ball in the air. Seve, guys like that. Having to shape their shot and fight their way round.'

'Everybody has this fascination, sadly, with the length of a golf course,' said Noble Brian. 'But it doesn't have to be long to be different.'

Captain Hugh asked Noble Brian how he got into golf course design.

'I was a civil architect,' said Noble Brian, 'and I was just sitting scunnered one day, putting buildings up that took for ever, and Edinburgh College of Art at the time did this golf architecture programme. It was backed by the European Institute of Golf Course Architects, so I did that course.'

And the rest, as they say, is history.

Noble Brian wanted to know how many regular members Harris had, besides the 700 life members from around the world.

'We've 80 regular members,' said Captain Hugh. 'Percentage wise, it's probably on a par with other courses.'

'And how much is regular membership?' asked Noble Brian.

'It's £80 per head.'

'£80 per head!' Noble Brian nearly fell off the bench. He was thinking of upping sticks and moving to Harris.

'You need to keep it affordable for people who are just starting,' said Donald.

As well as having attractive rates, at Harris they had a knack of coming up with fresh ideas, novel concepts that drew attention to the club, getting them in the papers.

Askernish wasn't the only Hebridean course able to drum up press interest.

'One thing that's raised the profile of the club,' said Captain Hugh, 'is the Harris tweed jacket. Our answer to the green jacket.'

'I burst out laughing when I heard that,' said Donald. 'I thought it was one of the best ideas.'

'I've only won the tweed hat so far!' said Bill, still jacketless.

'It made the national news,' said Captain Hugh. 'It was a great boost. It's exactly the kind of thing that we have to do here to keep our heads above water, think of innovative ways of heightening the profile of the club. Our Open championship went from about ten players to 80 with the publicity.'

Harris also had its Faldo connection. Nick Faldo has never won the Harris tweed jacket (though he's won the green version a few times) but he has played Harris. Faldo has said that, on a good day, Harris golf course is paradise.

'He came here to practise for the Open on a links course,' said Captain Hugh. 'That's the story.'

'That was about 1991,' recalled Donald. 'I was still a junior when he was here. The club was only going five or ten years. Then for somebody of that stature to come.'

Faldo left a signed £5 note. Each year the members compete for the Faldo Fiver.

The wind outside was still making a racket. I wondered if the course saw much action during the winter months.

'We have a winter league,' said Captain Hugh. 'We

trundle up on a Saturday morning, weather permitting.'

'That's a time to come up!' laughed Bill. 'Teeing off and you have to lean over just to stand still. Great fun!'

'The wind's quite strong a lot of the time,' said Captain Hugh. 'But you get days where it's absolutely glorious.'

'There's no better place to be when the sun's out,' said Donald.

I looked out the window. The sun was out. It was just a wee bit windy.

'Right,' said Captain Hugh, standing up. 'Will we go and play a few holes?'

We left the calm of the Bunker for the outside chaos.

'What do you think of the wind?' shouted Bill as we pushed towards the first tee.

I nodded. My legs were trembling. Either it was nerves or the wind was making me unsteady on my feet. Looking back, it was a combination of the two.

'I wouldn't go anywhere else!' shouted Captain Hugh, pointing towards the peaks of north Harris.

'Some days you could look at that all day,' smiled Donald.

I took in the mountains, then looked down the fairway to the frothing sea. I felt alive and giddy and wondered where my ball would end up. That depended on the wind and my ability to cope with it.

'It's a different experience every time!' yelled Bill. 'The wind can change this course totally!'

Wind is fine for surfing – and the surfing is great in the Outer Hebrides, especially off Lewis – but it can play havoc with your golf. Days without wind were rare in these parts. The weather perhaps isn't the Outer Hebrides' strong point and it has the capacity to change at any moment, so you grab those good moments while you can and are grateful for them. Was this a good moment? Well, the sun was still out.

I watched both Captain Hugh and Bill, seemingly unaffected by the wind, fire off big drives down the fairway. Clearly they'd done this before. Noble Brian had no trouble matching them, having battled with the wind growing up and golfing on the east coast. He had the game and the experience to deal with this.

It was my turn. As far as I was concerned, it was about hanging on in the initial stages of this round. I had trouble maintaining any sort of stance. Not being blown over was my main concern. Stay on your feet and hit it, I told myself. Remember you're Scottish – you can play in any weather. My heart was pounding. Somehow I got off a half-decent tee shot and even emerged at the other end with a bogey.

Harris in the wind carried real embarrassment potential. It was a Hebridean rollercoaster of a golf course, proper heart in the mouth stuff. The crumpled landscape was built for golf. On the second tee, out on a point overlooking the shore, I removed the head cover from my driver and almost lost it to the sea. I snatched it up and stuffed it in my bag. There was no point in complicating matters.

I then confronted the difficulty of the drive. You had to carry the rocks and find the narrow strip of fairway. Noble Brian mentioned Pebble Beach and, nearer to home, Machrihanish in Kintyre. All I saw was a tall order. I played it safe, aiming well right and not being greedy, seeking refuge in safety and accuracy, instead of courage and distance. And much to my relief, I found the fairway. Job done, I was able to relax for a moment. Captain Hugh and Bill both confronted the challenge of the shoreline head on and won. And Noble Brian outdrove everyone.

Waves broke on the rocks beneath the green as Noble Brian and Donald discussed the best spot for a bunker. Donald was tapping into Noble Brian's knowledge. Noble Brian was being the wise architect. It left me in peace to focus on my putt. I'd taken three shots on this short but tricky par four and was still just off the green. I called on my dad's putter to rescue me. I decided to be confident. No more cowering in the wind. With a sense of purpose, I drew back the putter and sent the ball on its way. It travelled ten feet, struck the pin and went in.

'Go on, Gary!' cried Bill. Captain Hugh cheered. My word, that felt good. How much would my dad have enjoyed being here on Harris, playing a round with Bill and Captain Hugh? I think Captain James would have had a great time.

I was one over par after two holes and this pleased me, given the trying circumstances and my shortcomings as a golfer. But I took one look at the next hole and thought about heading back to the Bunker. The third hole at Harris is the definition of an uphill struggle, the fairway rising for ever with no sight of the green. Wind against made it seem even more impossible. I scrambled a double bogey six, for which I was thankful.

'Tough hole today,' said Captain Hugh. I tried to imagine it ever being an easy hole. Perhaps if they turned the wind off. But it kept coming. Standing on the fourth tee I felt like I was in a wind tunnel. It was all I could do to stay on my feet. How I was going to stay on my feet and swing a golf club, I had no idea.

'There's a bit of a breeze here!' yelled Bill.

Noble Brian's hat flew off during his backswing. I ran down the hill after it. When I handed it back to Noble Brian he was laughing. Not because his hat had fallen off during his swing, but because he'd just hit a four iron 140 yards. And he had hit it well too. I have vague memories of my own drive and don't know how many shots it took me to get to the green. I holed a monster putt though. 'Still working,' said Noble Brian, nodding at my dad's putter in my hands. 'If you hole any 40-feet putts with it, it'll be a magic putter.'

This was like no other round of golf I'd ever experienced. It was hair-raising and exhilarating. When the wind wasn't pinning us back, we were covering the course at a considerable pace. Captain Hugh and Bill didn't hang around and it was up to Noble Brian and I to keep up. It's not like we were slowcoaches either. It was the great American golfer Walter Hagen who once said, 'Never hurry, never worry and always remember to smell the flowers along the way.' The Scotsman's version of that would be, 'Hurry. Worry. Never stop.'

Captain Hugh told me he used to be a PE teacher. I wasn't surprised and could imagine him putting his pupils through their paces. He'd been retired for nine years now and played golf once or twice a week.

After several holes of being blown about, the wind died down a little. Then, as if on cue, the sun – which had been absent for the past half-hour – broke out, lighting up the course and making everything look golden and even more stunning.

'Absolutely terrific,' beamed Bill. 'Brilliant.'

'It's an amazing place to be,' said Donald. 'It's special.'

They weren't talking it up either.

A huge black dog crossed the golf course. 'The Hound of the Baskervilles,' said Bill, who was really coming on to a game now. Once the hound had vanished, Bill struck another sweet iron shot.

'How the hell are you playing off 18?' demanded Donald.

'I'm playing for the jacket this year!' laughed Bill.

On the sixth green, I sank another long putt for my par.

'Dear God,' said Noble Brian. 'That putter's loving these Harris greens. Without it you'd be like He-Man before he turns into He-Man. You know, "I havenae the power!"'

'Aye, I've holed a few big ones today,' I laughed.

'The pressure's on now!'

I wasn't sure what he meant. I must have looked at him blankly.

'The match!' said Noble Brian.

It seemed that we weren't on the same wavelength.

'Me and you against Hugh and Bill!' said Noble Brian. 'You've just holed for a half!'

'Someone might have told me.'

'I just did. Wake up!'

I hadn't known this was a contest. It was news to me that we were competing against Captain Hugh and Bill. I'd thought we were just playing with them, but the competitive aspect of the round had been established somewhere between the Bunker and the first tee. I either hadn't heard or hadn't been listening. I blamed it on the wind. It was probably just as well I'd been golfing in ignorance because I'd have crumbled by now had I known this was a match.

Having said that, I coped pretty well with the next hole, a par three. One OK seven iron, one tidy chip and one short putt later, I'd bagged another par and ensured another half for my team.

'We'll have to review this man's handicap,' said Captain Hugh.

'Maybe you could award me one?' I suggested.

The sun went away again and the sky darkened. There was a definite change in the air. Captain Hugh shouted for us to take cover and dived behind his golf trolley. Donald kept on rolling his cigarette and Bill laughed as an angry Hebridean sky fired hailstones at us. Noble Brian and I dithered about, wondering what we should do, until there was nothing for us to do, since the hailstones had ceased as suddenly as they'd started. The clouds cleared and the sun said hello again.

I joined in with Bill's laughter. Well, you had to, hadn't you? There was no point in cursing extreme weather. Better to grin and bear it. How on earth had we ended up here, trying to play a fiendishly difficult game in slapstick conditions? Oh right, it was my idea.

'It can be idyllic some days,' said Captain Hugh, who had got back on his feet, dusted himself down and played his next shot. 'In the evening the wind usually drops and it's calm. The worst is heavy rain and wind. In the winter the ninth hole is just covered in sand. It's like one big bunker. Desert golf! We get to tee up.'

Bill laughed at the mention of desert golf, but the fact was he lived here and had the opportunity to play this amazing golf course anytime. Bill was originally from Central Scotland. Having been made redundant in the 1980s, he'd come to Harris for a break. The holiday turned into something more. 'I spoke to the man at the caravan park and he offered me a long let on a caravan. Fifty quid a week. I took it. Went back and moved everything up here.' Bill had been 27 years on the island with his family. 'Another three and I'll be a local!'

Donald had been back here five weeks since leaving his previous job in Stornoway. He kept on referring to the plan in his head. His vision for the golf course. He ran his ideas past Noble Brian who was only too happy to offer advice regarding course matters. The pair of them spent much of the round pointing around the course. But when you listened to Donald it wasn't just the golf course, because here was a man enthralled by Harris in general.

'Harris got me in the end,' he said, looking out to sea. 'Bitten by the bug. It's great, magical. Harris is a different place than you'll ever find. It's so friendly. There's hardly a vehicle passes that's local that doesn't wave. You don't get treated as an incomer either if you move here.'

'Once you've done 30 years!' laughed Bill.

Captain Hugh and Bill beat us in the end, but Noble Brian and I had won by coming here. It had been a short nine holes, but what the course lacked in length it made up for in difficulty. A golf hole didn't have to be long to

be difficult. There hadn't been an easy hole out there,
certainly not with the wind blowing. The challenge had
more than equalled the setting. I couldn't have gone
another nine holes, done this all over again, but I was
thrilled with the nine I had experienced. It had been an
immensely enjoyable (if gusty) round of golf on the wild
and wonderful west coast of Harris. And we'd shared it
with good people.

Back in the calm of the Bunker, Captain Hugh told us
about some surprise visitors they'd once had. 'Wealthy
Italian tourists, business people, one of them a billionaire. They were on a ship nearby and the ship's captain
phoned up to enquire about a round. We offered a minibus,
but they turned up in helicopters. Landed on the course.
They played their round and the wife of one of them got
soaking wet. We found her an old smelly pair of trousers
through the back and she put them on and they left in
the helicopters. One helicopter came back later with the
trousers washed and pressed. The billionaire is a life
member.'

Harris golf course had made a lasting impression on
someone who had everything. It wasn't surprising. It must
be one of the most beautiful golf courses in the world,
and one of the most welcoming. Two reasons to make the
effort. And a life membership for less money than a lot
of clubs charge for a year is another good reason to keep
coming back.

Captain Hugh offered us a lift down to Leverburgh, at
the bottom of the island, from where we were supposed
to be catching the teatime ferry over to North Uist. Captain

Hugh said that there was a pub at the pier at Leverburgh and suggested he join us for one before returning to the golf course. 'Weekly medal tonight at half-six!'

We said goodbye to Donald, leaving him with his golf course and his plans, and Noble Brian and I got in the back of Captain Hugh's campervan, our bags by our feet and my head resting on what appeared to be a cocktail cabinet. 'Keep an eye on the whisky!' said Captain Hugh to Bill who had strapped himself into the front passenger seat.

As we headed down the coast towards Leverburgh, Captain Hugh told us about some of the places he and his wife had been in the campervan. Portugal, Ireland, going on trips for weeks at a time. It all sounded wonderful. I wondered if, on his travels, he'd come across anywhere more beautiful than Harris.

At one point Captain Hugh stopped at Bill's house. 'Drop you off here Bill and pick you up for the medal?'

Bill wasn't having any of it. 'No, no.' He was up for the pub with us!

The Anchorage pub was handily placed. You could drink up and be on the ferry in a matter of seconds. We ordered beers and golf was the initial topic of conversation, or more precisely fussy golf club rules, specifically dress codes. Like having to turn up in a collar or risk being thrown off the course.

'It's these archaic rules that stop people from playing,' said Noble Brian who was on the Guinness. 'Tiger Woods doesn't wear a collar.'

Captain Hugh mentioned the relaxed dress code at

another island club, whose captain had told him, 'As long as your bollocks aren't hanging out you're all right.'

Having sorted out dress codes in golf clubs, we moved on to lobsters, naturally.

'Did you hear about the lobster that was caught the other day?' asked Bill. 'They couldn't fit it in a box. They had to put it on a lead and walk it to Stornoway.'

Captain Hugh chipped in with his own lobster tale. It was a big one too.

'Huge lobster,' he said, his hands wide apart. 'The guy caught it, left it on the boat and forgot about it. And when he came back the next day ...'

'It was gone?' I asked, my head swimming with beer and lobsters.

'Aye,' said Captain Hugh. 'The boat had vanished. Lobster ate the boat.'

I half choked on my pint. This was like my dad and the One o'Clock Gang. Natural storytellers with a sense of the absurd. Captain Hugh and Bill were as good company in the pub as they had been on the golf course.

Too soon, Noble Brian and I were on the ferry. As the ferry doors were closing, the wrong announcement was made over the speakers. 'Welcome to Harris.' I wished it was so, but we were just leaving. We'd not been long on the island, but what a time we'd had. You could say it had been a whirlwind trip.

Sollas Golf Course,
Middlequarter, North Uist
Route Plan of the 9 hole 'ghost' golf course

G

Traigh Iar /
Vallay Strands

beach

beach

dunes

dunes

dunes

dunes

crofting land

crofting land

crofting land

crofting land

dunes

dunes

dunes

TO A865 &
TO MIDDLEQUARTER

Sollas Golf Course
Bennecroy
Lochmaddy

SCORE CARD

HOLE NO.	PAR	YARDS
1	4	253
2	4	339
3	3	211
4	4	240
5	3	88
6	3	171
7	4	407
8	3	163
9	3	189
TOTAL	31	2061

Chapter 4

No Solace at Sollas
– North Uist

We must have spent all of five minutes on the tiny island of Berneray, where the ferry arrives after crossing the Sound of Harris. Berneray is one of Prince Charles' favourite islands. It's where he learned all about crofting, the Prince dipping sheep and picking tatties. We'd barely time to get our bags off the ferry and onto the waiting bus, which carried us over the causeway to North Uist.

Our bus driver Catherine was cheery but perplexed by the weather they'd been experiencing lately. It had been more barmy than normal on North Uist. 'There's something going on,' said Catherine, 'when you turn up in a T-shirt and sunglasses and your passengers are wearing raincoats.'

She hoped we'd have decent weather for our golf tomorrow. We were playing a round on Benbecula in the afternoon, but first, in the morning, we were going to play North Uist's nine-hole course. It wasn't marked on my golf map of Scotland, but I'd learned of its existence while carrying out my pre-trip Internet research. I'd figured that since we would be passing through North Uist anyway, we might as well check out the golf course.

From what I'd gathered, the course was maintained by a bunch of volunteers with permission from local crofters to use the land. It sounded basic, but nevertheless intriguing and I was keen to try it out. I hadn't been able to get hold of a contact number and although I'd discovered an e-mail address I had so far received no reply.

Therefore I was somewhat reassured by the fact that Catherine knew of the golf course. 'My dad plays golf,' she said. 'He never gets any better, but he loves playing!' She kindly offered to get more information on the course from her dad and pass it on to her colleague who'd be driving the morning bus that went round the island. He'd get us near the golf course. Catherine would also include bus details for us getting to Benbecula in the afternoon. She was a real star.

Catherine dropped us off in Lochmaddy at the Uist Outdoor Centre where Noble Brian and I were spending the night in one of their bunk rooms. The centre offered courses in sea kayaking, scuba diving and other non-golf-related activities. There were a couple of guests milling about the centre. With no one at reception, we helped ourselves to sheets and pillows from the linen cupboard and grabbed a room before heading out to see if there was anywhere in Lochmaddy serving dinner.

We didn't have to look far. Lochmaddy's newest hotel, Tigh Dearg, was yards from the centre and being bright red you couldn't miss it. *Tigh Dearg* means 'red house' in Gaelic. We entered an upmarket bar-restaurant that could have been in Glasgow.

Nearing the end of a long day that had started on Skye

with a bus journey, and was followed by the ferry to Harris, a bus to the golf course and the windiest round ever, an impromptu session in a pub and another ferry and another bus, Noble Brian and I decided to push the boat out, treating ourselves to scallops and chips and a bottle of wine. The bunk room in the outdoor centre that night was as good as a room in a five-star hotel, with both of us sleeping the deepest of sleeps.

There was no one around to take our money in the morning, so we popped it through the letterbox at reception, as instructed. Golf bags and other bags over our shoulders, we went in search of a coffee and got as far as Tigh Dearg. The man who served us asked where we were golfing. Sollas, I told him. That's where the course was on North Uist. The man smiled and described the course as rustic. 'You're in for a tough day,' he added. Oh well.

Noble Brian and I left the hotel and waited for the bus in the rain. A white van splashed by, with the words 'Scottish Water Emergency Hotline' written on the side of it. The rain became lighter as the man who'd served us in the hotel whizzed past on a bike. 'It'll dry up now!' he cried. 'That's the good news!'

'A mobile weather forecast,' marvelled Noble Brian.

Eventually the bus arrived. We paid the driver and he handed over a brown A4 envelope. We sat down and opened it. It contained a full dossier on the golf course, as promised by Catherine. There were directions on how to get to it once the bus dropped us off, and a basic hand-drawn map, with the note, 'Course is re-designed every few years

due to ploughing. Not sure what the present state is!' I
didn't like the look of that exclamation mark.

We weren't long on the bus. Before we knew it we were
being dropped off in the middle of North Uist, otherwise
known as the middle of nowhere. In every direction there
were fields, and a few scattered houses. I consulted the
dossier for how to get to the golf course:

HOW TO GET THERE

Walk down from Middlequarter junction on sandy track.
You will reach T-junction.

Take the track to left for first tee.

Well, there was a track fitting the description of a sandy
track so we set off down it, not so much carrying our bags
as wearing them. We'd grown used to them, but they still
weighed a bit. After walking maybe half a mile, we came
to the end of the sandy track. According to the dossier,
we now needed to turn left. So we did, and we walked
on a bit, and on a bit further, turned back, walked a little
more and stopped.

No sign of a golf course. Just a ploughed up field with
rusting pieces of farm machinery. I fished from the envelope the hand-drawn map of the course.

First tee, first hole 252 yards.

We scanned the field for any sign of a golf hole. A flag,
a tee, something. Nothing. I checked the course layout
again. It was a short course, plenty of par threes, one of
them just 88 yards. On paper, the course measured 2,061
yards in total. Except that there was no course. Clearly
there wasn't. It was just a ploughed up field in North Uist
with two golfers standing in it.

The rain started to fall. Noble Brian put up his brolly and we huddled under it. Of course, I hadn't thought about bringing a brolly to the Outer Hebrides. I must have been banking on days of uninterrupted sunshine. I offered to hold the brolly for a bit, but Noble Brian said it was OK. We both sighed at the same time. We stared out across this churned up field, trying to imagine what it would look like with some golf holes. I considered teeing up a ball and hitting it, but I couldn't be bothered. It was too wet and muddy. The game was a bogey.

The birds were giggling at us, the cows in the next field were laughing and the sheep over there were in stitches. These creatures knew how ridiculous we looked, standing in a muddy field next to broken machinery, a brolly between us and our golf clubs at our feet. And the people in the distant farmhouses were looking at us through binoculars and calling their friends and saying 'you'll never guess what?' And now everyone on North Uist knew about the two tourists who'd turned up in a field at nine in the morning looking for a game of golf.

Maybe they were all in on it. Catherine, her dad, Mobile Weather Forecast Man, the bus driver who'd dropped us off here. The dossier was a fake and that website I'd been on, the one that described a golf course on North Uist, was a spoof. What a masterful set up. Trying to quell my growing paranoia, I went back to the dossier for information on the next bus out of here.

CONNECTION TO BENBECULA

Walk back to Middlequarter junction to connect with Royal Mail Postbus at 11:15. This will take you to Clachan.

Connect on to DA Travel at 12:20, which will take you to Benbecula Golf Course.

So, two hours until we got picked up. In the meantime, we could try our hand at some ploughing.

Noble Brian remembered that we'd passed a small store, shortly before the bus had dropped us off.

'How long before?' I asked.

'Ach, maybe a mile or two.'

Our options seemed to be to hang about the field for the next hour or two, or walk to the store and see what entertainment we could find there. The lure of the store, with its food and beverages and warmth, was strong. We started back up the sandy track, weighed down by our golf bags, small bags and the disappointment of not having found a golf course. I also had to stoop to remain under the brolly because Noble Brian was holding it. We could have swapped round and had me holding the brolly, but we didn't want to make things easier. No, we wanted it all to be difficult.

The one or two miles to the store felt more like five miles but at least it passed the time. And the rain had softened to drizzle. The store turned out to be a small Co-op, with as many trolleys parked outside as you'd find outside a large town supermarket. We didn't bother with a trolley, though in hindsight we could have put our golf bags in it. We walked the couple of aisles trying not to knock any items off the shelves with those golf bags. Grabbing some bread, cheese, ham and some soft drinks, we moved towards the till. There wasn't much of a queue.

I said to the cashier that we'd been looking for the golf

course but hadn't been able to find it. She didn't seem to know too much about the course, but her colleague sweeping the floor did.

'The golf course is in a bad way,' said the young boy. 'Some of the flags are out.'

Well, that was one way of describing it.

Noble Brian and I took our purchased items and went across the road to the handily placed bus shelter for a makeshift picnic. I looked at my watch. Ten o'clock. Could we kill an hour in the bus shelter? Noble Brian took a bite of his carefully constructed ham and cheese sandwich and began tackling a newspaper crossword.

'13 across … five letters … '

'Camel,' I suggested.

The drizzle had petered out. Still, I found myself shivering from the efforts of our fruitless morning as I listened to my chattering teeth. To make matters worse, a bunch of midges had turned up in the bus shelter. Not interested in catching the bus, they just wanted to get at my ears and neck. What a day we were having. We might have just been denied a round of golf due to the lack of a golf course, but the prospect of an afternoon round on Benbecula was not something I was relishing. All I wanted was a hot bath and an afternoon nap.

Noble Brian gave up on his crossword and took the rest of his sandwich across the road to a distinctive dyke shaped in a circle. The dyke had a gate, which Noble Brian opened and closed behind him. He was now enclosed in a stone pen and appeared to be reading a plaque while munching on his sandwich. It felt slightly odd, him over there in his stone pen and me standing in the bus shelter, so I went over and joined him, hoping the midges wouldn't follow me.

I stood with Noble Brian in what was called the Commemorative and Picnic Area. The plaque told of the sad story of Sollas, the settlement we'd come to in the hope of finding a golf course.

Back in the early 19th century, many people locally worked in the booming kelp industry. Lord Macdonald of Sleat derived a large portion of the income of his estate from the harvesting of this thick seaweed, which was used for glass and gunpowder among other things. But by the late 1840s, the demand for kelp had fallen and the tenants of Sollas and other neighbouring settlements were finding it difficult to pay their rents. In 1849, police were called over from the mainland to evict the crofters. Arrests were made and the communities were cleared, more than 600 people in all forced from their homes, many ending up abroad.

This was a memorial to 19th-century feudal oppression, a reminder of the brutal clearances and of displaced islanders scattered across the world. We learned from the plaque, wet with raindrops, that all ten crofts in Sollas today, except one, were occupied by descendants of the original crofters.

Until we'd read this, all I'd recognised were some fields and the occasional house, but there had been much heartache here. Sollas. It even sounded a sad place. We'd come here to find a golf course that wasn't there, but it was no great hardship. All we were required to do was wait for the next bus and we'd be gone.

When it arrived, it was our first post-bus on the islands, the driver having the additional duty of dropping off and picking up mail as well as passengers. The only other passenger on the post-bus besides ourselves was a lovely elderly woman. We told her about our doomed attempt to play the golf course.

'But there isn't a golf course on North Uist,' she said.

If only we'd met her earlier. Hopefully there would be a golf course on Benbecula.

Benbecula Golf Club

Route Plan of the 9 hole golf course

G n

benbecula airport runway

TO BALVINACH BENBECULA AIRPORT

TO NORTH UIST (A865) →

B892

airstrip taxi way

pond

telecomms

rough grasses

rough grasses

rough grasses

rough grasses

Clubhouse

fence

fence

fence

fence

fence

fence

1
2
3
4
5
6
7
8
9

CONTEXT PLAN

ATLANTIC OCEAN

BENBECULA AIRPORT

GOLF COURSE

beach

dunes

SCORE CARD		
HOLE NO.	PAR	WHITE YARDS
1 THE FENCE	3	134
2 LONG	4	390
3 SUNAMI	4	323
4 TOWER VIEW	3	162
5 AIR AIS	3	180
6 RANSOMES	4	295
7 CNOC ROLUM	3	179
8 CURRACAG	4	312
9 AN TOM	3	214
TOTAL	31	2189

Chapter 5

Drying out at the Airfield – Benbecula

Arriving on Benbecula is like arriving in Venice. No? Towards the end of the train journey to Venice, the land disappears and all that is left, it seems, are the tracks across the water, with Venice before you. Crossing the causeway to Benbecula on the bus, with sea on either side, reminded me of the train journey to Venice. It's just that instead of making for St Mark's Square, we were going to Benbecula Golf Club.

Straight away, Benbecula looked greener and brighter than North Uist, which had mostly seemed brown and melancholy. A marked improvement in the weather could only partly account for the transformation.

North Uist is small, but Benbecula is tiny. It's a blink-and-you'll-miss-it kind of island, four miles long and as flat as a pancake that's been stamped on. You can see for miles in Benbecula – roughly four miles. You wouldn't want to be agoraphobic living here.

Not long after we'd crossed the causeway and just short of Balivanich, Benbecula's main town, the bus dropped us off by the golf course. This one existed, no doubt about it. There were the telltale signs of yellow flags fluttering in the breeze.

Noble Brian and I walked over a cattle grid and followed a wide tarmac path towards a distant building that we figured was the clubhouse. It quickly dawned on us that the path on which we were walking was an old runway or a taxiway. The present runway, with a plane coming in to land, was next to the golf course, on the other side of a perimeter fence. Noble Brian taxied in front of me before coming to a stop next to the building we'd thought was the clubhouse but now that we were here didn't look much like one. Though Archie, who was standing out front waiting for us (we'd said early afternoon or thereabouts), was able to confirm it was the clubhouse.

'It's an old generator building belonging to the RAF,' he explained. 'We managed to lay our hands on it a couple of years ago after our old clubhouse was blown away. We lost half of it one night. The damage was quite something.'

Benbecula is an island with a long-held military presence. An RAF base had been established on this site during the Second World War. Then, in the late 1950s, an Army base was built at Balivanich to serve as headquarters for the missile range on South Uist. Nowadays the airport deals largely with commercial flights, while the number of military personnel on the island has reduced in recent years, causing extra concerns for the local economy.

I looked out across a golf course of flat grassland. It was the most rudimentary course we'd yet encountered, if you didn't count Sollas. But I was still tired from our long morning of hanging around in the rain on North Uist so my first response to Benbecula golf course was 'this'll do me'.

'It's very basic,' said Archie. 'It's an ideal course for starting golf. Until the wind gets up – then it really is enjoyable! And the wind does really whip up here. Some of it's ridiculous when it's coming in off the sea. America next stop – we get all their wind. Makes it quite interesting.'

For the time being it was just a light wind, which was enough for me. I really didn't fancy being blown about another island golf course after Harris.

Archie's car was parked under an interesting canopy, fishing nets hanging off either side of the clubhouse. 'Everything's quite rough and ready,' said Archie, explaining that the salmon nets that protected cars from stray golf balls were from the local fish farm. 'They throw them away after a period of time. They're absolutely ideal.'

'We've got a place out the back for the machinery,' said Archie, pointing behind the clubhouse. 'Full of starlings. Bloody birds. All the machinery's white. We go in there to get a machine and go "oh no". I spend most of my time down here cutting the grass. I normally play four or five holes at lunchtime. I love it here. It's too nice to miss. In the summer it's the best place in the world. I've been all over the place and there's nothing like it. The peace, absolute peace.'

Archie loved Benbecula like Donald loved Harris.

'I first came here in 1963,' said Archie, who was English. 'I was in the Forces. I was backwards and forwards and I managed to talk them into sending me back up twice, because I got married up here in 1964 and we always wanted to come back. I managed to wriggle my way into two more three-year stints.'

Eventually he was able to turn it into something more permanent. Archie took us into the clubhouse where calendars and fixture lists filled the walls and tea bags and cups sat on a counter. We sat down and Archie told us a bit about the history of golf on Benbecula. It all began back in the 1960s, when visiting American troops decided they fancied a few holes of golf, so they built them.

'The Americans were the big units back then,' said Archie. 'You had two or three thousand flying in and they decided they were going to play golf. And they said, "Right, we're doing a five-hole golf course in the middle of the runway." Which they did. Only five holes, but nevertheless it was very enjoyable. And if planes were landing, you had to pick up your ball and get off. That's how the golf started here. Then the airport went to civil air and the course was gone.'

But golf would come back to Benbecula, as Archie explained to us.

'In 1984, a guy was posted in. A Regimental Sergeant Major by the name of John Ransome. He was a good golfer – loved his golf – and at that time in the Forces, if you could prove that more than ten people in the unit were interested in golf, or any other sport, then they would contribute money towards it. Being a Regimental Sergeant Major, in about six months he had money to develop the area. He decided to fit a course around the football pitch that was there. A few of us got together and planned it. I didn't play golf, but I enjoyed cutting and looking after the ground. They just told me where to cut and I cut.'

And Archie had been cutting every since. That the club had kept going, with less military personnel around, was down to the combined efforts of a dedicated few. 'It's all voluntary,' said Archie. 'Thursday night is ground maintenance night. I'll lay all the rakes out and hopefully someone will come and grab one and take their turn.'

The club had a few dozen members. 'Not bad for the catchment area,' said Archie. 'The population is getting smaller and smaller, which is detrimental to the island, but, on the other hand, in the summer we've got a lot more visitors now. Especially since the ferry prices were reduced. It's increased traffic, improved tourism tremendously. Hopefully they'll all come down here with a tenner!'

It was time for Noble Brian and I to hand over our tenners. Archie showed us the honesty box outside and we deposited our money. Archie then had to go and pick up his wife and drive her to work. The course was ours. The clubhouse was ours. Archie was leaving it open for us so we could store our extra bags there. Where in the world would visitors be entrusted with a clubhouse? Even if it was an old RAF generator building. As Archie got into his car, he asked us which other courses we'd been playing. We didn't mention the North Uist debacle, but we told him about our epic round on Harris.

'Harris?' grinned Archie. 'The first time I went over I wondered why everyone I was with was carrying extra bags. I just had my trolley. Well, it poured down from the moment we got there, and with the wind as well I was

absolutely saturated. It was something else. We only played
about four holes! It was that bad we had to abandon our
round. So we got in the car and they took us right down
to the pub at the end of the pier.'

'The Anchorage!' I said.

'That's the one. And we were there till nine o'clock at
night when the ferry decided to sail. I had the same pair
of jeans on and I sat on a radiator for a couple of hours.
Everyone else was as dry as a bone. They'd all been there,
done it before. I don't think I even had a towel. But that's
typical Harris. I just couldn't get over it. The guys are
really lovely people. You playing Askernish?'

'Tomorrow,' said Noble Brian, who couldn't wait to
play Askernish.

'Hope you have strong legs!' said Archie. 'It's a long,
long way. A bit too much for me. It will be lovely once
it's done.'

Archie drove off down the old runway and left us with
Benbecula Golf Club. We walked under the salmon nets
to the first tee.

Benbecula's opening hole is called the Fence. The fence
runs down the right side of the fairway. Luckily there was
a field beyond the fence and not the runway because Noble
Brian shanked his tee shot over the fence – and then some.
'Good work,' I said. The most remarkable thing was that
from his field of dreams Noble Brian made the green. As
rescue shots go, it was a cracker. I didn't play the hole
very well at all, although I at least kept my ball on the
course. Quite frankly, the pair of us were exhausted from
our golfless morning on North Uist. All that trudging

about in the rain had made us dog-tired. My bones ached, and despite the fact the sun was shining, I just couldn't get warmed up at all.

The second hole ran parallel to the runway. My playing partner didn't want to be shanking this tee shot over this particular fence, or he'd be needing permission from air traffic control to retrieve his ball, and they weren't going to give it to him. A sign on the airport perimeter fence carried a warning to the effect of 'don't go on the runway'. We weren't really thinking about going on the runway. We'd had a hard enough day as it was. Noble Brian hit another poor drive, but at least he had access to his ball for his second shot. My effort from the tee wasn't any better.

Noble Brian sighed. 'I left my game in Harris.' I'd no idea where mine was. When I swung my club, it felt weird, like the swing wasn't my own. I smelled defeat on this golf course and the saltiness off the Atlantic, hidden behind dunes after the runway. Between the second green and the third tee we passed a derelict building whose walls were half torn off. This was the former clubhouse. We peered in and saw a battered armchair amid the debris.

The main feature of Benbecula's third hole was the old runway. It ran to the right of the fairway. Noble Brian sliced another tee shot, his ball hitting the tarmac and bouncing 40 feet in the air. My own woeful effort trickled to a stop on the runway. I opted not to attempt that second shot because I valued my clubs too much.

Planes took off, but my game didn't. We struggled on, the nine holes feeling more like 18. We saw that Archie was back, out cutting the course. You couldn't keep him away from this place. A path cut across the eighth fairway and with the clubhouse in the background I was reminded of the 18th hole at the Old Course at St Andrews. I mentioned this to Noble Brian, suggesting that all that was missing was the Swilcan Burn and bridge. Noble Brian suggested that I was delirious. Still, the eighth turned out to be our favourite hole on the course. I holed an unlikely putt from off the green. Holing any putt here was an achievement, given that the greens hosted so many things, including daisies, mushrooms and animal droppings. It all added to the rustic charm of the place.

Noble Brian meanwhile had notched three pars in a row and had rediscovered his form. I told him to hold on to it, that he didn't want to be turning all crap again.

I played a memorable final tee shot, an absolutely horrible slice with my ball trampolining off the tarmac and landing at the wrong side of the clubhouse. The bounce on the hard surface had added a good 50 yards to my drive, getting me pin high on a par four. The only problem was I couldn't see the green for the clubhouse. I could have tried to hit over the clubhouse with the salmon net protecting Archie's car, but I didn't imagine that such a shot could possibly come off in my incapable hands. So I picked up my ball and dropped it somewhere more sensible and within sight of the pin. I pitched onto the putting surface, my ball coming to a stop next to a bird's egg. I moved my ball again and putted out as another plane was taking off. Benbecula had been a singular golfing experience, which was exactly what we were after.

We fetched our other bags from the clubhouse. Archie was out on his grass cutter at the far end of the course. We left him to it and walked back down the tarmac to the main road.

'All that's eccentric about Britain,' said Noble Brian, meaning Archie and not us. 'This golf course is an example of the sheer bloody-mindedness of people getting things done, albeit it was the Americans who started it.'

I looked over again at Archie. He had found his spot. It was a particular kind of beauty that he couldn't be parted from. Although I'd had a tiring time on the course, a reaction to a muddled morning, I understood the attraction of this place with its incredibly flat and lush terrain and a huge blue sky carrying a breeze off the sea.

Noble Brian and I walked with our bags on the edge of the road in the direction of Balivanich where we needed to catch our next bus that would take us over another causeway to South Uist. It was only about a mile's walk at most into Balvanich. Every time a car came towards us, we moved on to the grass verge. We had to do it quite a lot. It must have been rush hour in Benbecula, the school run or something. At one point we passed a riding school, with just a pony in the field.

'Fancy a go?' I asked Noble Brian.

'It would only accentuate my shortness,' he replied.

Now all I wanted was to see Noble Brian riding a pony.

Balivanich happens to be the second biggest town in the Outer Hebrides after Stornoway. It didn't seem very big, but it did have a cash machine. We topped up and waited on the bus. Soon we were on our way in what was a minibus, the driver stopping at a shop at one point to pick up something for her tea. Noble Brian and I got out too and grabbed a couple of soft drinks from the fridge. Climbing back into the minibus, Noble Brian managed to bang his head on the top of the door. He then did the same thing offloading his clubs when we reached Lochboisdale, our final destination. Banging your head twice on the top of a minibus is a fair achievement, especially for a man of Noble Brian's stature.

We were planning on spending the night in Lochboisdale, South Uist's biggest village, though we hadn't got round to booking anywhere. It was six o'clock, the tourist office was closed and Lochboisdale wasn't as big as I had imagined. It wasn't that I'd expected some sprawling metropolis, but Lochboisdale seemed to amount to little more than a pier and a tired-looking hotel. We made enquiries at the hotel about the possibility of a room and were told we could have one … for £100! Maybe in London, but Lochboisdale? We ended up outside the hotel, picking out B&Bs from my guidebook and phoning them. On the third call, we were able to secure a room at a B&B a couple of miles back down the road. Yet another chance for us to stretch our legs. We were used to lugging our bags about the Outer Hebrides by now. Two more miles didn't amount to much in the grand scheme of things.

We'd been walking for about a mile when a car drew up alongside us. The driver leaned out the window.

'You'll be Tiger Woods, then?' he said to Noble Brian.

Before Noble Brian could answer, a truck pulled up alongside the car. Driving the truck was the son of the man who'd just asked Noble Brian if he was Tiger Woods. Now both father and son were offering us a lift to our B&B. We went with the son, since we could chuck our clubs in the back of his truck. We waved cheerio to the dad and joined Colin in the front of the truck.

He was heading home for his tea before going out to the pub to watch the Champions League Final. Noble Brian and I had forgotten all about the football. Travelling around the Outer Hebrides we'd forgotten about most things. Colin said that the pub showing the football was walkable from our B&B. So that was our evening sorted. Check into B&B. Go to pub to watch football.

Colin dropped us off at the excellent Lochside Cottage where we were welcomed by the wonderful Morag who showed us to our comfy room before serving us tea and biscuits in the conservatory overlooking the loch. Already sitting in the conservatory enjoying Morag's hospitality were two other guests, Englishmen up in South Uist on business. They were working at the rocket range, but they didn't elaborate. We told them we were playing some golf courses, but didn't expand much on that. Not because we felt any need to be secretive, more because we figured they wouldn't be that interested. Apart from not talking about the rocket range or the golf, we had a very nice chat over a cup of tea.

Noble Brian and I set out on a nice South Uist evening to watch the football at the pub. It felt good to stretch our legs, even if that was all we'd been doing all day. It was a more enjoyable walk than the one to the store on North Uist in the morning. The pub was part of the

Borrodale Hotel and there was a mobile cinema in the car park. The pub itself was fairly busy. We said hello to Colin who had given us the lift earlier and tipped us off about the football and we also met Ali, a Scot living in London who was up here on holiday.

Ali was a PE teacher and was recovering from a bad knee injury. He had torn his cruciate ligament and this trip to the Outer Hebrides was part of his rehabilitation. He was cycling round the islands, enjoying the fresh air and scenery while building up the strength in his knee. Noble Brian had ripped his cruciate ligament once and he and Ali swapped experiences over a pint. Ali was loving his time in the Outer Hebrides. He'd felt the need to escape from London for a bit and was really glad he'd come here. Each night he'd been pitching his tent wherever he wanted to. We asked Ali what had been his favourite island so far and he was emphatic in his answer. Barra. He'd been enthralled by the place. 'So beautiful and so friendly.' Noble Brian and I would be on Barra later the next day, after playing Askernish in the morning.

A few pints and much good conversation later – we'd barely watched the football – Noble Brian and I set off back to the B&B. Ali passed us on his bike, waving. We hoped that he would manage to find his tent. He had pitched it on a patch of grass somewhere and it was getting pretty dark.

As we walked by the side of the road, Noble Brian and I talked about Askernish. We were both looking forward to playing it in the morning. Of all the island courses, it was the one Noble Brian was most excited about, the lost

Old Tom Morris course that had been rediscovered. Noble Brian's excitement was rubbing off on me and I sensed that tomorrow might be special. I just needed a good night's sleep first.

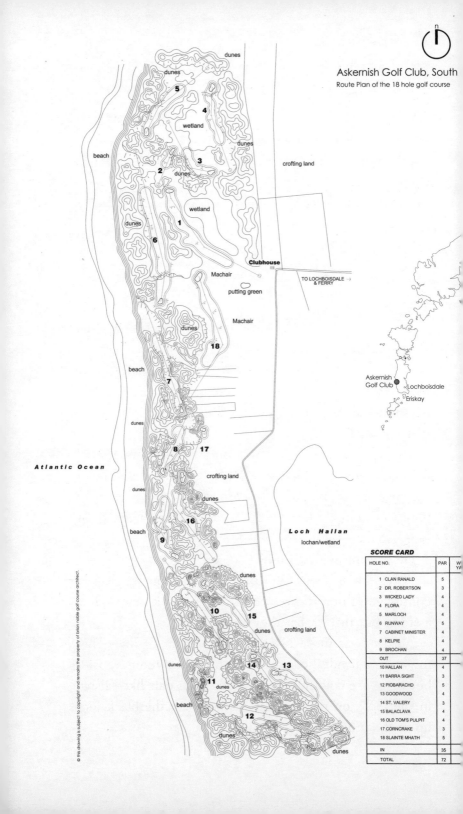

Askernish Golf Club, South
Route Plan of the 18 hole golf course

dunes
dunes
5
4
wetland
dunes
3
2
dunes
1
wetland
dunes
6
beach
crofting land
Clubhouse
TO LOCHBOISDALE →
& FERRY
Machair
putting green
Machair
dunes
18
beach
7
dunes
8
17
Atlantic Ocean
dunes
16
crofting land
dunes
9
Loch Hallan
lochan/wetland
dunes
10
15
dunes
crofting land
dunes
14
13
11
dunes
beach
12
dunes
dunes

Askernish Golf Club
Lochboisdale
Eriskay

© this drawing is subject to copyright and remains the property of brian noble golf course architect.

SCORE CARD		
HOLE NO.	PAR	W YA
1 CLAN RANALD	5	
2 DR. ROBERTSON	3	
3 WICKED LADY	4	
4 FLORA	4	
5 MARLOCH	4	
6 RUNWAY	5	
7 CABINET MINISTER	4	
8 KELPIE	4	
9 BROCHAN	4	
OUT	37	
10 HALLAN	4	
11 BARRA SIGHT	3	
12 PIOBARACHD	5	
13 GOODWOOD	4	
14 ST. VALERY	3	
15 BALACLAVA	4	
16 OLD TOM'S PULPIT	4	
17 CORNCRAKE	3	
18 SLAINTE MHATH	5	
IN	35	
TOTAL	72	

Chapter 6

Skirmish with Askernish – South Uist

Our preparation for Askernish was perfect: a good night's sleep followed by one of Morag's magnificent cooked breakfasts. Sausage, bacon, black pudding, etc. Morag even moved breakfast time forward to cater for us. Not only that, but her husband Alisdair had offered to give us a lift to the golf course.

On the way there – it was only a couple of miles – Alisdair told us about some other guests they'd had recently who'd played Askernish. 'They came back and they were bloody knackered,' said Alisdair. 'They say it's long … they say it's tough.'

He had me worried now.

'They say it's an Old Tom Morris course,' Alisdair continued. 'I'm not sure if there's truth in it or not, if it's a story, but that's what they're saying.'

Alisdair was more of a fisherman than a golfer. There might be a handful of golf courses in the Outer Hebrides but there are countless lochs to fish. Alisdair liked fishing in the lochs on the machair, 'rather than the black lochs up in the moors'.

We reached the turn off for the golf course. A sign said RAON GOILF. AISGEARNAIS. Golf Course. Askernish. Well, that was my translation of it. The Outer Hebrides is the heartland of Gaelic culture. About one per cent of the Scottish population speaks Gaelic, with the majority of Gaelic speakers living in the Outer Hebrides. I hadn't really heard much Gaelic so far. It had mostly been English with a Hebridean lilt.

At the end of a long road stood the tidy little clubhouse. It looked like it had just been put up the day before. There didn't seem to be anyone around. It was eight o'clock in the morning. Alisdair left us to it and drove off back down the road.

Noble Brian and I stepped onto the clubhouse porch and tried the door anyway. It was locked. Peering in the window we saw a modest lounge with chairs, tables and a wall-mounted TV, plus a kitchen area. We were going to have to leave our extra bags on the porch while we played our round. This didn't bother us. We had become very trusting since leaving the city. Our bags would still be there when we got back, we were sure of it.

We walked over to the first tee. It was raining lightly and fairly misty and it seemed to suit Askernish, this mystical course with the intriguing story. On one side of us were the dunes and the sound of the Atlantic, on the other the hills, blurred by the mist. It seemed like it was just us and the golf course. And really it was just us and the golf course.

'Nice easy par five for starters,' said Noble Brian. The first fairway was long and immensely inviting. It had an epic feel to it. I focused on my drive and watched with satisfaction as my ball bounced down the left-hand side of the fairway. Walking down the hole, it felt like it had an energy of its own. I was hypnotised, I couldn't deny it. The fairway curved towards the green. 'An appropriate use of land,' said Noble Brian. The golf architect was in golf heaven.

For my second shot, I punched a five iron down the middle. I wasn't quite there yet, but I was getting closer to the green. 'That'll do you handy,' said my playing partner. We trudged contentedly towards the flag. I didn't quite manage an opening hole par on the heavily contoured green, but it had been a wonderfully natural hole to play. It boded well for the rest of the round.

'Lapwings giving it laldy,' said Noble Brian, commenting on the quality of birdsong that filled the air. The golf architect was an ornithologist. South Uist – in fact much of the Outer Hebrides – draws a lot of birdwatchers for the varied birdlife, but it is wasted on me. The only bird cry I'm able to recognise is the seagull. Beyond that I'm struggling.

Having completed the first hole at Askernish, we were introduced to Dr Roberts, a testing par three. I landed just short of the green and was faced with the most mind-boggling putt of my life. I had never encountered so many angles, never had to think about so much with one putt.

'You've got a hell of a shot,' said Noble Brian. 'I wish you the best of luck from there.'

In the end I read it pretty well. I just didn't hit it firmly enough.

'Should have had your porridge,' said Noble Brian.

If I'd eaten a bowl of porridge as well as Morag's cooked breakfast, I wouldn't have made it onto the course this morning. My second putt slipped by the hole and I tapped in for a bogey. I wasn't annoyed in the slightest at three-putting such an intimidating green.

Next up was the Wicked Lady, a short par four. With the wind in my face and my eyes watering, I topped my tee shot and ended up with a six.

Dreich and misty, I wouldn't have wanted it any other way. Us and Askernish. I'd totally fallen under its spell. We lacked scorecards, but the course was guiding us. It had an irresistible flow, inviting you to take each shot as it comes and savour the moment and the opportunity of hitting off the soft machair. It may not have been so much that magic had been worked on this course as the land itself was magical and it had just taken someone to see it.

'There's no attempt to define things,' said Noble Brian, enthralled by these early holes. 'There's very little green-keeping. It's as it was. I think it would be a shame if they worked on it and tried to make it like a championship course.'

The course was presented in a rustic manner and it was wonderful. Noble Brian liked that there were no yardage markers and you had to rely on your eyes. 'Think and see. That's the problem with Skycaddie technology and GPS. You know the exact yardage. It takes the fun out of it. Here there's nothing.' Nothing but guesswork, yet it all made sense.

When I'd woken up in the morning, my first thoughts

had been about my dad. It's not that I always woke up and thought about him, but I had this morning for some reason. And I was thinking about him now. The sad stuff mainly. The immediate aftermath. The doctor delivering the news. Me trying to be strong for my mam. Having to meet my brother when he arrived at the hospital. Having to phone my sister in Australia, to wake her up in the middle of the night and tell her the news. Having to phone one of my dad's sisters. Having to cope with the hardest hour of my life. Not that it was easier for anyone else.

Now with my dad's putter in my bag, my melancholy mood matched the mist. But I wasn't being sad. I was remembering being sad. The worst of the grief had passed. It had been more than 18 months. When I thought about my dad now, it was more often than not with a smile. And that's what I did now, smiled. Better to smile at his being than dwell on his passing.

I chipped out of the rough. 'Back on the cut stuff!' said Noble Brian, never far away with an encouraging word on the course. I seemed to be doing OK. The course required thought, but it wasn't that tough. 'For those that are accustomed to links golf,' said Noble Brian, 'it's as you were.' We were here and we were coping.

I rammed home a 20-foot putt for my par. 'That putter travels far too well,' said Noble Brian. I totted up my score so far – 6-4-6-4. Level 5s for the first four holes at Askernish. Not blistering form but not bad for a man with no handicap playing a demanding golf course. Noble Brian described his round so far as 'steady rubbish'.

The next hole played towards the sea, a short par four

but with the now strong wind possibly adding another 100 yards. Flashback to Harris. Stand firm and shape a decent golf shot. I just about got away with it. Once on the green, I rolled a ten-foot putt into the middle of the hole for my bogey – 6-4-6-4-5. Far from a calamitous sequence for someone of my limited ability. I was somewhere between hanging in there and rising to the challenge.

The sixth was an absolute monster of a hole, not much shy of 600 yards. How could this be? It was called the Runway and the long straight fairway had the look of one. (I later learned that there had once been an airfield at Askernish, part of the reason why the earlier golf holes had been lost over time. The Runway then must have been a runway.) I topped my tee shot, making the longest hole of my life even longer. The flag looked like it was at the other end of the golf course and not at the end of this hole. I got there eventually.

Six holes down and it had just gone nine o'clock. We'd been on the course an hour and were making excellent progress. Then we came to the seventh tee. 'Now we're talking!' cried Noble Brian. Evidently the first six holes had just been the warm up. After the Runway, you took off.

We stood in awe on an elevated tee, looking out to the grey Atlantic, and down below, way down below between ancient dunes was the fairway, inviting us to give it a go. 'It's as dramatic a golf shot as there could be,' said Noble Brian. 'I've never seen a tee shot like it. You'd never get bored hitting that shot.'

This stupendous golf hole was called the Cabinet Minister

and we entered into a debate with it. I lost, but Noble Brian emerged victorious. 'Green like a ship's prow,' he said, walking off the most dramatic golf hole I'd ever played with a par.

The Cabinet Minister was followed by another epic hole among the giant dunes. This was a different golf course entirely, the scale more huge than anything I'd ever experienced. These were the lost golf holes that had been brought back to life and into play. And I wanted to relish them, I truly did, but the high winds and the sheer proportion of everything had knocked the stuffing out of me. I was overwhelmed by this golf course and, I have to admit, intimidated by it.

I was left without a golf game. I'd been coping adequately up to a point but now I felt the brute force of Askernish and was flailing amid the increasingly difficult conditions. Another tee; another mammoth hole. The sea at my back, before me a yawning pit. 'Make sure you carry it,' warned Noble Brian. It required all my strength for me to do so. Noble Brian could barely believe where he was playing. 'As a place to play golf, you could hardly find anything better.' This was golf in the raw, golf as it used to be, on the most natural and thrilling of coastal landscapes.

On the tenth tee, I pulled a hipflask from my bag. 'If you want to join me on this one.' I poured Noble Brian a dram. He raised his cup and made a toast to Old Tom Morris. I toasted the moment, losing some of my whisky to the wind.

'It's good to sprinkle the course with a drop,' said Noble Brian.

'I'd rather sprinkle my throat with it,' I said.

I looked at my watch and saw it was ten o'clock. It had taken us an hour to play those last three holes, an indication of the scale of them. We were slowing down and soon, I imagined, if the course continued in this fashion, we would come to a halt and someone would have to come out on a tractor to collect us.

We plodded on. The fairway felt spongy underfoot. The machair was soft, but not that soft. I looked down to find myself standing in the biggest pile of cow shit.

'I'm surprised you missed it,' said Noble Brian.

'I didn't miss it. I'm in it.'

'Ach, it wouldn't be the islands if you didn't stand in cow shit.'

It wouldn't have been so bad if I'd been wearing golf shoes, but of course I didn't have a pair of golf shoes. The shoes I was playing in were the only shoes I'd brought to the Outer Hebrides. And if I'm being honest, they were more trainers than shoes. I managed to wipe off most of the cow shit by dragging my feet across the machair. But another problem was the dampness of the course. I'd been spending a fair amount of time in the rough too and water was beginning to seep through my trainers and now my socks were wet, which didn't make for a pleasant golfing experience. And we still had lots of holes to play. I tried to ignore my wet feet but wondered if I was going to end up with a cold after this.

On the middle of the fairway, past the cow shit, I found a ball that was neither mine nor my playing partner's.

'Maybe it's Old Tom's,' said Noble Brian, 'and he's playing with us.'

If Old Tom was playing a Titleist 1, then perhaps it was the case.

The 11th hole was Barra Sight. Presumably you could see Barra on a clear day. This wasn't a clear day. What was clear though was the size of the challenge that this stunning par three presented. Between the tee and the green was a deep gully. It was like having to hit across the Grand Canyon and then scale Everest. The wind coming towards us off the sea wasn't aiding my chances of making the green either.

In fact, I'd already written off my chances. I was behaving like a defeated man. I tried to talk myself out of this defeatism. The past few holes hadn't been easy on me, sure, so here was a chance to start afresh. Play a memorable tee shot befitting this incredible hole and move on from there. Eliminate everything but the green. The gully isn't there. Believe that and you'll reach the other side.

None of that helped. I didn't even come close. My ball was swallowed up by the pit, plugged somewhere down there in the thick rough. I was never going to find it. 'Hit another one,' said Noble Brian. I had neither the heart nor the energy. I stepped aside and let him go for glory. The bold Noble Brian absolutely Evil Knieveled it, his drive clearing the Grand Canyon, avoiding all that unnecessary mess down there, his ball landing on the green without a doubt. What an effort from the wee man with the big swing.

When we got over there, he had the chance of a birdie, which he fully deserved to make after that tee shot. 'Come

on, give us one,' said Noble Brian, leaning over his ball.
'Give us one on this crazy tour.' Alas, he missed, but he
said his par felt like an eagle. Noble Brian had flown like
a sea eagle on the epic 11th at Askernish. He had impressed
me once more with his brilliance. At this stage, resigned
as I was to struggling for the rest of the round, I was taking
comfort in my friend's performance.

The next hole was downwind at least, but that threw
up its own problems. Literally. As we stood on the elevated
tee looking out to sea, the wind strengthened and picked
up sand from the beach below and flung it in our faces.
We coughed and spluttered, rubbing our eyes and laughing.
We'd been sandblasted. 'Can't see America today,' mumbled
Noble Brian, squinting at the ocean with a mouthful of
sand.

I turned to face the fairway and was further disheart-
ened by the prospect of another brutal par five. This one
was even longer than the Runway. Fear mixed with the
smell of seaweed. The only relief came from being able to
step down off the tee and out of the wind, after yet another
poor tee shot. As far as the rest of the hole went, it didn't
go well.

I should have taken to swearing. I had every right to.
Golf can provoke all manner of profanity and there's nothing
wrong with cursing on the course, airing filth on the fairways, as long as you replace your divot. It's a passionate
sport, no doubt about it. If you can't use foul language
when you're slicing and hooking and topping, when the
golfing gods are conspiring against you, then when can
you? It's an infuriating game. But despite all that I was

having to put up with at Askernish, I didn't start swearing. I kept a lid on it. I just suffered.

By the 16th, another beast of a hole called Old Tom's Pulpit, I was a broken man. My game had gone to pot, my nerves were in tatters, my feet were soaking wet and the clubhouse was too far away for comfort. Let there be an end to this. Just let me be. A skied tee shot and my heart sank once more. I soldiered on; the happiness of the first few holes a distant memory. What had happened to me since then? For the average golfer playing below average, Askernish is unforgiving.

I'd lost another ball and ended up walking most of the 16th hole. Nearer Old Tom's Pulpit, the dramatic raised green, I dropped another ball and swung a nine iron at it. My ball shot up into the air and dropped into the pulpit, stopping next to the pin. It was my first decent shot in possibly an hour. A shot to savour too. Something to keep me going. It was the way of golf. Hit enough bad shots and you expect the next one to be bad. You approach it fearing the worst. And suddenly there is nothing to look forward to any more. But play one good shot and you're as right as rain again.

On the 17th tee, we saw other golfers for the first time at Askernish. Two men, in tweedy old-fashioned golf gear, on the adjacent ninth tee.

'Morning,' said one of them. 'Not a bad day.'

'How you getting on?' asked Noble Brian.

'It's been good so far,' said the other man.

They sounded glad to be here. This tiny exchange, this reminder of where exactly we were, raised my spirits. The men were right. It wasn't a bad day. How could it be? This was a morning to celebrate, despite my game being down in the dumps. Noble Brian sighed.

'Don't tell me you're feeling down, are you?' I asked.

'Nah,' said Noble Brian. 'How can I be down about anything?'

He was getting to play Askernish, testing golf in the most amazing location, the highlight being those holes I'd struggled so much with, the large-scale ones through the tumbling dunes. This was a very special place to play golf and Noble Brian was making every minute of it count.

My colleague hit a fantastic drive on the 17th and mine wasn't too shabby either. I was due that. My mood had officially improved. Golf, it's an emotional game. When we reached the 18th, my heart, for a moment, sank again. Par five, 509 yards. Not another one. This course didn't get any easier. I was hoping to be able to saunter home. Where was the fairway though? We looked around and could not see one. Then it dawned on us that the fairway had just never been. The 18th fairway at Askernish consisted of a white carpet of daisies. It was beautiful. I smacked a big tee shot, my best of the day, into the distance and we treaded on this magical white carpet.

'The daisies just lead you home,' said Noble Brian. 'I like that.'

Follow the daisies and they'll lead you home. It was an unexpected end to a round that had been full of the unexpected.

'Do you not feel like Julie Andrews?' asked Noble Brian as we traipsed through the daisies.

I warned him not to start singing, or else the hills of South Uist would be alive with the sound of swearing.

After four hours of being pummelled by a gargantuan golf course and battered by the wind, getting my feet soaked and my face sandblasted, being at breaking point and then giving up point, I finished off with a five, making my par on the final hole.

'He salutes the crowd!' said Noble Brian. 'His dinner will taste good tonight!'

I'd lost a lot of golf balls and my bag was lighter. My mood had lightened also, partly because we were done. I tried to tell myself that we had been fortunate to have such a morning. We'd pretty much had Askernish to ourselves. And it had had me for breakfast.

'It's amazing,' said Noble Brian. 'It was there for us to do as we will.'

I hadn't done very well, but I knew what he meant.

'My feet are soaking,' I said.

'You'd better watch you don't have trench foot,' said Noble Brian, standing like a sensible person in his waterproof trousers and golf shoes, shaking his head at an ill-prepared idiot in his jeans and trainers.

We walked back to the clubhouse. Well, I squelched back to the clubhouse. Our bags were still sitting on the porch. The clubhouse remained locked, with no one about. I sat down on the porch and took off my trainers and my wet socks. I stood on the porch in my bare feet for a while, giving them a bit of an airing. I wasn't caring. I just wanted to be comfortable.

A farmer went by on a tractor, his collie dog sitting

beside him. The farmer waved. He appeared to be laughing, possibly at me standing about in my bare feet. I put on a fresh pair of socks. The problem I had – well, one of my many problems – was that if I put on my wet trainers again, my new socks would get wet. So I paced about the porch in my socks, wondering what to do, and thinking about the bottom half of my jeans also being wet because I hadn't worn waterproof trousers and had spent quite a lot of time in the rough. I really needed to get some proper golf gear. Noble Brian meanwhile had managed to change out of his golf shoes and put his other shoes on over dry socks. And, of course, he'd removed his waterproof trousers to reveal a dry pair of trousers. Why couldn't I be more like that?

I was still standing about in my socks when a mint green campervan came up the road and parked in front of the clubhouse. A young couple jumped out and said hello. Noble Brian and I introduced ourselves. They were David and Jules, newly-weds on their honeymoon. They lived in London, had got married in Edinburgh and now they were here, exploring the Outer Hebrides in a campervan. I couldn't think of a better idea for a honeymoon.

Jules explained that she had family from North Uist. She and David had been touring the islands and had stopped here because David had seen Askernish featured on a TV programme recently and wanted to see the course for himself. And here they were. At least I'd put on a fresh pair of socks for them.

'So where's the first tee then?' asked David.

'Well,' said Noble Brian, 'if you want a recommendation,

follow that path up to the seventh tee.' He pointed David and Jules in the direction of the Cabinet Minister. They thanked him and set off up the path. They were going to be greeted by some view.

Noble Brian and I began getting our bags together. I looked up at one point and smiled, seeing David and Jules in the distance. She was standing on the seventh tee swinging an imaginary club and he was taking a picture of his new bride. Once they were done, they ran back down the path to the clubhouse. David was satisfied that he'd seen some of Askernish. He'd seen the very best of it.

The newly married couple were heading north but offered us a lift down to the main road from where Noble Brian and I would catch the next bus heading south. We jumped in the back of the happy honeymooners' campervan. This was our second campervan in two days. This one was a bit tidier than Captain Hugh's. In fact, it was immaculate. I felt quite bad sitting down in my wet jeans and wet trainers.

As David drove down to the main road, a car passed us, heading in the direction of the golf course. Noble Brian and I looked out the back window of the campervan and saw a woman get out of the car, step onto the porch and go into the clubhouse. Impeccable timing. Now we were leaving, it was open.

'I never got a scorecard,' sighed Noble Brian.

David asked if we wanted to go back. Noble Brian and I looked at one another. 'Nah, we're fine,' said Noble Brian.

After we'd waved David and Jules off, we stood at the bus stop. My clean socks were now saturated and changing into yet another pair of socks seemed pointless. I was a right mess. Nothing good could come of this. Only something bad, like being bedded with the cold. We were supposed to get to Barra this afternoon and play another nine holes before the day was over. Today's plan had seemed manageable enough on paper, but after that skirmish with Askernish ... oh boy.

The bus arrived. It was the same driver who had dropped us off at Benbecula golf course yesterday. 'Where is it now boys?' he asked, opening the boot for us to put our golf clubs in.

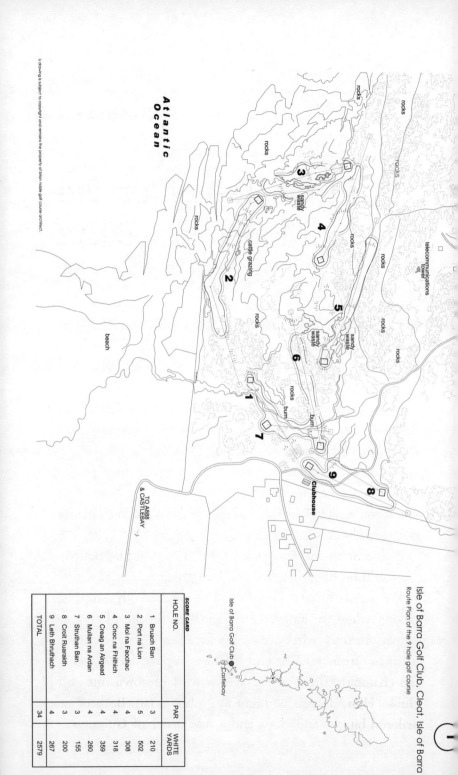

Isle of Barra Golf Club, Cleat, Isle of Barra
Route Plan of the 9 hole golf course

Atlantic
Ocean

beach

rocks

rocks

cattle grazing

sandy waste

sandy waste

rocks

rocks

rocks

rocks

rocks

rocks

rocks

rocks burn

burn

telecommunications tower

Clubhouse

TO A888 & CASTLEBAY

Isle of Barra Golf Club
Castlebay

SCORE CARD

HOLE NO.		PAR	WHITE YARDS
1	Bruach Ban	3	210
2	Port na Lion	5	502
3	Mol na Faochac	4	308
4	Cnoc na Fhithich	4	318
5	Creag an Airgead	4	359
6	Mullan na Ardan	4	260
7	Struthan Ban	3	155
8	Croit Ruaraidh	3	200
9	Leth Bhruthach	4	267
TOTAL		34	2579

Chapter 7

Go Tee off on the Mountain – Barra

We journeyed south on the bus, 'Still Crazy After All These Years' playing on the radio. I sat with chattering teeth and wet feet. Eventually we ran out of South Uist, the bus crossing the causeway to tiny Eriskay.

From Eriskay we were catching the ferry to Barra. But first we were going to pop into Eriskay's only pub, Am Politician, for a pint and a bite to eat. The bus driver approved of our plan. 'Best pint of Guinness on the islands,' he said as he helped us get our bags from the boot. 'See when you walk in?' he said. 'They'll all stop talking. They're not sure about strangers over here.'

Noble Brian and I must have shown signs of hesitation. 'You'll be fine,' laughed the bus driver.

We needn't have been concerned. Nobody stopped talking when we entered the pub because the place was empty. Instead what we got was a smile and a warm welcome from Julia behind the bar. 'Which one of you is the champion then?' she asked as we laid down our golf clubs. 'Him,' I said, nodding at Noble Brian. Both of us ordered burger and chips and a side order of Guinness.

Am Politician is named after the SS *Politician*, a ship that foundered off Eriskay in 1941, carrying a cargo of whisky. The islanders ensured the crew were safe, then set about salvaging some of the whisky. You can't let good whisky go to waste. A game of hide and seek ensued, with police and customs officers descending on the island and the locals stashing away the liberated whisky. The whole episode was immortalised in Compton Mackenzie's whimsical novel *Whisky Galore*, which was in turn made into the memorable film *Whisky Galore!*

Pictures of the SS *Politician* hung on the walls of the pub. One picture had the words, 'Never in the history of human drinking was so much drunk so freely by so few.'

As Noble Brian and I got stuck in to our burgers, Julia brought over two bottles of whisky. She wasn't trying to get us drunk ahead of our ferry. No, this whisky wasn't for drinking. These were actual bottles brought off the SS *Politician*. Noble Brian and I were suitably impressed.

I held one of the bottles in my hands. It looked like whisky all right. Dark golden, but with some sediment at the bottom, maybe soil. Perhaps 70 years ago some islander lost this bottle in the hills. It possibly wasn't his first bottle. The bottle I held had White Horse (Glasgow) embossed on the glass. Noble Brian was examining the other bottle, marked Spey Royal, and he looked like he was about to open it. He put the bottle down and took a consolation sip of his Guinness.

Julia also brought over a framed Government of Jamaica 10 shilling note. The SS *Politician* had been bound for Jamaica and New Orleans and was carrying plenty of currency as well as whisky. 'Everyone talks about the whisky,' smiled Julia, 'but there was money – and bikes too.' I half expected her to go behind the bar and bring out a bike covered in seaweed.

Julia had completed her studies in Edinburgh and was back on Eriskay, enjoying the summer, working behind the bar. 'Meeting all kinds of people,' she smiled. A family walked in and Julia went off to serve them.

Noble Brian held up both bottles of whisky and grinned. 'This is our retirement here!'

I picked up the framed 10 shilling note.

'We could go to the Caribbean!' said Noble Brian.

I looked out the window and saw grey sea and grey sky.

'We are in the Caribbean,' I said. 'It's just a bad day of weather.'

Both of us fancied a second pint, but we needed to get going, otherwise we'd miss our ferry. The bus driver had told us about a short cut between the pub and the pier. It involved a walk across a beach, instead of us having to follow the road round. Julia confirmed the short cut and pointed us in the right direction. We thanked her and slung our bags on our backs and set off for the pier.

The beach was the most beautiful stretch of white sand and we golfed the length of it, stopping now and again to hit shots off the sand. Only later did I learn that the beach was the same beach Bonnie Prince Charlie had landed on from France. I don't imagine he had golf on his mind.

We soon got to the pier and there were quite a few people waiting about for the ferry. We got talking to some of them, including members of Barra's horticultural society who'd been over for the day selling their plants.

One lady, not one of the gardeners, couldn't understand us. She understood what Noble Brian and I were saying, but, to her, what we said made no sense at all.

'You're playing golf on Barra tonight? And getting the ferry to Oban in the morning?'

I confirmed that this was the plan.

'Well, I've heard of crazy golf, but that's just daft!'

'I know, I know,' I said.

When Noble Brian mentioned that we hadn't booked anywhere to stay on Barra yet, the lady and the members of the horticultural society and just about everyone else waiting for the ferry sprang into action. People started calling out the names of other people on Barra who ran B&Bs. And one old man, leaning on his walking stick, seemed to know all the phone numbers.

'What's Mary's number?'

'624,' said the old man.

'And what about Margaret'?'

'583.'

'And what's Moira's number?'

'294.'

'Good job you swallowed the phonebook!' said the woman who'd decided we were crazy golfers to the old man with all the digits at his fingertips.

'What's Peggy's number again?

'498.'

The old man knew every number on the island. He was the human face of directory enquiries.

I tried all the numbers but either got no answer or was told that they were fully booked. Someone shouted out another name and the old man provided the number. I punched it into my phone.

'Are you vegetarians?' asked the woman who knew we were nuts.

'No,' I said, answering on behalf of two proud meat eaters.

'Well, that's good. He'll probably be out killing something at the minute.'

'Sorry?'

'He's got the slaughterhouse next to his guest house.'

I tried the number but there was no answer. Our potential host for the night must have been out slaughtering some animals.

But from all these phone calls, the picture had emerged that Barra was busy. It hadn't crossed my mind that we might have difficulty finding somewhere to stay. Until we'd arrived at the pier, it hadn't crossed my mind for us to find somewhere to stay. We'd been too busy dealing with Askernish and getting as far as this. Barra is a small but fairly popular island and we just hadn't prepared for this. Maybe we'd be sleeping on the golf course.

Soon we were on the ferry, sailing across the Sound of Barra. Between the sound of the waves and the noise of the boat's engine, I was struggling to keep up my end of the conversation I was having with one of the ladies from the horticultural society.

'So you're playing the golf course?' she shouted.

'Yes,' I yelled back. 'I hear there are cows on the course!'

'Just don't touch the fences!'

'OK! Maybe there'll be some members there!'

'Aye, there'll be a lot of heifers!'

Either she was insulting the members or she hadn't heard me.

I carried on talking, or at least shouting. I shouted about Duncan the Welder. Duncan was our contact for Barra Golf Club. Noble Brian had exchanged a couple of e-mails with Duncan, ahead of our trip. Unfortunately, Duncan wasn't going to be able to meet us because he was going to be on the mainland at the time of our visit. But he had passed on Noble Brian's number to his brother Murdo. We hadn't heard from Murdo and we didn't have his number. I shouted all this to the lady from the horticultural society. And she spun round and called out to everyone else on the ferry.

'Does anyone have the number for Murdo the Welder?'

The old man called out Murdo's number.

Noble Brian gave it a go but it rang out.

Where was this evening going? All that had been on my mind this morning had been Askernish. But now it was teatime and we still had to get to Barra, get to the golf course and I had a vague idea where it was and I knew that a bus met the ferry and that the bus went round the island, so ... if we got to the golf course it was only nine holes ... but after that, what were we going to do? Where were we going to stay? And how were we going to get there? And it was six o'clock and we'd be catching the ferry to Oban in little more than 12 hours. I thought I'd planned this Hebridean trip to perfection. Now my plan was unravelling. And my feet weren't dry yet. Despite the good efforts of our friends on the ferry, it looked like we had an accommodation problem. We needed to get that sorted out before anything.

As the ferry bounced up and down, my eyes settled on an advert for the most westerly hotel in Britain, which happened to be on Barra. I bit the bullet and called the number and a woman answered and quoted me an eye-watering rate for a twin room for the night. I ran it past Noble Brian. The room was expensive. We wouldn't be in it that much. But with a golf course still to find and play, locating somewhere to stay the night would at least be one problem solved. 'Take it,' said Noble Brian. I told the woman we'd take it. We had secured shelter for the night. We could get on with our game of golf – once we'd found the course – and after our round head to the hotel, wherever that was. The woman on the other end of the phone said that the hotel was a couple of miles from the golf course. Ach, if there wasn't a bus when we came off the course, which there probably wouldn't be, we'd walk it to the hotel. What were two more miles, right? My trainers and socks had dried up a bit. And that round at Askernish was a long time ago. A few hours ago.

'Golf at this bloody time of night?' asked the bus driver after we'd got off the ferry.

'Afraid so,' I said.

'Do you go anywhere near the golf course?' asked Noble Brian.

'I could drop you at the turn-off,' said the driver. 'From there it's a good mile or more up the road. Or I can drop you off at the graveyard, in which case it's a couple of fields and a wee climb. More of a direct route. About a quarter of the distance.'

Graveyard, couple of fields and a wee climb it was then. Good grief.

'A commando yomp,' sighed Noble Brian. 'We might as well.'

We sat back and enjoyed our early evening bus journey to the graveyard. The bus stopped once, picking up a man who sat down opposite us and introduced himself.

'They call me Kubota Joe.'

We said hello to Kubota Joe. He wore a baseball cap, an earring and a big grin. He told us he worked in the local quarry. I braced myself.

'Went for four days and came out five-and-a-half years later,' he said. 'There's a machine in there from 1925 and it's still working.'

Noble Brian asked Kubota Joe how he liked living on Barra.

'My sister's married to a millionaire, I'm married to Barra,' he smiled.

'So you like it, then?'

'Ach, Barra's too slow for me. I want to speed up! I'm going for a night out in Castlebay! Why not, eh?'

I could think of no reason why not.

'So you're off to play golf?' asked Kubota Joe.

Noble Brian and I nodded.

Kubota Joe leaned forward. 'Watch the wind doesn't get you at the corner.'

Just then the bus driver called our stop. 'Here you go

lads.' Noble Brian and I said cheerio to Kubota Joe and thanked the bus driver.

We stood with our bags at a small cemetery. Beyond it were a couple of fields and then a hill. A pretty big hill. Rocky looking too. Somewhere up there was Barra golf course, according to the bus driver.

Noble Brian and I walked past the cemetery and through the first field, sheep scattering in all directions, then climbed over a stile and walked through the second field. At this point we caught up with a road that seemed to wind its way up the hill. We started following the road, finding it hard to believe there was a golf course up here. I thought of the postcard of Barra golf course at Franco's cafe, in particular the image of that white beach, and wondered now where on earth we were heading.

We continued our climb and eventually, surprisingly, came to a golf course. It didn't look much like a golf course, more a rocky hillside with some flags sticking out of it. This was our final golf course in the Outer Hebrides. At least it wasn't North Uist. At least there were flags. We approached a blue shipping container with the words 'golf scorecards' painted on it as well as an arrow pointing towards a white box. Noble Brian reached inside the box. 'It's like opening Davy Jones' locker,' he said, pulling out a couple of scorecards and an envelope. We each placed a tenner in the envelope that Noble Brian dropped into a second black box, the honesty box.

I looked at the scorecard. 'All greens are protected by Electric Fences. Care should be taken not to touch the wire.' I would be taking great care on this golf course. We

were able to locate the first tee without any great difficulty, with 'first tee' chalked on a piece of slate on the
ground. I teed up between the piece of slate and a rock.

'Better watch you don't break your wrists,' said Noble
Brian.

I gazed down on most of the golf course and the sea.
And a beach, perhaps even the one in the postcard. Even
under a cloudy sky and next to a choppy sea it looked
stunning. As far as the hole went, there were two greens
down below. You had to hit over the first one towards the
second one. Either that or this was the shortest and most
vertical hole in existence. We double-checked the scorecard, which seemed to confirm that the furthest green
was indeed the one we should be aiming for. I smacked
my ball into the air and it sailed off somewhere.

The greens on Barra are square and surrounded by those
wire fences mentioned on the scorecards. My ball, after
a couple of shots, sat in front of a fence post. I considered my options. I could just about putt under the fence
and onto the green, but there was a strong chance my
putter would connect with the fence. And as well as the
warning on the scorecard there was a sign on the fence
saying ATTENTION ELECTRIC FENCE. It also said ELEK-
TROZAUN SCHRIKDAD, which sounded even more
dangerous. There were further warnings in other languages.
Just to stress the point there was a handy picture of a hand
being zapped by electricity. Taking everything into account,
I picked up my ball and walked through the gate onto the
green. Then dropped my ball where I felt like it and had
a putt. Once Noble Brian was also done putting, we walked

out the gate. That was fun. It occurred to me that they should introduce gates to the Open. 'After you, Tiger.'

We'd trouble finding the second tee. We looked around for a piece of slate with 'second tee' in chalk but couldn't find one. Instead we began the hole from where we thought it might begin. Of more concern to me than not being able to find the tee was the number of cows on the fairway. There were at least a dozen of them. The thought of hitting one of them bothered me less than cows terrified me in general.

I was once chased by a cow. Oddly enough at a place called Covesea, pronounced 'Cowsea', near Hopeman. My mam grew up at Covesea. Anyway, one day I was walking along the lovely coastal path between Hopeman and Lossiemouth when I passed a field of cows at Covesea. And one of the cows took a run at me. Fortunately a fence stood between us. But I started to run away from the cow anyway, sprinting along the path, the cow giving chase along the line of the fence. It did cross my mind at the time that this was a ridiculous situation, me being chased by a cow. Cows don't chase after people. But this one did. And it looked like it was about to vault the fence and flatten me. I kept on running and didn't dare look back until the field and the tormenting cow were out of sight. Cows worried me, and this fairway was packed with them. I voiced my concerns to Noble Brian.

He laughed. 'Och, what are they going to do? Charge after us?'

This was exactly what I was thinking.

Fretting about cattle, I played my tee shot and convinced

myself that I'd hit one of the cows. Now we had to walk past them, with me having struck one of them. As we made our way – I did my best to always ensure that Noble Brian was between me and the bovine menace – it appeared that the cows weren't minding our presence. Perhaps that's what they were up to, lulling us into a false sense of security, before charging at us. I couldn't decide whether it was best to walk slowly or really fast. So I varied it, walking slow and fast, stopping quickly to play my next shot. Once we'd got past the cows, I breathed a sigh of relief. Though why I'd believe they were the only cows on the golf course, I don't know.

The third tee, which we were able to find, had the most beautiful backdrop. It was the epic beach I'd admired from afar on the first tee. And it was the beach I'd been thinking about. I'd finally made it into the postcard at Franco's cafe. But my joy was short-lived. This fairway was clogged up with cows to an unbelievable degree. They also surrounded the green. I tried my best in trying circumstances. Nearer the green, I even managed a nice chip. Nice enough until my ball bounced off a rock and shot off at an angle, my good work scuppered. While I was looking for my ball, a nearby cow rose to its feet. What did that mean? I tried to stay calm and interpret this sudden movement. Was it about to charge me? Was this Covesea all over again? What were my options? I could make a run for the gate and get inside the green. Or I could sprint to the shore. Cows couldn't cope on pebbles. The cow lay down again. I gave up searching for my ball and tiptoed towards the green.

The wind had picked up and I was reminded of what Kubota Joe had said on the bus. 'Watch the wind doesn't get you at the corner.' And here we were, at the corner. Kubota Joe had spoken of the wind as if it might pick us up and toss us into the Atlantic if we weren't careful. Actually, here was I being tormented by cows and weather on a rocky hillside masquerading as a golf course, while Kubota Joe would be sitting in the pub right now. Who was the wiser? The only possible answer was Kubota Joe.

Once we got past the third hole, the course was pretty much free of cows. But the fifth hole was mindboggling. It was like no golf hole I'd ever encountered. We were required to hit up through a rocky gully. There was no fairway as such. (None of the holes really had fairways, but this was an anti-fairway.) There was very little grass. It was mainly boulders. This round of golf had become a mountaineering expedition. We hit more in hope than anything else as we scaled this insane golf hole and eventually came to an area of sandy waste, the biggest natural bunker I'd ever seen. Somewhere beyond it was the green. My mind had been well and truly scrambled by this bizarre golf course. I wasn't sure whether I should be admiring it or damning it.

As with Askernish, the natural landscape determined the golf course. But Barra wasn't Askernish. Not with all of these narrow gullies and exposed rocks. You could argue that there had never been a golf course here. Or you could try to put yourself in the frame of mind that, yes, this was a golf course that you'd carried your clubs to at the end of a long day, and that this golf course, which didn't look like any other golf course, was hummocky. Hell of a hummocky. And bouldery. And bewildering.

The game we were engaged in was called golf on the rocks. And the only way to tackle this haphazard golf course was in a haphazard manner. Except that we were seriously flagging. We had got up this morning, played 18 holes at Askernish and got soaked (well, I'd got soaked), jumped on the bus to Eriskay, gone to the pub, golfed across a beach, caught the ferry to Barra, jumped on another bus and commando yomped across fields and up a hill to reach this astonishing golf course. And I could have lain down when we got here, but for the fact we were here to play nine holes on Scotland's most westerly, wild and most surreal golf course. In high winds. And if this was golf as it used to be, then, boy, they had a hard time of it back then.

I'd stopped counting my shots. The only thing I was counting was the number of holes we had left. I wanted this to be over. Noble Brian wanted it to be over. We ditched the order of holes and just started hitting towards the shipping container, aiming for any green that brought us closer to it, not caring if it was the next green or not.

We did play the final hole in a conventional manner. I overshot the green, my ball landing next to the shipping container. I chipped back, got inside the fence and three-putted. The round over, now all we had to do was get down off this bloody hill, walk through the fields and hope some islander would stop and give us a lift to our hotel. Otherwise who knew how long we'd be walking for tonight.

It was still blowing a gale and it had started to rain horizontally. Noble Brian and I had the Barra blues. Before we set off, we warmed up with a dram behind the shipping container, sheltering from the wind and the rain. 'The golfing graveyard,' said Noble Brian, observing a discarded pencil bag on the ground. We got our own stuff together and began our descent of the mountain, commando yomping through the fields towards the graveyard, sheep running in all directions again. We were cold, we were hungry and we were in dire need of a beer. It was coming on for nine o'clock and we were miles from our hotel.

I shouldn't have doubted Barra. Just as we reached the road, a passing car stopped, reversed and the driver leaned out his window.

'Where are you heading?' he asked.

'The Isle of Barra Hotel,' I said.

Robert Ross introduced himself and told us to throw our clubs in the boot. We jumped into the back of the car. Robert's daughter was in the front passenger seat playing the recorder. While she practised a tune, her dad asked us how we'd got on at the golf. 'The course is challenging, isn't it?' We had to agree with Robert there.

Robert Ross, our hero, our saviour, dropped us off at the hotel, his daughter still playing the recorder as he drove away.

The next morning we caught the ferry from Castlebay to Oban, a journey that took seven hours with the ferry swinging by Lochboisdale on South Uist to pick up more passengers. Among them was Ali, the PE teacher we'd enjoyed a few pints with the night before we'd played

Askernish. That night was only a couple of nights ago, though it felt more like a week ago, given all we'd packed in since then.

Ali had thoroughly enjoyed his time cycling round the Outer Hebrides, building up the strength in his knee, enjoying the scenery and pitching his tent wherever. But perhaps the highlight of his holiday had been a trip to the mobile cinema in the car park of the Borrodale Hotel. Ali had gone last night and likened it to a sort of movie Tardis. 'You step in and there's these rows of seats and an aisle and all of that.' The cinematic experience had been such that he had forgotten he was in a truck and stepping back out into the car park after the film had proved pretty disorientating.

The film was some edgy thriller and so Ali's imagination was running wild as he walked in the dark to a nearby phone box to call his girlfriend. As he dialled the number he saw some movement out of the corner of his eye. Ali swung round, but there was nothing. After all, it was dark outside. He spoke to his girlfriend and asked her to call him back. As he waited, he turned to the side to see an old woman with her face pressed up against the glass. Ali got the fright of his life and jumped out of the phone box.

'Did I scare you?' shouted the old woman.

'Of course you scared me,' said Ali. ('My heart went through my arse,' Ali explained to Noble Brian and me.)

The phone had then rung.

'That'll be for me!' shouted the old woman, going into the phone box, picking up the phone and shouting 'hello!' to Ali's girlfriend. Ali was eventually able to talk to his girlfriend. Once he came off the phone, the old woman had gone.

He laughed as he finished telling the story. He hadn't been laughing at the time.

As the ferry sailed south in the morning sunshine, the sea as calm as it could ever be, we stood on the top deck and Ali spoke of his love of Scotland. He had both a great appreciation and great knowledge of his country. Living in London, Ali felt his friends back home didn't get out often enough and see Scotland, that they took it for granted. Ali thought that we should all see more of our country. Noble Brian and I heartily agreed. What a time we'd had in the Outer Hebrides. If you're ever feeling jaded about golf, or life in general, I can't think of many better places to go.

Sometimes people's love for their homeland grows when they leave. Ali would probably love Scotland as much if he did live here, but I thought of my own feelings towards Scotland and recalled the time my wife and I had moved to Spain for a bit, choosing to live in Madrid. We didn't know how long we were going to stay, and after several months, much as we loved the city, we knew that we would return to Scotland. They say absence makes the heart grow fonder and the biggest thing I learned in Spain was that I loved Scotland. And my wife felt the same way. If I was told that I could never leave this country again, I might even be all right with that, especially with the summer I was having.

Standing out on deck in the sun, my ears were itching. Over the past few days, they'd got a bit burnt. It hadn't always been sunny on the islands, but just being out on the golf courses, walking from place to place with the wind blowing, was enough. I was pretty red about the face, especially the tips of my ears. I'd been wearing a hat too, just not one that offered great coverage. An old base-ball cap that did nothing for my ears. Noble Brian's ears were looking quite normal. He'd been wearing a proper hat. I had to get myself a proper hat.

Wanting to stay out on deck and enjoy the Scottish scenery, but not wanting my ears to burn further, I reached into my backpack and brought out a cagoule I hadn't worn yet on my travels. I'd been making do so far with a light jacket I was fond of, but that wasn't exactly waterproof. The cagoule had a hood that would cover my ears. So I might look silly standing in the sun with a cagoule hood up, but I looked silly anyway with red ears. I put the cagoule on. It was slightly on the small side, a bit short in the arms. You see it was my wife's cagoule. I explained this to Noble Brian and Ali.

To Ali, the great outdoors man with all the proper outdoors gear, the cagoule was insufficient for the Scottish climate as well as being ill-fitting. 'You wouldn't last five minutes in the rain wearing that.' Ali shook his head at the golfer going round 18 islands with all the wrong clothes. 'Some guys have all the gear and no idea,' said Ali. 'You've got all the ideas and no gear!'

At least my trainers were now completely dry. I vowed to be better prepared next time. I'd get a cagoule of my own and a pair of golf shoes and a pair of waterproof trousers and a proper hat that would cover my ears and some sun lotion and some insect repellent. Whether the insect repellent would work or not. My neck was covered in midge bites. I'd a few on my ears too. Sunburnt, midge-bitten ears. What a state I was in. Why wasn't Noble Brian covered in midge bites? I decided it must be a height thing. Midges didn't fly low enough for Noble Brian.

The ferry was passing the Small Isles of Rum and Eigg. Both looked gorgeous, but neither of them had golf courses. I wondered which island we'd tackle next?

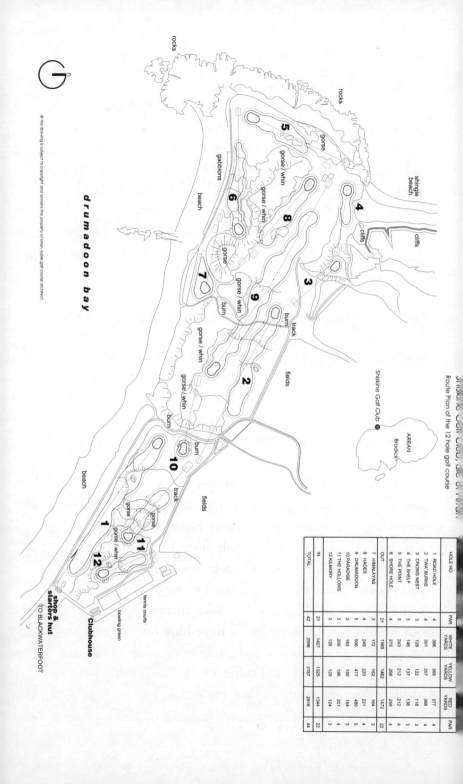

Shiskine Golf Club, Isle of Arran
Route Plan of the 12 hole golf course

HOLE NO.	PAR	WHITE YARDS	YELLOW YARDS	RED YARDS	PAR
1 ROAD HOLE	4	366	368	377	4
2 TWA BURNS	4	391	357	368	4
3 CROWS NEST	3	128	122	118	3
4 THE SHELF	3	146	137	138	3
5 THE POINT	3	243	212	212	4
6 SHORE HOLE	4	275	266	299	4
OUT	21	1589	1462	1472	22
7 HIMALAYAS	3	172	162	164	3
8 HADES	4	249	220	221	4
9 DRUMADOON	5	506	477	480	5
10 PARADISE	3	163	150	164	3
11 THE HOLLOWS	3	209	196	201	4
12 KILMORY	3	128	120	124	3
IN	21	1427	1325	1344	22
TOTAL	42	2996	2787	2816	44

drumadoon bay

ARRAN
Brodick
Shiskine Golf Club

Clubhouse
shop & starters hut
TO BLACKWATERFOOT
tennis courts
bowling green

Chapter 8

In the Shiskine Sunshine
– Arran

Once I'd been back in Glasgow a few days and my wife had stopped laughing at my red ears and red neck, I sat down with my golf map of Scotland and tried to figure out where I wanted to go next. Somewhere not as far away as the Outer Hebrides. Another day trip like Bute would do. There was one obvious destination. It had to be Arran. An hour on the train then an hour on the ferry and I'd be there.

I phoned Noble Brian and told him it was Arran. 'Magic,' was his response. Then I went out and bought all those accessories I'd lacked in the Outer Hebrides. I got myself a pair of golf shoes (my first pair since I was a teenager), a cagoule I could call my own, a pair of waterproof trousers, some insect repellent that claimed to tackle midges, and some sun lotion. Plus, for the sake of my ears, I fished out my dad's old fishing hat, a navy blue bucket hat that looked more Stone Roses than golf course. Still, it did the trick. Never again would I suffer on an island golf course. Well, in any other aspect than my game.

The day of our Arran adventure arrived. Noble Brian

travelled through from Edinburgh, and from Glasgow Central Station we took the train down to Ardrossan on the Ayrshire coast. As the ferry left Ardrossan harbour, an announcement was made to all passengers. 'The cafe is now open for breakfasts, teas, coffees and alcoholic beverages.' Ten in the morning and we were being urged to start drinking. Noble Brian and I kept it sensible and ordered a couple of CalMac breakfasts. Having devoured the last of my black pudding, I flicked through a free copy of an Arran tourist brochure. The editorial contained the following warning, 'Arran can be addictive and all visitors should remain vigilant lest they succumb to a serious attack of Arran-itis. Symptoms start with a mild feeling of well-being, which can develop into extended periods of euphoria in extreme cases. There are many well-documented cases of people deciding to stay on the island permanently, two hours after stepping off the boat. So tread carefully and avoid strong drink for the first 24 hours as this will significantly increase the chances of catching the malady.'

Hmm. We'd better watch ourselves. To be honest, I was already wary of Arran. I'd been once before on my brother's stag-do which, as his best man, I'd organised. My brother broke his collarbone, dressed up as Batman. He jumped over a fence in a beer garden (thinking he was Batman) and landed awkwardly. He spent the rest of the night in the corner of the pub with an ice pack on his shoulder. Earlier that day I'd led an ill-advised expedition up a glen in soaring temperatures with one of the stag party ending up with sunstroke and the rest of us not feeling too great either. I considered the stag-do to be a raging success. It certainly provided a few anecdotes. But I was wary of Arran. Funny things – painful things – have happened to people on that island in the Firth of Clyde.

It is beautiful though. Arran is often described as Scotland in miniature, and here I go repeating that. The Highland Boundary Fault runs through the island, as it does on Bute, but the effect on Arran, with its jagged peaks, is far more dramatic. Approaching Arran on the ferry you can't help but be thrilled. The journey to Arran is a big part of the experience. On a good day, Arran puts me in mind of Tahiti. And I can say that since I've also been to Tahiti. There really isn't much of a difference.

Arran, very beautiful and very accessible, is one of Scotland's most popular islands, and it has no less than seven golf courses. Though there was never any doubt that we would be playing Shiskine, the 12-hole course that my friend Johnny had so often spoken of in glowing terms. It was high time I tackled the Crow's Nest.

Noble Brian and I got off the ferry at Brodick with our golf bags – no extra bags necessary on this single day trip, though we'd both brought a full set of clubs – and jumped on the next bus to Blackwaterfoot. Over the picturesque String Road we went, from the east to the west of the island. The sun was shining. Maybe the sun always shone on Arran. It had done so during my brother's stag-do, perhaps a little too much. From the bus stop in Blackwaterfoot it was just a five-minute walk along the shore road to Shiskine golf course. We were greeted in the club shop by Hamish who'd been expecting us. I'd called ahead and arranged a tee-time. This wasn't the Outer

Hebrides. The golf courses on Arran get busy during the summer.

Hamish, the club champion, introduced Noble Brian and me to an elderly man who had been standing behind us and who I had thought was just waiting in the queue. Far from it. The man was Colin Bannatyne and he knew everything about Shiskine. Colin was the club historian and had written a book about the course. I'd said to Hamish on the phone how I was travelling round Scotland playing lots of different island courses and here was Colin to tell me all about Shiskine.

Colin wondered if we'd mind him walking round with us. We didn't mind at all. In fact, Noble Brian and I were thrilled at the prospect of having someone as knowledge-able as Colin show us round. Besides, he seemed such a nice man. A real gentleman, with a kind manner and a soft voice. I asked Colin if he'd rather play with us than just walk round, but he gently declined the offer.

'I have a big eyesight problem nowadays,' said Colin. 'I have great difficulty in playing. I can see the ball at my feet, but I can't see it after that. I depend on my playing partner to spot the ball for me. So, no, I'm quite happy to go along with you, but I would just be getting in your hair if I was attempting to play at all. I still play, but with a very tolerant partner.'

'I hope you can tolerate us,' I joked, before quickly correcting myself. 'Well, me.'

I glanced out the window and remarked on how busy the course looked.

'The same holiday crowd come back year after year,'

said Colin. This made me think of my friend Johnny and his family.

'How much is the membership here?' I asked Colin.

He didn't know. He was an honorary member. After all, he'd written the book on Shiskine. Colin handed me a copy and I thanked him. He spoke of the work it had entailed, the piecing together of history to tell the story. 'I just had to really drag through all the old minutes and so on and eventually the story emerged. I got very absorbed in it for a bit.'

Arran born and bred, Colin had spent much of his working life away from the island, before returning 25 years ago and retiring. Colin loved the island, especially Shiskine golf course. 'I've been golfing off and on for the past 87 years,' he said.

It was nearing noon, our tee-off time. Hamish asked if we'd like to play off the white tees. Noble Brian did. Not wishing to make life more difficult for myself, I decided to stick with the yellow tees. 'Have a good game!' said Hamish.

Noble Brian, Colin and I stepped out into the Shiskine sunshine. A welcome breeze was coming off the sea. 'We get a fair amount of wind,' said Colin. 'It takes a wee bit tricky at some of the holes.'

I was just loosening up, taking a couple of practice swings – trying to do things by the book and give myself the best chance of a decent start to my round – when I heard a 'Hello Gary!' It was Rodger Baillie, the Scottish sportswriter. I knew Rodger from my spell in sports journalism. We'd covered some of the same matches and press conferences and I'd always enjoyed bumping into him. Here I was bumping into him now. Rodger was on holiday with his wife, enjoying the good weather and playing a bit of golf. It was good to see him. Now I had a decent sized audience. Rodger, Colin and Noble Brian, and quite possibly Hamish looking out the window.

I knuckled down to business, feeling several pairs of eyes on me. I wanted this to go well. As much as I can hit a good shot, I know how bad I can be. I was quite capable of making a right hash of this. I had to stop thinking I would. Be positive. Easy swing, steady head, eyes on the ball. Much to my relief, I sent a solid drive down the middle of the fairway. Rodger liked it and said so. 'Shot, Gary!' Colin was complimentary too. That was all I needed. It didn't matter that Noble Brian then whacked his ball miles past mine from the back tee. I waved cheerio to Rodger and off we went on a round I was very much looking forward to on a lovely summer's day.

I couldn't see the green for my second shot, since it was tucked over the hill. But I had Colin to guide me. He told me the line and I more or less followed it. We walked on, Noble Brian and I trying to keep up with Colin. He was a sprightly figure for his age, covering the course at a brisk pace in his light jacket and baseball cap.

I couldn't help thinking about my dad. And the years without him on the golf course that were still to come. I'd imagined him golfing his way into old age. It never occurred to me that he wouldn't get there. I put my sadness to one side.

A family out pony-trekking waved to us from a path by the shore. I looked across the course and saw again how busy it was. There were a lot of lady golfers in colourful gear. Shiskine felt more like a holiday golf course. Port Bannatyne, Skye, Harris, Benbecula, Askernish, Barra, none of the other courses had had that feeling. North Uist hadn't had a golf course, never mind golfers.

On the second tee, we met two ladies on the adjacent 11th tee. One of them was from Dundee, the other from Drymen. They were here for some holiday golf. I said to them that I was looking forward to playing the Crow's Nest. 'You'll like that one,' said one of the women. Her friend laughed. The Crow's Nest had been a notable feature in their round.

Shiskine's second hole was called Twa' Burns. Funnily enough, a couple of burns ran across the fairway, one just before the green. Noble Brian pondered his tricky approach shot.

'I think you can probably carry it,' said Colin.

'I think you've probably jinxed me,' said Noble Brian.

But he didn't crash and burn. In fact, he came up trumps, landing his ball right next to the pin. I had a go at clearing the burn and thinned it but somehow my ball bounced over the water.

'The Jesus chip,' said Noble Brian.

I was past the burn and just short of the green, perhaps 20 feet from the flag. I called on my dad's putter. I struck it too hard, but fortunately my ball struck the pin and stopped dead. 'I'll give you that,' said Colin, throwing me back my ball.

We moved on to the third hole. The time had come and the question was this: could we conquer the Crow's Nest?

The Crow's Nest at Shiskine involves the ultimate blind shot. The hole consists of a tee, a hill and somewhere up there, guarded by bushes, a hidden green. It's the Prieshach in reverse and my brain was struggling to comprehend it at first. Then I just accepted that what I faced was 120 yards of sheer uncertainty and one of the daftest and most daunting tee shots I'd ever encountered. It reminded me of a certain crazy par three at Cullen on the Moray coast where you had to fire your ball over a huge rock with an arrow on the rock saying 'this way'. The Crow's Nest was that kind of hole, one where you simply hoped for the best. It was just how my friend Johnny had described it. I wasn't disappointed.

'Anyone who's played this course always remembers this hole,' said Colin.

It was fixed in my memory and I hadn't even played it yet. The other aspect of the Crow's Nest was the cliff rising beyond the hill and the hidden green, making the hole look even more improbable.

'We're back on Barra,' groaned Noble Brian. 'Just hitting at a rock.'

We had to wait a bit before we tackled the Crow's Nest as there was a party ahead of us. We could see the tops of their heads as they putted out. Even if we had not been able to see the tops of their heads, there was no sign of the safety flag. Only when the safety flag was visible could you tee off. (We had been issued with a full page of instructions along with our scorecards. The various notes about signals, flags and bells spoke of the many blind shots on this idiosyncratic island course. Although with Colin around, we didn't have to refer to them.)

The safety flag appeared at the top of the Crow's Nest. The golfers in front of us had finished the hole and moved on. We were good to go. There was no sight of the pin, even though it would have been put back in, but Colin kept us right. 'You don't want to go left of the steps.' A set of steps ran up the hill to the green.

Don't go left of the steps … don't go left of the steps … I wasn't going left of the steps. I had limited control over which direction I hit the ball at the best of times, but I convinced myself I was going to succeed and that, surely, was half the battle, wasn't it? Mind over matter. The hill didn't matter. Just drop that ball on the green.

I caught it well, finding enough elevation, though my shot had a slight draw on it. Don't go left of the steps … don't go left of the steps … certainly I was threatening the green. The ball vanished over the bushes. Colin thought it was OK. Well, if Colin thought it was OK, then it must be OK. I couldn't wait to get up there and see where my ball was, but first I had to watch Noble Brian make his bid for the Crow's Nest. He played the shot as if he'd played it before. He was definitely on the green. Colin was very impressed.

I climbed the steps after Colin. There was no way of finding yourself in front of him. As soon as we hit our shots, he was off. I hoped I'd have such stamina at his age, if I reached anything like his age. The man was a marvel.

'Whoa!' said Colin, giving me the Crow's Nest seal of

approval. Yes, there was my ball, beside a bush but on the front edge of the green. Noble Brian had done even better, his ball on the heart of the green. We were looking for a pair of birdies. Neither of us managed it. We both needed two putts to get down. Still, I was chuffed to bits. I could say I'd conquered the Crow's Nest.

Though not quite like Colin had once conquered it. 'One of the highpoints of my golfing career was when I found my tee shot in the hole. That was about 25 years ago.' He made it sound just like yesterday.

I asked him if he'd ever had any other holes-in-one.

'I've had three at the 12th. The 12th is about the easiest hole on the course.'

'So you've had four holes-in-one!' said Noble Brian.

'Well, that's over a good number of years.'

Now that we were in the Crow's Nest, we had to get back down. And that's where Shiskine's next hole came in. The Shelf. Johnny hadn't told me about the Shelf. Or if he had, I hadn't been listening at the time and was still picturing the Crow's Nest.

Noble Brian, Colin and I stood on the fourth tee, the cliff rising above us, the green way down below, and beyond it Kilbrannan Sound, and after that the outline of the Kintyre Peninsula. After the ultimate blind tee shot, the most spellbinding view. It seemed that all you had to do was knock your ball off the Shelf and it would land on the green. Now this hole reminded me of the Prieshach.

'There are really no difficulties here,' said Colin. 'You just have to get the ball off the club.' It sounded easy enough and it looked easy enough.

'I could do with a hole in one here,' said Noble Brian, which I thought was asking a bit much. His tee shot was good, but he didn't find the hole. He was on the green. I found the green too, the ninth green. I hooked it a bit.

As we climbed down off the Shelf, Colin explained that neither this hole nor the Crow's Nest had been part of the original course. These two epic golf holes had once just been waste ground. 'Shiskine didn't start out as a 12-hole golf course,' said Colin. 'There's been a fair bit of evolution.' It had started out as a nine-hole course in the late 19th century. Within a couple of decades the course had been extended to 18 holes, with six of the newer holes on higher peaty ground. Before long those holes were abandoned, the land reverting to wilderness, leaving Shiskine with the unique 12-hole layout it has today. And it was all in Colin's book.

The fifth tee was out on a point. We had to cross a small wooden bridge to reach it. Colin explained that the tee, once just a rock, had been built up by his brother in the 1960s. 'He had the local haulage business and carted 200 tons of sand to make that tee,' said Colin.

When we came to the sixth hole, Colin declared it his favourite hole on the course. Shore Hole was a classic links hole, a short par four by the sea, the fairway full of hillocks. It was the sort of golf hole that looked like nothing had ever been done to it, a golf hole that just was. I was reminded of Askernish. Noble Brian, who had played many more courses than I had, was reminded of a course closer by, Prestwick on the Ayrshire coast.

Colin gazed down the fairway. 'I've probably had more

birdies here than any other hole on the course.' So his favourite hole had also been kind to him over the years. Left of the fairway was rough, to the right was a fence, then the sea. A sign on the fence read DANGER COASTAL EROSION – KEEP OFF. They weren't kidding. Colin said that the fairway had once been 15 yards wider. One day those 15 yards had simply collapsed onto the beach.

We tackled Colin's favourite golf hole and Noble Brian played it very well indeed. He was born to the links. I tasted the salt tang of the sea air as I looked for my ball in the long grass, having hooked my drive. All I found were bits of dead seagull. I gave up on my ball and joined Colin. I asked him how often he played these days.

'Usually three times a week. Less in the summer when the course is so crowded. At my age, all my playing partners seem to be dropping off.'

The next hole, Himalayas, involved a blind approach to the green, a black and white post at the top of Everest – a different Everest from Askernish – indicating the way. You had to keep your wits about you on this course, but I climbed Everest and got down in two for my par.

White sand streaked the wide fairway of the eighth hole, Hades. The holes at Shiskine had such wonderful names. Everything seemed to play in the course's favour. I'd fallen head over heels for the place. I knew I'd want to come back here and play again.

The ninth hole was the only par five on a very short course, even for 12 holes. 'Big hitters can get on in two sometimes,' said Colin as we stood on the tee, 'but most human beings have to play their second short of the burn.'

Noble Brian birdied the hole and I made par, which pleased me greatly. I usually ran out of steam on the par fives, so this five felt like an eagle.

We enjoyed the tenth hole, a sweet par three fittingly called Paradise, and then, at the penultimate hole, Colin, our energetic spotter, paced to the top of the hill to tell us when we could hit.

It was getting pretty hot out on the course and I was recalling my brother's stag-do, me leading everyone up that unshaded glen in punishing sunshine. I found the sun lotion in my golf bag and began applying it like mad. I also had my dad's bucket hat on, so I was Mr Prepared. And I was wearing my new golf shoes. They felt good. Golf shoes were a good idea. As for my new waterproof trousers and my cagoule, I wasn't needing them today. But their time would come. This was Scotland after all.

We were nearing the end of our round at Shiskine with Colin. What a time we were having on this quirky little course next to the sparkling sea. The Crow's Nest had provided a great deal of the quirkiness, the Shelf had been exhilarating while Shore Hole was just a classic golf hole.

Shiskine's final hole was a bit of a nothing hole, a flat par three with no standout features, distinctly ordinary after the out-of-the-ordinary that preceded it. 'It can be anything from a driver to a putter, depending on the wind,' said Colin. Of course, this was the hole he had aced no less than three times. Today was a day for an easy seven iron. After putting out, Noble Brian and I shook hands with each other and with Colin and thanked him.

Back in the club shop, Hamish asked if we'd enjoyed

our round. We couldn't deny that we had. Hamish described the course as 'old school architecture', a description that Noble Brian happily agreed with. The rolling landscape was used to wonderful effect and lots of quirky natural features helped make the course memorable.

Colin was going to leave us now. We said cheerio and I hoped I'd come back to Shiskine one day and see him again. It was something to meet such a gracious man, someone so tuned in to his golf course that he had written its story. You can't beat local knowledge and no one knew Shiskine like Colin. It was a real pleasure sharing our day on Arran with him. Shiskine would have been fun anyway, but it was more fun in the company of Mr Shiskine. Colin's presence had made it extra special.

Noble Brian and I had coffee and rolls with sausage in the clubhouse, the names of past club presidents – including Colin – on the wall. Noble Brian was intrigued by framed correspondence from the original course architect, Willie Fernie, which was also on display. I asked Noble Brian for his verdict on Shiskine. 'Holes that are worthy of a better course and other holes, well, nice idea,' he said. 'A fun course.' I'd found Shiskine to be a bundle of fun. The key was to be open-minded and relaxed enough to enjoy this curious 12-hole course on the west coast of Arran. I was already thinking of future family holidays here. Some places just have that effect on you.

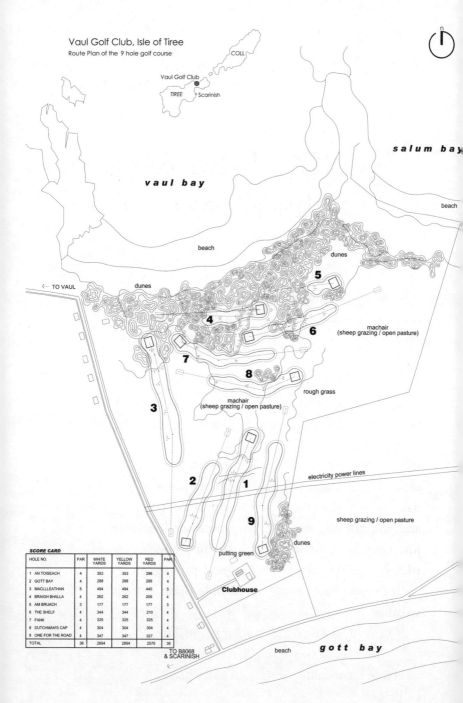

Vaul Golf Club, Isle of Tiree
Route Plan of the 9 hole golf course

COLL

Vaul Golf Club

TIREE ● Scarinish

salum bay

beach

vaul bay

beach

dunes

← TO VAUL

dunes

5

4

6

machair
(sheep grazing / open pasture)

7

8

rough grass

3

machair
(sheep grazing / open pasture)

electricity power lines

2   1

9

sheep grazing / open pasture

dunes

putting green

Clubhouse

beach   gott bay

TO B8068
& SCARINISH

SCORE CARD

HOLE NO.		PAR	WHITE YARDS	YELLOW YARDS	RED YARDS	PAR
1	AN TOISEACH	4	353	353	296	4
2	GOTT BAY	4	288	288	288	4
3	MACLLLEATHAN	5	494	494	440	5
4	BRAIGH BHALLA	4	262	262	209	4
5	AM BRUACH	3	177	177	177	3
6	THE SHELF	4	344	344	210	4
7	FANK	4	325	325	325	4
8	DUTCHMAN'S CAP	4	304	304	304	4
9	ONE FOR THE ROAD	4	347	347	327	4
TOTAL		36	2894	2894	2576	36

Chapter 9

The Land Beneath the Waves – Tiree

'Ominous looking,' said Noble Brian, peeking through the curtains of our Oban hostel room and seeing dark clouds over Mull.

We'd last been in Oban a few weeks ago, passing through the busy west coast port after our journey round the Outer Hebrides. Now we were back with our latest plan of action. Four islands – Tiree, Iona, Mull and Seil – in the space of three days. After which, I'd have done 12 islands (I was still counting North Uist. We'd been there, with our golf clubs). By the time we came off the course at Seil in three days' time, I'd have achieved two-thirds of my overall target, and we still had much of the summer left. Noble Brian just needed to fit in his trip to Bute and he'd be on 12 islands too. We were making good progress.

'It doesn't look good,' said Noble Brian, scowling at the weather.

'Oh well,' I said. 'It'll be sunny on Tiree.'

'What makes you think that laddie?'

'Tiree's sunshine central. It's about the sunniest place in Britain.'

I'd done some research.

'How do they measure that?' asked a sceptical Noble Brian.

'Sunglasses,' I explained. 'How long the locals have to wear them in the course of an average day.'

'Cannae be. Don't believe it.'

'It's true.'

'Sunniest place in Britain,' said Noble Brian shaking his head. 'I'll hold you to that.'

We left the hostel with just our golf bags since we'd be back there later tonight. Both of us had gone back to a half-set of clubs, though I'd managed to pack my sand wedge this time. We made our way along Oban's seafront to the ferry terminal. My dad once fished out of Oban when he worked the fishing grounds off the west coast years ago. My granda too. I wondered what they would have made of me leaving Oban harbour with a set of golf clubs.

At the ferry terminal, two pipers were talking to the woman at the ticket desk. They were heading over to Mull to compete in the annual Highland Games, but they had a dilemma, which they were explaining to the woman. Their problem was that they were a piper down. Their friend had slept in. He was on his way. The woman pointed out that the ferry to Mull was about to depart. The pipers consulted one another and decided that they'd wait on their dozy friend and catch the next ferry. Noble Brian and I stepped forward and got two tickets to Tiree.

Once on the ferry, we only had one thing on our minds – the CalMac breakfast. We ditched our bags and marched to the cafe where we said yes to everything. Yes to sausages, yes to bacon, double yes to black pudding and yes, why not, to fried egg and beans. Adding two slices of toast and a mug of coffee to our trays, we sat down and tucked into our morning banquet.

As we ate, Noble Brian asked me geography-related questions as if he thought I was a geography teacher or something.

'How much between the islands?'

'Eh?'

'Coll and Tiree.'

'Oh. About two miles.'

I'd done some reading on the Inner Hebrides, which Tiree and its near neighbour Coll were considered part of, so I was actually in a position to educate my unlearned friend. I warmed to this role of educator and informed my ignorant colleague that while there were no rabbits on Tiree, there were plenty on Coll.

Noble Brian looked up from his plate.

'Why's that, then?'

'I don't know.'

I hadn't expected to have to give a reason. I thought one up anyway.

'They just haven't swum across yet.'

'Well they couldn't swim across, could they?'

'No, probably not.'

'How did the rabbits get to Coll in the first place?'

'They must have parachuted in.'

There was a slight pause as Noble Brian and I pictured the same thing. Rabbits raining down on an island.

'There are hares on Tiree,' I pointed out.

'But no rabbits?'

'No.'

I took a sip of my coffee. I had a question for Noble Brian.

'What's the difference between a hare and a rabbit?'

'Is this a joke?'

'No, serious question.'

'They're sort of the same, aren't they?'

'Hares and rabbits aren't the same. They're as different as cows and sheep.'

'Cows and sheep?' Noble Brian frowned.

'Aye, cows and sheep.'

'You don't get milk from a sheep.'

'Aye, you do. How do you think we get sheep cheese?'

'Sheep cheese?' Noble Brian put down his fork. 'That's about the most disgusting thing I've ever heard.'

'You mean to say you've never had a sheep cheese and tomato pizza?'

'Ach, you're putting me off my breakfast.'

'You're telling me you've never tasted sheese?'

'Sheese?'

'Sheep cheese.'

'There's no such thing.'

'What about manchego?'

'Ach, away ye go.'

From rabbits to sheep cheese in three easy hops. It was the kind of early morning conversation made possible by a late night in an Oban pub. Noble Brian and I put our plates and our differences aside and stretched out in our seats, adopting the CalMac breakfast recovery position.

When we were ready, we rose from the table and went out on deck. The ferry was making its way up the Sound of Mull, just as we'd sailed down it a few weeks back with Ali. It had been much sunnier then, though these clouds looked to be clearing. The sun would be shining by the time we reached Tiree, I was certain of it. Just as I was sure about the existence of sheese.

We sailed westward and after some time stopped at Coll. I didn't see any rabbits bouncing about. Coll seemed a rugged island, very rocky, if not quite eastern Harris. Soon we were on our way again and before too long we had reached Tiree.

Tiree looked nothing like Coll. For a start, it was very green. It was also very flat. Tiree's Gaelic name is *Tir fo Thuinn* – The Land Beneath the Waves. From the pier, I could see a long white beach. Adding to the instant magic of this low-lying island was the clearness of the water. Tiree put me in mind of a coral atoll. And there I go again with my South Pacific comparisons.

But there was real beauty here and I was struck by the rare quality of the light. Everything seemed, well, brighter. Standing on the pier in the sunshine (we couldn't very well have turned up at one of the sunniest spots in Britain with the sun not shining) I felt completely relaxed after our long journey. I let Tiree wash over me for a moment. Then we went looking for the bus that would get us to the golf course.

Angus the bus driver said they'd been getting more golfers

on the island recently. Tiree is better known for its windsurfing. As well as being one of the sunniest spots in Britain,
it is one of the windiest. The wind didn't seem all that
strong today, more of a gentle breeze. Let it stay that way,
I thought. We'd come here to play golf, not take to the
waves. Although looking at that stunning blue sea, I did
want to be in it.

The bus, carrying us and a few other passengers, travelled along the road with fields and the occasional white-
washed house to our left and the gorgeous big bay I'd seen
from the pier constantly on our right. Angus stopped at a
hotel to let off a panicky Englishwoman. She was worried
about catching her ferry tomorrow. Angus assured her he'd
come and pick her up. The woman got off and a man
stepped on the bus. He wasn't going anywhere. He just
wanted to arrange getting picked up later. Angus essentially ran a combined bus and taxi service. But Angus wasn't
too happy with the man, reminding him that he'd twice
asked to be picked up recently and on both occasions had
failed to be there when Angus turned up. Angus had also
heard the man had been using a rival bus service. The man
apologised and Angus agreed to pick him up later, on the
basis that he'd be there. The man, having been let off the
hook, thanked Angus and got off the bus, and we were on
our way again.

Soon Angus turned off the road at a red phone box and
we had arrived at our destination. The first thing I noticed
was the number of sheep. So it was that kind of golf course.
I looked back across the bay and could see the ferry still
at the pier. Noble Brian and I decided that we'd walk back

after our round. It was only a couple of miles at most, the sun was shining, it was a nine-hole course and we had hours until our ferry back to Oban. We thanked Angus for dropping us off and told him we wouldn't need picking up. He wished us a good round and off he drove.

Inscribed on a slab of stone close to the first tee were the words Vaul Golf Club. Noble Brian and I crossed a cattle grid to get to the small clubhouse. It was closed. But what did that matter? What were we going to do in a clubhouse? We were here to play golf. We each put £15 in the honesty box and took a receipt. We saw that a week ticket would have set us back £40. Now there was a golf break. While the fortnight ticket was even better value at £50. While we were getting ready, a truck arrived, three men jumping out and grabbing their clubs from the back. They waved us on. They were in no hurry. Time for us to tee off on Tiree.

'Look!' said Noble Brian, pointing down the opening hole. Sheep filled the rough at either side of the narrow fairway. 'They're helping us. They're defining the fairway.'

'Aye, but they're not doing that to help us. There's more grass in the rough.'

'Aye, so if the sheep are eating the rough, why's there rough? They're just nibbling, and helping us at the same time.'

I wasn't going to argue with him. This conversation was heading the way of the rabbit conversation.

It really was a very narrow fairway though. Like the fairways at Muirfield, if you blocked out the sheep and telegraph poles. Noble Brian felt that Tiree could be a US

Open venue. Well, it was nearer America than most Scottish golf courses.

The thought of Muirfield returned me to my first golfing memory. I was seven years old in the summer of 1980 when my parents took me to Muirfield to see the Open. Tom Watson won but all I remember was me trying to get Seve's autograph. My dad brought me forward and I held out my notepad and pen. Among all the other notepads and pens. Seve eventually gave me his autograph. Then he walked off with my pen, barging my mam out of the way. Unintentionally I think. In any case, she remained a big Seve fan.

Somehow I found Tiree's tight first fairway with as good a drive as I could have hoped for. I thanked the sheep. Noble Brian's tee shot was just as accurate and twice as long.

The sky appeared bigger in Tiree, and that wonderful light had such a calming effect. This was a beguiling island. Tiree seemed to agree with me and I decided that this should be one of those rare days when I golfed without a care in the world.

The only sound was that of bleating sheep. As with Barra, the greens were surrounded by fences that kept off the livestock. But I was far happier having to contend with sheep than cows. Much less of a menace, in my opinion.

'What did you make?' asked Noble Brian as we exited the gate at the first green.

'Six.'

'Ach, never mind. Put it down to ferrylag.'

I didn't mind and wasn't too tired either. The moment

we'd landed on Tiree I'd felt lifted and ready for the day. All I'd done was play a hole badly after a good tee shot.

The sheep had fairly left their mark on the second tee. It was covered in their shit. As Noble Brian tried his best to avoid it – an impossible task really if you wanted to tee off – he wondered where the course stood from a health and safety point of view.

'One piece of advice,' said my colleague.

'What's that?'

'Don't lick your golf ball.'

'I'm not in the habit of licking golf balls.'

'I wouldn't anyway.'

I didn't come close to finding this fairway, hooking my ball into the rough. Not that I had any trouble finding it. The rough at Tiree was very forgiving. The sheep saw to that with their focused nibbling. You tended to be left with a good lie.

Noble Brian was thoroughly enjoying his round. He'd found a new category of golf course – farmyard links. That it was different again to anything we'd encountered delighted him. He hadn't wanted to come all this way to be faced by the familiar. Every island course we'd played had given the golf architect something to chew on.

I wasn't playing very well, but the sunshine and the breeze – Tiree in a nutshell – were of comfort, as was the scenery. We had come to the fourth tee on the north side of the island, having gone shore to shore (it hadn't taken long). I could have gazed at that beautiful beach all day. You could hit your tee shot, but would you ever want to leave? I wanted to put down my clubs and go and sit down on the sand, take off my golf shoes and have a paddle in the Atlantic. And I should have done. We'd all the time in the world. I think what prevented me was the learned order of a round of golf. You finished one hole and moved on to the next. You didn't interrupt your round with a trip to the beach.

I may not have gone paddling, but I did live up to the wondrous setting with a big drive, my ball disappearing over the hill. Noble Brian bashed his monster tee shot into the distance, then started finding fault with this gorgeous golf hole. He wasn't happy with its direction. In the golf architect's eyes, the hole should have continued through the dunes and not veered away from the shore.

'You leave those dunes alone,' I told him. 'They're lovely.'

'*That* could have been the hole,' sighed Noble Brian, pointing his driver across the dunes. 'It's a missed opportunity.'

'We've got the best of both worlds. Nice dunes and a nice golf hole.'

'Ach.'

At the end of the fourth hole, a perfectly good golf hole that didn't need the likes of Noble Brian tampering with it, I considered my below par performance so far and acknowledged that I was quite a lot over par. I'd started out 6-6-6-6. The number of the golf beast. I really wasn't doing well at all, and I couldn't have cared less.

'I'm feeling a bit jiggered,' said Noble Brian. He said jiggered was his favourite word. That and scunnered. But he wasn't scunnered. He was tired, but happy.

At one of the holes I didn't bother with the gate to the green and simply climbed over the fence. They weren't electrified and this one was fairly low. Noble Brian followed me, but with his shorter leg span had to push down on the top wire to get over. The fences on this golf course were clearly designed to keep both the sheep and Noble Brian off the greens.

On the final hole, I overhit my putt and my ball stopped short of the cup thanks to a pile of something that an animal other than a sheep had left behind.

'You used the shit well there,' said Noble Brian.

'Thanks.'

He reminded me not to lick my golf ball. And I pointed out once again that I didn't lick golf balls. Then we shook hands.

Nine islands down. I had reached the halfway point.

We walked over to a gate to get to the clubhouse. The gate had a sign on it. KEEP GATE SHUT. ANY PERSON FOUND LEAVING GATE OPEN WILL BE SHOT. SURVIVORS WILL BE SHOT AGAIN!

Whatever you do when you've finished your round on Tiree, close that gate. If you don't, the sheep will get through. Worse than that, you'll be taken out. As warnings go, it was a strong one. We figured it was tongue-in-cheek, but we closed the gate anyway, just to be on the safe side.

I lay down on the grass next to the clubhouse and stared at the clear blue sky. When I'd done staring, I got up and cleaned the sheep shit off my golf shoes. I was so glad I'd bought a pair of golf shoes. I'd never have managed this course in a pair of trainers.

Noble Brian and I set off on our walk back to the pier. We walked by the side of the road for a bit, stopping for a pint at the hotel where the bus had stopped earlier. We sat in the beer garden overlooking the bay. You couldn't have wished for a better spot for a drink after a round of golf.

After our pint, we crossed the road and went down onto the beach, our plan being to walk the rest of the way across the sand. I was reminded of our walk to the pier on Eriskay. And Noble Brian couldn't resist having another crack. He started hitting golf balls across the beach and was sensible enough to stop when we came within range of a family out walking their dog.

At the end of the beach, we had to clamber up some rocks, climb over a stile and walk across a field. Ahead of us – just up from the pier – was a striking looking structure, which we went and investigated. It turned out to be An Turas (the Journey), an award-winning ferry shelter once voted the best building in Scotland. A long white-walled enclosure ending in a glass box offering a fantastic view of the bay. Noble Brian and I did the decent thing, merging golf and architecture, and putted the length of the building.

There was still some time until our ferry, so we wandered up the road until we found a shop. We bought sandwiches and drinks and had an impromptu picnic at a lovely location, picked by me, overlooking a tiny beach. 'Aye, great spot chief,' said Noble Brian, pointing out the public toilets behind us and the two sewage pipes that flanked the beach.

Back at the pier we met Angus, sitting behind the wheel of his bus, ready to take more people to wherever they needed to get to. I asked him about the beach at the back of the golf course, the one I'd wanted to leave the fourth tee for and go in the water. It was called Vaul Bay. Of course, the golf course was called Vaul. I said to Angus how amazing the beach was. He was glad we'd enjoyed our day and said that the next time we visited the island we should try windsurfing.

I could have lingered longer on Tiree, this laid-back island with the endless sky and remarkable light. I'd been wooed by the Land Beneath the Waves, but it was time to go.

Noble Brian and I sat out on the back deck of the ferry as it made the long journey back to Oban. We stopped once more at Coll and saw a couple being escorted off the boat. I recognised them from the queue at boarding on Tiree. They'd seemed quite tipsy then and now they looked even more drunk as they stumbled up the slipway together. The woman had had a walking stick at the pier on Tiree, but she didn't have it now. She was leaning on the man, but he could barely walk because of the state he was in. It was as much a case of her supporting him. They broke off and stood looking at one another. They were arguing. The man snapped. In a strop, he threw his mobile phone to the ground, some of it bouncing off the slipway into the sea. He seemed to realise what he'd done. He stood with his head in his hands, the woman shouting at him. The two were in a bad way. Where did they go from there?

We left the bickering, blootered couple; the ferry heading off into the calm evening, towards the Sound of Mull. In a few hours' time we'd be back in Oban. My mind was already turning to the morning and the prospect of a game of golf on Iona.

Iona Golf Course, Isle of Iona
Route Plan of the 18 hole golf course

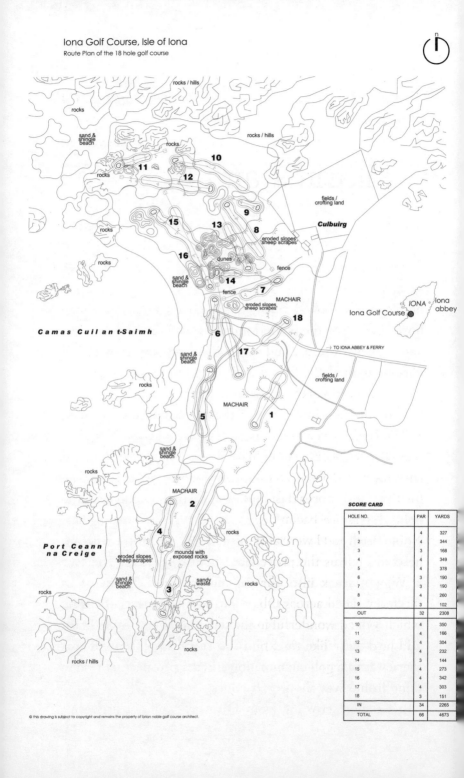

n

rocks / hills

rocks

sand &
shingle
beach

rocks / hills

rocks

11

rocks

12

10

fields /
crofting land

Culbuirg

15

13

9

8

eroded slopes
'sheep scrapes'

16

dunes

14

fence

sand &
shingle
beach

fence

7

MACHAIR

Camas Cuil an t-Saimh

eroded slopes
'sheep scrapes'

18

IONA Iona
abbey

Iona Golf Course ●

6

rocks

sand &
shingle
beach

17

→ TO IONA ABBEY & FERRY

rocks

MACHAIR

5

1

fields /
crofting land

sand &
shingle
beach

rocks

MACHAIR

2

rocks

4

mounds with
exposed rocks

*Port Ceann
na Creige*

eroded slopes
'sheep scrapes'

sand &
shingle
beach

sandy
waste

rocks

rocks

3

rocks

rocks / hills

rocks

© this drawing is subject to copyright and remains the property of brian noble golf course architect.

SCORE CARD

HOLE NO.	PAR	YARDS
1	4	327
2	4	344
3	3	168
4	4	349
5	4	378
6	3	190
7	4	190
8	4	260
9	3	102
OUT	32	2308
10	4	350
11	4	166
12	4	304
13	4	232
14	3	144
15	4	273
16	4	342
17	4	303
18	3	151
IN	34	2265
TOTAL	66	4673

Chapter 10

Pilgrims and Flag Pins
– Iona

Noble Brian looked through the curtains of our Oban hostel room for the second morning in a row. It was overcast, but the forecast said no rain. We'd settle for that. We checked out of the hostel and, this time carrying all our bags, walked along the seafront to the ferry terminal where we boarded the first ferry of the day to Mull.

The captain welcomed us on board. Not personally, but over the speakers. Though he knew how to talk to his passengers, wholeheartedly recommending Mariners Cafe for the CalMac breakfast and even listing some of its highlights. 'Ayrshire bacon … Stornoway black pudding …' Noble Brian and I were at the counter with our trays before he could tell us the provenance of the beans.

We got stuck into our captain-approved breakfasts as the ferry sailed across Oban Bay past the Isle of Kerrera, which looked wonderful in the morning light. Noble Brian said he'd quite like to explore Kerrera. I pointed out that there wasn't a golf course. Noble Brian said that not everything in life was about golf courses.

It's a short crossing from Oban to Mull and it wasn't

long before the ferry was docking at the pier at Craignure.
We were playing the local golf course later in the day –
the Mull portion of this 18-islands adventure – and spending
the night in Craignure. But first we had to get to Iona and
back. A bus ran from Craignure to Fionnphort at the western
side of Mull. From there, we'd catch the ferry to Iona.
We had a busy day ahead, one that involved two rounds
of golf (18 holes on Iona, nine holes on Mull) and we
wouldn't have wanted it any other way.

As we looked for our bus we thought that surely it
wasn't the one with the bagpipe music blaring and the
driver standing by the door wearing tartan trews. Quite
a few people coming off our ferry were heading straight
for that bus. But it turned out not to be ours. It was bound
for nearby Duart Castle. 'It's like being put in a shortbread tin and piped to a place of historic interest,' said
Noble Brian.

Our bus – a bog-standard bus without bagpipe music
and with a driver who wasn't tartaned up – duly arrived
and Noble Brian and I boarded with a few other tourists
who weren't lugging golf clubs about. The bus travelled
along a bendy road through magnificent mountain scenery.
I hadn't realised how grand scale Mull was. Though I was
keeping one eye on the road. The journey was quite frantic
at times, the bus driver challenging most oncoming traffic
to a game of chicken. Farmers in their tractors, holiday-
makers in their campervans, sheep in their fleeces ... the
bus driver took them all on and won. He was less confronta-
tional with the bus full of nuns that squeezed past us.

As our bus skirted a lovely bay, I spotted something dark

in the water and got pretty excited about it. Noble Brian couldn't believe the fuss I was making over what, to him, was a rock being washed by a wave. 'Either that or it's a mutant rock,' he said, laughing. I assured him that it hadn't been a rock, that it had been a dolphin or some other marine mammal. Noble Brian asked if I was needing glasses.

We reached the tiny pier at Fionnphort with the two of us still arguing over what I'd witnessed in the bay. The clouds were beginning to clear and it had the makings of another beautiful day in Scotland. The Scottish summer, it does exist. I'm telling you.

As we walked onto the ferry with our golf bags and other bags, one or two of the ferrymen nodded at us. Daft buggers, they were probably thinking.

Imagine my delight when I discovered on the ferry a wall chart of Commonly Sighted Cetaceans Around the Hebrides. I studied it in detail, determined to find a match for the object I'd seen in the bay earlier that most definitely wasn't a rock.

Minke whale ... common dolphin ... killer whale ... bottlenose dolphin ... Atlantic white-sided dolphin ... white-beaked dolphin ... harbour porpoise ... that was it! A harbour porpoise.

According to the chart of Commonly Sighted Cetaceans Around the Hebrides, the harbour porpoise, Britain's smallest cetacean, is commonly sighted in coastal areas and especially around headlands and estuaries. They are extremely fast swimmers (mine was probably taking a breather), easily missed (not by me they're not), rarely leap out of the water (yep, mine wasn't leaping) and, upon surfacing, will only show a small part of their back and fin (that's about as much as I saw). They also don't normally approach boats. It didn't say anything about buses.

'Harbour porpoise,' I said, showing Noble Brian the picture of a harbour porpoise.

'No. *That's* what you saw.' Noble Brian was pointing out the window to a rock by the shore. It was clear to me that Noble Brian didn't know the difference between a rock and a harbour porpoise.

Mull to Iona is the briefest of ferry journeys, the Sound of Iona being only a mile wide. Noble Brian pointed out Staffa to the north. I was tempted to suggest it was a whale.

We arrived on Iona, walking up the slipway with all our bags. Some of our fellow ferry passengers were already getting on another boat that was taking them over to Staffa to see Fingal's Cave. Others were heading off to visit Iona Abbey. Iona is a tiny island with an international reputation. Every year thousands of Christian worshippers make the pilgrimage to this sacred isle where St Columba founded his monastery in 563AD. Not many visit Iona for the golf.

It occurred to me how focused my island hopping was on golf. Well, of course it was. But I did feel I'd like to revisit some of these islands someday and enjoy what they had to offer besides fairways and greens.

Iona's golf course was on the other side of the island, which meant it wasn't far at all. A mile's walk, if that. Noble Brian and I went to the post office to pick up some scorecards. I'd read on a website that that's where you got them.

A woman stood behind the counter sorting out parcels. I asked if she had any scorecards for the golf course.

'There,' she said without so much as lifting her head.

We looked around the room. Noble Brian spotted the scorecards. He took two. 'Thanks,' he said to the woman. She didn't respond. We left the post office, glad we hadn't needed to post anything.

Before we set off for the golf course, we wanted to find somewhere to dump our extra bags. It wasn't going to be the post office. We asked at a cafe and the owner pointed us to a hut next to the public toilets. The unlocked hut contained other bags so we threw ours in, fairly confident they wouldn't get pinched on Iona, of all places.

We began our walk across the island, enjoying the sunshine as we headed along a quiet road past fields of sheep. Only two cars passed us and it was the same car twice, the woman behind the wheel giving us a cheery wave on both occasions. She surely wasn't related to the woman in the post office.

The road began to climb and once we reached the top of the hill we could see the Atlantic and another island off to the northwest. It was Tiree, where we'd been yesterday. After walking a little bit further, we came to a gate with a sign that said West End Common Grazing. Beyond the gate, red flags fluttered in the breeze, against a backdrop of a blue sea and matching sky. There were sheep on the course, but we'd come to expect that. As the sign said, common grazing. This was crofting land that also happened to be golfing territory. It was a question of us sharing our round with the sheep. There were no cows as far as I could see.

The first tee was easy enough to find, though there wasn't much sign of a fairway. In fact, at first glance, the golf course was one big field. Not so much farmyard links like Tiree as, well, farmyard. The rudimentary scorecards provided us with some clues as to the layout of the course. Luckily, Noble Brian was here with his golf architect's instinct to figure out the rest. He had his uses.

The tee was absolutely covered in sheep shit and I congratulated myself again for investing in a pair of golf shoes. An old man came and sat down on the bench by the gate, gazing out to sea. He wasn't interested in us teeing off.

Noble Brian pointed to where he thought the first green might be and I knocked a solid drive over the brow of the hill.

'Your best of the day,' said Noble Brian.

'Thanks.'

The hole was a par four, but when I got to my ball, there was still no sign of a green.

'It must be over that next hill,' said Noble Brian.

I trusted him and hit a satisfying five iron. I was in dangerously decent form. We walked on and Noble Brian was proved right, the green tucked behind the second hill. It wasn't much of a green, to be honest. There wasn't a great deal of distinction between it and the fairway, and the flag was in shreds. Either the weather had done that to it or the sheep had got at it, climbing on each other's backs, creating sheep pyramids in order to reach it. No, it was probably the weather.

'Cracking piece of land for a golf course,' said Noble

Brian looking out across the machair. 'It's a pity they couldn't define it more. You could be constantly mowing and rolling these greens.'

It was rustic, but at the same time there was something wonderful about it. We could have been playing in any century. I hoped that the pilgrims to Iona had found what they were looking for, because we'd found what we came for. The golf was basic, but good for the mind and heart. A peaceful game beside a sparkling sea. I felt full of the joys of golf as Noble Brian's second tee shot struck a rock and bounced over a fence into a field with more sheep.

The third hole, a par three, was dramatic to say the least. Uphill to a raised green that dropped off steeply on all sides. Between the tee and the green was a vast sandy waste area, and behind the green, rising cliffs. The view from the green, taking in the entire course and the shore, was superb. I struggled with the hole – but loved it.

A huge rock dominated the fourth fairway and the green was behind the rock, giving us a choice of tee shots. Aim left towards the beach or go right and approach the green from that direction. Noble Brian went right. I fancied being nearer the beach, but didn't quite get near enough, leaving myself with a ridiculous blind shot over the rock. There was a lot of head scratching and laughing going on as we made our way round this singular golf course.

At one point, we met a young man out walking. He was a student at St Andrews, enjoying a break on Iona. He said he was leaving soon and sounded like he wanted to stay. He couldn't believe we had scorecards – that a course like this would have them – and asked to have his picture taken swinging a club on the tee.

Noble Brian obliged. Then Noble Brian produced a gigantic drive.

'You nailed it!' shouted the student.

Noble Brian nearly nailed a sheep too. It was doddering along on the 'fairway' minding its own business, the business of nibbling grass, when Noble Brian's ball shot an inch or two over its head. The sheep knew nothing about it and carried on nibbling.

It was my turn and I totally topped it, my ball going all of ten yards. At least the student didn't shout, 'You topped it!' He was too polite to acknowledge the fact that I'd made a pig's ear of my tee shot. The student said cheerio and wandered off, while Noble Brian and I discussed the near miss with the sheep.

'What do you do if you hit a sheep?' I wondered.

'I don't know,' said Noble Brian. 'I think we should contact the R&A and ask them "what do you do if you kill a sheep?"'

'I think it's the farmer you'd need to contact. I mean, it's his sheep.'

'I didn't kill a sheep.'

'No, not this time.'

A couple of holes later, we bumped into the student again. He'd been joined by his girlfriend. The size of the crowd had doubled and I willed myself not to repeat that earlier travesty of a tee shot. Thankfully, I caught this one perfectly. In fact, it was a huge drive by my standards, finished off with a slight and very satisfying draw.

'Nice draw,' said the student.

'It wasn't intentional,' I said, trying to play it down and be all modest while the big beam on my face made me look very pleased with myself.

Noble Brian and I continued to get a lot of satisfaction from our round on Iona and the 11th hole in particular was a heap of fun. It involved a blind tee shot with the bowl beyond the hill being there to gather a good drive. Noble Brian cracked his second shot off another huge rock in the middle of the fairway. I managed to avoid it and as I walked towards the green I was no longer interested in whether my ball had made it onto the putting surface or not.

I had become distracted by what lay to the right of the green. Holding my full attention was one of the most spectacular beaches I had ever set eyes on. It was perfect in every way. I dragged myself away from the perfect beach and muddled on, dealing with the rocks, dodging rabbit holes and climbing over stiles.

The penultimate hole required us to hit across the public path that ran from the gate at the top of the course down to the perfect beach. I waited as a family walked past. Once they were out of harm's way (I'd accounted for slice potential too) I sized up the challenge of the drive. It appeared that I had more chance of hitting a sheep than missing one, such was the number of them in front of me. Somehow I didn't strike any of them, and as I approached the ball for my second shot, the sheep made way for me. They're very considerate towards golfers, sheep. More so than cows.

The final hole was really short and we both made the green. Noble Brian actually said he would have been embarrassed to have made his first hole-in-one on Iona, that he'd much rather save his first hole-in-one for a more illustrious course. I said I wasn't that fussy. I didn't care where my first hole-in-one came, if it ever came at all. I'd have welcomed one there and then.

The closest I've ever seen anyone come to a hole-in-one was my friend Johnny at the Prieshach. We were playing with my dad and it was Johnny's first time at Hopeman. The sun was shining and Johnny's ball was heading straight for the pin. I smile every time I think of Johnny, my dad and me running forward on the tee, clubs in the air in anticipation, roaring as Johnny's ball slipped an inch past the hole. I remember it like it was yesterday.

It took me two putts to get down on Iona's final green, which was no mean feat on this course. I'd little faith as I struck what proved to be my final putt from six feet. It was the only putt of any length I'd holed during the round. The greens here were unreadable, too many variables, too many animal droppings. I could see the hole, but could never quite visualize my ball dropping in. So it was nice to finish with a putt for my par.

Noble Brian and I shook hands and I reflected on the fact that Iona was my tenth island. I'd made a start on the inward nine, so to speak. 'You're approaching Amen Corner,' said Noble Brian. I now had fewer islands ahead of me than behind me.

We took our time walking back to the village. When we got there, we went to get our other bags from the hut.

As we were grabbing them, we heard the noise of an engine. We turned round to see a nun on a quad bike. She stopped and asked Noble Brian if he wouldn't mind lifting a sack of maize from the hut and putting it in her trailer. Noble Brian dealt with the sack, which was almost the size of him, and the nun thanked him. 'That'll be your good deed for the day!' she said before motoring off.

We went and enjoyed a pint on a terrace by the shore. In that setting and in the sunshine, after a walk across the island and back and 18 holes, it was an award-winning pint. 'The Holy Grail of pints,' said Noble Brian, eyeing his glass. We stuck to just the one, as we'd more golf to play on Mull before the day was over. There was no let-up and no complaints either.

Craignure Golf Club, Isle of Mull
Route Plan of the 9 hole golf course

Tobermory

MULL

Craignure

Craignure Golf Club

Scallastle Bay

Sound of Mull

rocks

rocks

beach

shingle beach

heather

gorse / whin

11th tee

gorse / whin

gorse

gorse

gorse

marsh

bracken / whin

bracken

woodland

bracken/whin

woodland

marsh / bog

woodland

burn

bunker

gorse

beach

shingle beach

gorse

bracken

woodland

river

A849

Clubhouse

safety fence

gorse / whin

shingle beach

shingle beach

gorse

gorse / whin

TO SALEN
& TOBERMORY

TO CRAIGNURE
& FERRY

1 2 3 4 5 6 7 8 9

SCORE CARD

HOLE NO.		PAR	MEN YARDS	LADIES YARDS	PAR
1	LOCHALINE	4	261	245	4
2	LOCHLINNHE	3	180	173	3
3	ALT CREICH	4	262	222	4
4	ININNMORE	4	358	281	4
5	DUN DA GHAOITHE	3	132	129	3
6	MAL NAN DAMH	4	435	400	4
7	GLAS EILEANAN	4	310	158	4
8	CNOC BHACAIN	3	177	172	3
9	TOROSAY	4	430	425	5
TOTAL		33	2545	2005	33

Chapter 11

The Allure of Craignure – Mull

Following another ferry and bus combo, we found ourselves back in Craignure by teatime. We walked the couple of hundred yards to our B&B. Handily, the owners of the Linnhe View also ran the golf course, something I'd been delighted to learn when booking the room.

On the front door of the B&B, a lovely old house overlooking the Sound of Mull and Loch Linnhe, was a note. 'Hi Gary, we are on the golf course. Please come in. You are in Room 1 up the stairs. See you around 5.30. Mary.'

We got settled into our room, had a cup of coffee and, before long, heard someone calling. Mary was back. We went downstairs and introduced ourselves.

Mary was happy that we'd made it. There had been some confusion over our arrival time. This confusion had been caused either by me being vague, or saying one thing and doing another. Mary had thought we were coming off the ferry from Oban. We had come off the ferry from Oban, except we'd done so first thing in the morning and since then had been to Iona and back. Mary and her husband Jim had been out at the golf course, taking turns to come back each time a ferry arrived from Oban. I apologised for being a dunderheid. Mary was fine about it though. She was just glad we'd got here.

She drove us the couple of miles to the golf course. She and Jim were busy preparing the course for Sunday's Open, the biggest competition of the year. The forecast wasn't looking great. 'It's been really wet recently,' said Mary.

Home for Mary and Jim was once Zimbabwe. They had left the trouble-torn country a few years ago and come to Scotland. 'It was a big adjustment,' said Mary. 'We knew Mull. We'd been over on holiday a couple of times with the kids and we definitely wanted to be in Scotland. We love Scotland.

'I look out every day and I think there are worse places to be. It's just wonderful. The winters are a bit grim. I don't like the winter much. It's quite cold and it's dark at four o'clock. But it could be worse.'

The idea of getting involved in a golf club had always appealed to Jim and he had become the chairman at Craignure. The club had a greenkeeper, Ronnie, who also worked on the ferries. Ronnie had looked after the course for years. He had thought about giving up the greenkeeping a couple of years ago, but had carried on, much to Mary and Jim's relief. Without Ronnie, Mary said, they wouldn't have managed. 'Everyone bows to Ronnie around here.'

We arrived at a golf course bathed in golden evening sunshine, the trees casting long shadows on the fairways. Jim was out on a tractor at the far end of the course by the water. I commented on the beauty of the setting. Mary told us about some of the wonderful wildlife. Two sea eagles were nesting near one of the tees. 'They've managed to rear chicks and I've been keeping an eye on them,' smiled Mary. 'I've called them Pitch and Putt.'

Noble Brian and I each gave Mary our £15 for the round. The club, like many other island clubs, operated an honesty box. Mary mentioned a group of rugby players who had played the course recently and left a penny in the envelope. She hoped that we would enjoy our nine holes, and left us to it.

I botched my opening tee shot, driving my ball straight into the burn. It didn't even bounce in. I never found the ball either. It was the first ball I'd lost all day. I'd played 18 holes on rough-and-ready Iona without losing a ball, only to lose one now. Noble Brian had no such trouble with the burn, clearing it by a mile. The wee man outgunned me every time. And he began his round on Mull with a birdie.

When booking the B&B a few days earlier and learning about Mary and Jim's connection with the course, I'd mentioned that I was travelling with a golf architect. On the drive over, Mary had taken me for the golf architect. This had delighted me. Noble Brian, the golf architect, was having trouble getting over it.

'Maybe I look like one,' I said.

'You look like you're off to a music festival,' said Noble Brian, nodding at me in my T-shirt and bucket hat. 'Or worse still, just back from one.'

Jim came by on his tractor and stopped to say hello. He'd a Saltire draped over the back of the seat. 'You've got the good weather!' he said. 'Find your way round all right?'

'No problem,' I said. Craignure was far from being Barra, or Iona for that matter.

Having just told Jim that we were coping fine, we somehow got the next hole all wrong, teeing off from the wrong place and turning a par three into a par four. The layout of the course was a little bit confusing. Still, standing next to the sea in the sunshine, I couldn't even begin to get annoyed.

I love playing golf on a warm summer's evening. It reminds me of my Hopeman childhood. And I enjoy that sense of squeezing more out of the day. We'd squeezed plenty from this day and it still had some way to go yet. We lingered on the green by the water, sailing boats bobbing up and down and birds swooping. I took my time with my putt. It didn't help any. I still missed.

On a third tee strewn with bird feathers, we turned our backs on the sea and hit towards the hills. Wherever you looked was a treat. Craignure reminded me a little of Sconser on Skye – a golf course wedged between the mountains and the sea.

The lush fairways were a pleasure to play off. In truth, they were a welcome break from the kind of fairways we'd become accustomed to on the islands, well those that had fairways anyway. Yes, it was nice to have good lies for a change.

'Keep left, avoid the bushes.' These words of advice came from Noble Brian on the fourth hole. I kept it left and found the fairway. My playing partner skied his tee shot. It wasn't like him. Noble Brian was left bemused by his ugly effort. Stuff like that happened to me all the time on the golf course.

The walk to the sixth tee turned into a trek. It was like walking through a jungle. A Mull jungle. Mary had mentioned this dense woodland walk. The upshot of it was that once we reached the tee we had to carry a mighty amount of rough in order to make the fairway. Looking down the hole, with the hills in the background, I was both thrilled and awed by the challenge. I wanted to meet it and did, smacking my ball into the sunlight. I didn't see it drop, but I knew it was good.

Neither of us had had any expectations for Craignure, probably because we had scheduled it after Tiree and Iona and both of those had seemed somehow more exotic, partly because of the greater effort required in getting there. I was enjoying my early evening round on Mull. For Noble Brian, the course was a little disjointed, with some crossover holes and long walks to tees. He felt the routing of the holes left a lot to be desired and had maybe been altered to make the course longer, but there were some good shots on offer and the big smooth greens were a joy to putt on.

The standout hole was the seventh, which also turned out to be my best hole. I held my nerve when faced with another tricky tee shot, and easily carried the water with my second, my ball landing just short of the green. I pitched to within a couple of feet and tapped in for a satisfying par.

I was pretty chuffed with myself. And then golf got me back on the next hole, the awful eighth. Still basking in the glory of my display at the previous hole, I stood on the tee, intent on walloping my ball towards the green, and instead shanked it into the sea. The minute you get things right, you're on the verge of getting them wrong.

Jim was waiting for us when we came in to give us a lift back. Ronnie the greenkeeper was around too and said hello. Jim asked how we'd got on. I said it had been fun, once I'd got over the disappointment of losing my ball to the burn with my opening shot. 'My first ever shot here went straight into that burn,' said Jim. It wasn't just me then. I'd make sure I got over it next time.

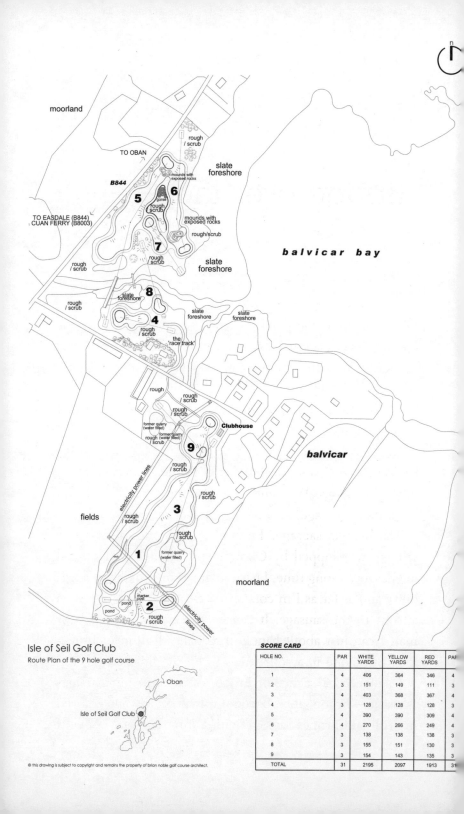

Isle of Seil Golf Club
Route Plan of the 9 hole golf course

Isle of Seil Golf Club

© this drawing is subject to copyright and remains the property of brian noble golf course architect.

SCORE CARD

HOLE NO.	PAR	WHITE YARDS	YELLOW YARDS	RED YARDS	PAR
1	4	406	364	346	4
2	3	151	149	111	3
3	4	403	368	367	4
4	3	128	128	128	3
5	4	390	390	309	4
6	4	270	266	249	4
7	3	138	138	138	3
8	3	155	151	130	3
9	3	154	143	135	3
TOTAL	31	2195	2097	1913	31

Chapter 12

Bridge over the Atlantic – Seil

We were up at the crack of dawn the next morning for the first ferry back to Oban. Ronnie the Craignure green-keeper was on the gangway in his ferry worker capacity as we boarded. He nodded, but didn't say anything. Perhaps it was the time of day, or maybe he thought we'd wrecked his golf course.

Noble Brian and I decided to forgo the CalMac breakfast on this occasion, both being of the opinion that it was time to downsize. We went instead for the streamline option of roll and sausage.

That's links sausage. Proper sausage. Not the square sausage worshipped by Glaswegians. Though I have lived in Glasgow a long time, I have retained my northern sensibility and as far as I'm concerned the square sausage is an affront to the sausage. It can be like chewing on a beer mat. I can just about handle it as part of a bigger breakfast. But alone in a roll? It has to be the links sausage.

I squeezed a sachet of broon sauce onto my sausages (sausage = broon sauce, bacon = tomato sauce) and enjoyed my roll and proper sausage with a mug of black coffee. I still felt peckish afterwards and considered ordering the CalMac breakfast, but I stuck to my guns and my health kick and didn't.

It was a ridiculously serene crossing back to the mainland. Barely a ripple in the sea, not a breath of wind, not a cloud in the sky. As we approached Oban, we were seeing it in the best of lights. It looked gorgeous, not something often said of Oban. But there, I've said it.

Yes, it was building up to be another beautiful day in Scotland. How lucky had we been with the weather on this trip? I hadn't had a chance to try out my new cagoule and waterproof trousers yet. The forecast for tomorrow was terrible, but we'd be home and dry by then. I hoped though that the forecast would improve for Mary and Jim's sake, for Craignure's big day. They deserved their Open in the sunshine.

Noble Brian and I left the ferry and waited at a bus stop on Oban's seafront for the 418 to Seil. I'd never heard of Seil until I came across it on my golf map of Scotland. It is one of the so-called Slate Islands, along with Easdale and Luing. These were 'the islands that roofed the world' during the 18th and 19th centuries when there was extensive slate quarrying on them.

Seil is the Slate Island with the golf course, and you didn't even need a boat to get there. Seil, like Skye, can be reached via a bridge, but a much older, more dramatic sounding bridge. I was pretty excited about crossing 'the Bridge over the Atlantic'.

The 418 turned up, the driver stepping off the bus to light a cigarette. He cut a somewhat dishevelled figure.

Wild hair, unshaven, bloodshot eyes. He reminded me of Father Jack in the classic TV comedy *Father Ted*. Maybe the 418 wasn't the bus to Seil. Maybe it was the bus to Craggy Island.

Noble Brian and I nodded at Father Jack who told us he'd had a hard week. He looked like he'd had a hard week. But that was him now, off duty for the rest of the weekend. We'd be getting another driver, said Father Jack, who then wandered off into the Oban morning. I was happy that Father Jack was getting his well-earned break, but in a way I wished that it was him driving us across 'the Bridge over the Atlantic'. It could have been some bus journey with Father Jack at the wheel. Perhaps it was for the best.

Our new bus driver turned up. He was young, clean cut and looked like he'd had a decent night's sleep. Noble Brian and I climbed on the bus with all our bags and sat at the back where we were hit by the smell. The bus reeked. It had the whiff of wet dog or something. But we refused to let this strong odour dampen our enthusiasm. We were heading for 'the Bridge over the Atlantic' and more island golf in the sunshine.

Some miles south of Oban we reached a turn off with the sign ATLANTIC BRIDGE. I could barely contain my excitement. Noble Brian, on the other hand, was remaining sceptical. To his mind, this bridge couldn't possibly live up to all the hype. If I was being honest, part of me was worried that the bridge crossing might turn out to be a non-event.

I shouldn't have had any concerns. 'The Bridge over the Atlantic' is fully deserving of its fancy title. OK, so you don't actually cross the Atlantic. The bridge spans a narrow sound. But it's a lovely old humpbacked bridge and crossing it on the 418 was a brilliant experience, like being on a fairground ride. With candyfloss, the moment would have been perfect.

Seil made an instant and positive impression on me. The island seemed to be one big lush garden. So green, so beautiful. Soon after the bridge, we were dropped off by the golf course. We walked up a road past a shop to the clubhouse, really just a tidy little shed. The shed was open and we went inside and got ready for our round. We left our other bags in the shed and left money for the green fees, picking up tags. I'd trouble tying mine to my bag. I often have trouble with these things. In fact, I find playing golf easier. I gave up with the tag and shoved it inside my bag.

As we were preparing to tee off, a man arrived, carrying his clubs and wearing tailored shorts in this nice weather. He said hello and explained that he was waiting on his regular Saturday morning playing partner and so we were fine to go.

Noble Brian teed up on the whites, as he had been doing so far, on those island courses that had medal tees. 'You want to play off the yellow tees,' said the man. It wasn't clear whether he was suggesting Noble Brian did or telling him to. In any case, Noble Brian smiled and carried on as normal, except that he topped his shot something awful. It was a terrible effort and terribly unlike him. The man saw it, but said nothing. I stuck with the yellow tees, took my time about it and fired a decent enough drive halfway down the fairway. And off we went. I looked back and saw the man taking practice swings by the shed, waiting for his friend to arrive.

Noble Brian lifted his head on his second shot, something he never did, the result being another dreadful strike. I asked what was up with him.

'Ach, I dunno,' he replied.

'Maybe you should've had the CalMac breakfast.'

'Aye,' said Noble Brian. 'There's nae ballast in my belly.'

The opening hole was a straight par four, with a small drowned quarry to the left. DANGER – KEEP OUT said a sign. I wasn't going anywhere near it. We putted out beneath power lines. They ran across the course, but still it seemed a daft place to put a green. Already I was spotting more warning signs. DANGER – OVERHEAD CABLES. This wasn't quite what I'd had in mind for this morning. I'd been looking forward to a relaxing round of island golf.

We took on the second hole, an uphill par three over a pond with the green hidden from view. I focused on the post at the top of the hill that indicated where to aim for, and blocked out the sign to my left that read DANGER – DEEP WATER.

We crossed a bridge over the water, the bridge showing the sign THIS BRIDGE IS FOR THE USE OF GOLF PLAYERS ONLY WHO CROSS IT AT THEIR OWN RISK. It was like some scene in an action movie. *Indiana Jones and the Golf Course of Doom.*

When we got to the green, I was happy to see my ball lying just short of the pin. I'd hit a nice seven iron for my tee shot. Noble Brian's ball was pin high. We rushed our putts beneath more humming power lines. It was most off-putting. I missed my birdie putt, but Noble Brian held his nerve to hole his.

The two of us stood on the elevated third tee, the fairway way down below. Noble Brian insisted on teeing off from the whites again, even though that put the power lines in the path of his drive. You couldn't miss them, and couldn't help thinking about them. Just in case we'd forgotten about them there was another sign saying DANGER – LOOK UP AND LOOK OUT FOR OVERHEAD ELECTRIC POWER LINES. CARRY RODS/POLES AT A LOW LEVEL AND PARALLEL TO THE GROUND. There was a useful drawing of a man lying on the ground, having been electrocuted. This golf course was making me nervous.

Noble Brian swung his club and I stood well back. His ball narrowly missed the power lines, sailing over them before dropping down to the distant fairway. The yellow tee was far enough forward at least for the power lines to be out of play. But still I was distracted, unable to concentrate at all. I topped my ball into the drowned quarry. Noble Brian rang the bell marked '1912 *Titanic*' to let anyone behind us on the second tee know that it was safe to tee off.

When we reached the green, which put us back near the shed and the first tee, Noble Brian delivered his damning verdict on a haphazard opening few holes full of hazards. 'Completely and utterly stupid.' He was furious. I was more anxious. It crossed my mind that we could just grab our bags from the shed and go. But instead we soldiered on.

It was quite a hike to the next hole. We had to cross the road and carry on down a dusty track past a pile of rubble. It was like walking through a building site. But when we got to the fourth tee we were met by an altogether more appealing scene. This next section of the course looked really pretty. Free of power lines and with a lovely setting next to the water with the odd fishing boat and sailing boat out there. I tried to put the opening three holes behind me. Perhaps this round of island golf was about to get better.

The fourth was a par three and Noble Brian sliced his tee shot onto the shore. He played a nice second off the seaweed though. However, his mood blackened when he reached the green. 'Why oh fucking why have they built a rockery?' I thought a rockery seemed a nice feature to have beside the green. It was better than a pylon. But the rockery did nothing but rile the golf architect. It was clear that Noble Brian had a zero tolerance approach to rockeries next to greens.

A group of four men waited on the next tee to let us through. I wasn't sure if they had overheard Noble Brian going to war with the rockery. If they had, they didn't mention it. All of us watched as Noble Brian smashed a huge and highly accurate drive down the fairway. The men complimented him on his shot. One of them asked where we were from.

'I'm from Aberdeenshire,' said Noble Brian.

'Plenty good courses there,' said the man.

'A lot of good golfers too in that part of the world,' said one of the other men.

'There's one less there today because he's here,' said the first man.

Noble Brian grinned as the man who had just acknowledged his golfing prowess turned to me. 'You just need to better that.'

No pressure then. I wasn't going to crumble in front of them and I didn't. I even surprised myself by matching Noble Brian for both distance and accuracy. It's also good not to mess up when someone has decided to let you through. We thanked the men and continued with our round. They seemed nice people. This game of golf on Seil was getting better, I was playing better and the sun was still shining. Noble Brian hit a hot streak, picking up two birdies in quick succession. This place wasn't so bad. The early holes were a distant memory. It was as if they belonged to another golf course.

We reached the eighth, the penultimate hole and the best one yet, a short par three over water. 'A bonnie hole,' said Noble Brian. There was no sign of a rockery next to the green either. I didn't quite connect with my tee shot, my ball falling short of the green and landing on the shore. 'Tee up another one,' urged Noble Brian. I tried again and this time caught it too well, my ball racing through the back of the green. 'Too much porridge,' said Noble Brian who fared much better, getting it right first time.

Once we'd putted out, I went to put the flag back in just as a man walked up to me. He'd been playing a nearby hole.

'I don't see any ticket on your bag,' he said, not bothering with a hello.

'Oh,' I said. 'I've got one. It's in my bag. I'll just get it.'

The man stood over me, saying nothing, while I rummaged about my bag for the ticket. I fished it out and showed it to him. 'There you go.'

He nodded and marched off, lord of his little kingdom. He hadn't cared where we'd travelled from to play the course, or whether we were enjoying our round. But he had succeeded in asserting his authority and had reassured himself that we weren't cheats who had sneaked on. He reminded me of what I didn't like about golf clubs. Officious, pompous, charmless types like him. The type that's often drawn to golf clubs, unfortunately.

'What was that all about?' asked Noble Brian.

'Och, his lordship wanted to see my ticket.'

I'd just played the best hole on the course and even that experience had been spoiled.

One more hole to go, one more hole and we were out of here. A sign pointed us in the right direction. We trudged back down the sandy track, past the rubble, wiping dust from our eyes. Shoulders slumped, golf bags feeling heavier and the increasing heat not helping either.

The only reason I could come up with for playing the final hole was that it brought us back to the shed, because you definitely didn't play the last hole for the fun of it. It was by far the worst on the course, the final kick in the teeth. If our other bags hadn't been in that shed, we wouldn't have bothered. We'd have just turned and walked back down the road to the bus stop.

Behind the ninth tee there was a row of pretty white-washed cottages that must have once housed quarry workers. Ahead of us was a rubbish golf hole. At least it was short. The only feature was a pylon.

'What's this hole called?' I asked.

'Pylon,' said Noble Brian.

I don't think it was called Pylon, but it certainly was a nothing hole, one to ensure that our round ended in disappointment. Both of us drove the green. Neither of us was made up about it.

'Let's get down in two and get the fuck out of here,' said Noble Brian. He putted just past the cup and tapped in for his par.

My turn. I was hesitant with my first putt and left myself with a testy four-footer.

'Miss this,' said Noble Brian, 'and you have to spend the rest of your days here.'

I looked up at him. He smiled. 'No pressure.'

I was fed up with this course. My confidence was shot. I knew I was going to miss. I lipped out, my fate sealed. Destined to spend the rest of my days on this golf course. Unless I wriggled out of it.

'You have no authority over me,' I said. 'You can't make me stay here. I'm coming with you.'

Noble Brian relented and let me accompany him to the bus stop.

It was boiling hot in the bus shelter, its clear roof intensifying the heat of the sun. It was like an outdoor sauna and I found it more comfortable standing behind the bus shelter in the company of wasps. I counted the minutes and seconds, waiting for the 418 to come and deliver us from Seil. I was pining for Oban. A bright double-decker shot past in the other direction, 'Sightseeing Glasgow' splashed on the side of the bus. Those tourists had come a long way from George Square.

The 418 appeared eventually and took us back across 'the Bridge over the Atlantic', which wasn't as much fun second time around. We had a nice lunch at a restaurant on Oban's seafront before catching the train back to Glasgow. We waved from the train at anglers out on Loch Awe. Everyone was having a good time in the Scottish sunshine. Save for a couple of hours on Seil, we'd had a good time too.

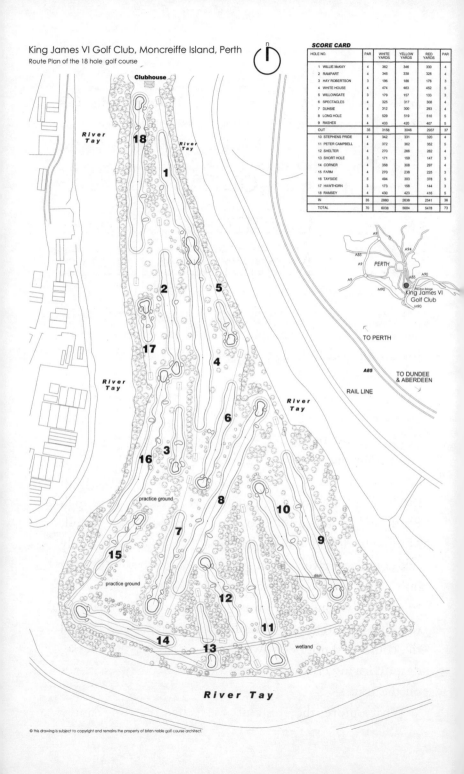

King James VI Golf Club, Moncreiffe Island, Perth
Route Plan of the 18 hole golf course

SCORE CARD

HOLE NO.		PAR	WHITE YARDS	YELLOW YARDS	RED YARDS	PAR
1	WILLIE McKAY	4	362	346	330	4
2	RAMPART	4	348	328	328	4
3	HAY ROBERTSON	3	196	186	176	3
4	WHITE HOUSE	4	474	463	452	5
5	WILLOWGATE	3	179	157	133	3
6	SPECTACLES	4	325	317	308	4
7	DUNSIE	4	312	300	293	4
8	LONG HOLE	5	529	519	510	5
9	RASHES	4	433	420	407	5
OUT		35	3158	3046	2937	37
10	STEPHENS PRIDE	4	342	331	320	4
11	PETER CAMPBELL	4	372	362	352	5
12	SHELTER	4	270	266	262	4
13	SHORT HOLE	3	171	159	147	3
14	CORNER	4	358	308	297	4
15	FARM	4	270	238	225	3
16	TAYSIDE	5	494	393	378	5
17	HAWTHORN	3	173	158	144	3
18	RAMSEY	4	430	423	416	5
IN		35	2880	2638	2541	36
TOTAL		70	6038	5684	5478	73

Chapter 13

Journey to the Centre of Perth – Moncreiffe Island

Just as we had followed our Outer Hebrides expedition with a day trip to Arran, so we sought a straightforward day excursion after our journey round the Inner Hebrides. Somewhere not too far away and easy enough to get to. Perth was just perfect.

Now anyone with a basic knowledge of Scotland will know that Perth is far from being an island. It's a city in the heart of the country. But the River Tay runs through Perth and in the middle of the river there's an island. Moncreiffe Island. And it has a golf course. It's the only self-contained river island golf course in Britain and the only access is via a walkway on the railway bridge. We had to check this one out. I was grateful to my friend Brian (another Brian) for mentioning it. His mam had played the course. I'd not been aware of the island or the course, despite having crossed that railway bridge countless times on the train.

What's more, the golf club was called the King James

VI Golf Club. If ever there was an island course to bring my dad's putter to, then this was it. I briefed Noble Brian and everything was arranged easily. He'd catch the train from Edinburgh, I'd get one from Glasgow and we'd meet up in Perth.

On the way up on the train, I read an article in the newspaper about a recent academic study on golf. According to researchers at the University of St Andrews (naturally), golfers who thought too hard about the game were harming their performance. The researchers had taken a group of good golfers and a group of beginners and got them to putt. Afterwards, some of them were asked to discuss their performance in detail and others weren't. They were all then asked to putt again. It was discovered that the putting of good golfers who'd talked about their putting deteriorated. Whereas the beginners, whether they'd discussed their putting or not, were largely unaffected. In other words, they were still crap. The results seemed to indicate that if you were a half-decent golfer, and thought about it too much, your game suffered.

It had to do with verbal shadowing, apparently. Talking causes the brain to focus more on language than on other skills. The thinking seemed to be that thinking too much undermines your performance. Empty your head and you'll play good golf. I was going to be as empty-headed as possible on Moncreiffe Island.

I stepped off the train at Perth to find myself surrounded by trainspotters with tripods. Golf meets trainspotting. I wondered which was the more ridiculous pastime. Pointing cameras at trains or trying to place a ball in a hole. Taking care not to knock over any of the tripods with my golf bag, I went and tracked down Noble Brian. He was waiting by the front door of the station. He said he'd enjoyed boarding the train in Edinburgh, with Waverley station full of commuters with briefcases and him carrying his golf clubs. The world was going to work, whereas he was heading off to play golf on yet another promising day.

We walked the short distance from the station to the riverbank. An information board next to the railway bridge explained the history of golf in Perth. The earliest mentions of golf in Perth came from cases of breaches of the Sabbath before the Kirk Session, the church ruling body. In 1599, four local men confessed to playing golf on Sunday afternoon. And in 1604, six boys were caught golfing on the Lord's Day and made to repent before the church congregation.

Noble Brian and I were fascinated to learn about the Battle of the Trees, which sounded like something straight out of Tolkien. The Battle of the Trees took place in Perth in 1861. The town council had decided to plant trees on a piece of land where golf was popular. A mob of angry golfers, having none of it, uprooted the trees. The council chose not to replant the trees and the golfers played on happily until the day the Ents passed through Perth on their way to fight Saruman and his Orcs and inadvertently trampled on the golfers.

I may have made that last bit up, but what is true is that people have been golfing on Moncreiffe Island since the 19th century. The course was designed by Old Tom Morris (yes, him again) and the King James VI Golf Club was named after the eponymous king who was a keen hacker back in the day and was said to have learned the game around Perth. Noble Brian and I now felt confident that we could appear on *Mastermind* with the history of golf in Perth as our specialist subject.

We climbed the steps to the railway bridge and set off across the walkway, the mighty Tay flowing fast beneath us and the railway tracks next to us on the other side of a fence. It was a novel experience and it got even more exciting when a train shot past heading for Edinburgh. Not that we were that into trains, just to make that clear. Noble Brian and I were too anal to be trainspotters. We were golfers.

But what an adventure this was proving to be. What a remarkable route to a golf course. Half the fun was in getting there. Halfway over the bridge we climbed down some steps and set foot on Moncreiffe Island. We walked under one of the bridge's giant arches, a sign pointing us in the direction of the golf course. It was a pleasant walk past some allotments, this island in the middle of the city seeming such a nice place for a spot of gardening.

The day was really warming up. I felt the sun on the back of my neck and cursed the fact that I'd managed to leave my dad's bucket hat and the sun lotion at home, yet had brought along my waterproofs. Clearly I'd anticipated rain rather than glorious sunshine. But I should have known by now that the sun shone when Noble Brian and I played golf. At least it had done on the last few islands.

We came to a colourful wrought iron gate with a yellow

flag and a green worked into the design. There were no
cars outside the clubhouse, but then how could there be?
A man was sweeping the front steps, the only sound besides
the brushing being the singing of the birds. It seemed so
peaceful and idyllic here, surrounded by all the trees. It
only made us look forward to the golf even more.

There were a couple of people in the clubhouse. One
of the members told us that the course occasionally flooded,
a consequence of it being in the middle of such a big river.
'At high tide, and when they open the dam at Pitlochry,
you get a lot of water coming down the river.'

'Plus,' said his friend, 'it's a shipping channel. When
these big boats go past, the water can come right over the
top at the bottom of the course. You don't want to be too
long at the 13th sometimes!'

I pictured Noble Brian and myself trying to shimmy up
a tree.

The men wished us a good round. 'You've got a nice
day for it,' said one of them.

It was approaching our tee time. We'd had to book our
round, this being Perth not Benbecula. Noble Brian and I
went over to the club shop where we met the resident
pro, Allan Knox. I said how we'd enjoyed the walk over
the railway bridge. 'It's a bit of a walk down here,' said
Allan, 'but it's unique. You get a lot of folk coming to play
here because it's an island.' We certainly fell into that
category.

On the first tee I mentioned to Noble Brian the newspaper article I'd read on the train, about researchers finding
that thinking too much harms your game. 'The best way

to play is to not think about it,' agreed Noble Brian. 'Otherwise your muscles and brain seize up.'

I bowed to Noble Brian's infinite wisdom and the findings of the boffins. I relaxed and emptied my brain. I swung my driver and produced a nice clean shot, my ball landing in the middle of the lushest fairway we'd seen on our island travels. It was one of the best tee shots I'd hit all summer. I thought to myself, 'I need to do more of this not thinking'.

The course was busy. The retired gentlemen of Perth were out in force and hard not to spot in their colourful golf gear. I was astonished by the number and variety of trees bordering the fairways. There was barely a cloud in the sky, the birds were still singing and I noticed I still had traces of sheep shit on my golf shoes from Iona.

At the second I chipped over a bunker and holed the putt for my par. 'I'm liking this course,' I said.

'Don't get too cocky,' warned Noble Brian.

'I can't afford to be cocky,' I reminded him.

But I was producing some of my best golf. With an easy swing, I hit a nine iron to the heart of a green. The fairways felt incredibly springy. I wasn't used to this. It was a bit of a treat. As were the smooth greens. It was great being able to read them and judge the weight of a putt and gain satisfaction from getting it right.

This island course wasn't wild or unpredictable. There were no livestock or rocks to contend with, no freak gusts of wind. This was golf with slippers on. Even the par fives, which I normally struggle with, weren't a slog. The course was flat. It made for a gentle morning round and I wasn't complaining. I'd been through Barra to get this.

Being here on Moncreiffe Island seemed to be doing my golf some good. Perth bills itself as 'The Perfect Centre' and here we were in the middle of the River Tay in the centre of Perth in the heart of Scotland. I felt suitably centred. The only problem I had was with the big orange thing in the sky.

'Come on clouds!' I said, feeling the heat and willing the sun to disappear.

'Height of summer and he's hoping for clouds,' sighed Noble Brian.

My colleague gave his initial thoughts on the golf course. 'This place doesn't have the happy amateurism of the other island golf clubs. It's more manicured, well tended, but it's not too stiff either. Do you know what it does have in common with all the other island golf courses?'

'Um, that it's on an island?'

'No! The lack of fairway bunkers.'

I hadn't noticed the lack of fairway bunkers, but I had noticed the number of greenside bunkers. They seemed to make up for the lack of fairway bunkers. The bunkers around the greens appeared to be kitted out with tractor beams, because my ball kept getting dragged into the sand. I was ending up in these bunkers with a remarkable regularity, escaping the clutches of one only to end up in another.

While I struggled to get out of yet another bunker – bunker shots aren't my strong point – Noble Brian delivered a lecture on the proliferation of bunkers in old school golf architecture, wittering on about something called the penal school. 'The first golf architects were the best golfers,' said Noble Brian, 'so they set up the golf course to their

liking and the lesser golfers couldn't get over these
barriers.'

At least I knew who to blame.

As we made our way round this mature parkland course
and I tried not to become acquainted with any more
bunkers, Noble Brian told me that he had played Gullane
No. 3 the other day and had really enjoyed the East Lothian
links course. Noble Brian had played many of Scotland's
top golf courses, whereas I really hadn't played any of
them. I asked him to name his top three courses in Scotland
and he offered me Royal Dornoch, North Berwick and
Cruden Bay.

'The thing about Cruden Bay,' said Noble Brian, 'is that
there are a lot of different types of shots you have to play.
It's the same with North Berwick. For instance, one hole
might be a short par four with the green sitting way up
high, and another one might be a par five where you can
play short. I like courses that make you think. And they're
not necessarily long golf courses. They're ones you'd go
back and play time and time again, rather than a place like
Carnoustie or Troon where you've got to be playing really
well every time to come away with an enjoyment of the
game.'

'Look! A tree rat!'

A squirrel had just scampered across the fairway and
shot up a tree. And I had decided that I was going to experience Royal Dornoch, North Berwick and Cruden Bay.
Once I was done with these islands.

My driving was becoming increasingly erratic. I kept
firing balls off into the trees. At least it offered me some

shade. Who'd have thought you would have to hide from the sun on a Scottish golf course? Some like it hot and some like it not. I'm in the overcast camp. I'd argue the heat doesn't agree with me.

My not thinking, on the back of that newspaper article, had gone right out the window. The heat was making me uncomfortable and now I was fretting about my deteriorating game. I spent the majority of one par four in the trees, half-heartedly trying to hack my ball out into the sun and ending up with a seven.

'Bit of a nothing hole,' said Noble Brian who didn't rate it.

'Let's just forget it then, eh?'

Despite my zigzagging along the course, going from one set of trees to the next, we managed to catch up with the group ahead of us. They, in turn, were being held up by the group in front of them. The delay suited me fine. I sat down under a tree.

'Are you suffering that much?' asked Noble Brian.

'Afraid so.' I was thinking about putting on my new cagoule with the hood up.

I didn't have to in the end. My prayers for adequate cloud cover were answered on the back nine. The weather turned dull and it was bliss.

It occurred to me, more than halfway round the course, that you'd hardly know you were on an island. You couldn't see the river for the trees. I would have liked to have seen more of the Tay, yet we'd only had a glimpse of it so far. I supposed that when the course flooded they saw plenty of it. One of the few sightings we had of the river was by the 13th green, where the man in the clubhouse had said the water washed over sometimes. It was low tide when Noble Brian and I passed through. You had to go right to the riverbank to even notice the water.

At the 15th hole, a short par four, I drove to within 30 yards of the green. I pulled out Captain James' putter on the King James VI golf course. As I lined up my ambitious 40-yard putt, I heard a shout of 'fore!' I spun round to see a man waving at me from the next tee. Clearly his sliced tee shot was heading straight for me. Any time now I was going to be struck on the head by a golf ball and denied my eagle opportunity. I darted about, dodging an invisible ball, covering my head with my hands as the ball crashed into a tree behind me and dropped onto our green.

'Sorry about that,' said the man, coming over to retrieve his ball.

'Ach, no harm done,' I said.

The most beautiful sight on the King James VI golf course – and it really is the most beautiful sight – is that of the three tall dark trees behind the 17th green which make the par three such a lovely hole to play. Noble Brian labelled them raven trees, but they may have been black maples.

We stood on the 18th tee, next to the raven trees, the clubhouse now in sight. I was already thinking about a pint.

'Come on,' said Noble Brian, urging me on. 'One last good drive down the last.'

After a good start, I hadn't played that great, but when had I ever? The most I can hope for from a round of golf are a few highlights and the avoidance of any major catas-trophes. My drive was heading right, towards the trees, and then it started to turn. Turn, turn, turn ... I made it onto the fairway. I'd enjoy that pint in the clubhouse now.

A greenkeeper was out on a tractor and it made me wonder how they got anything onto the island. The walkway over the railway bridge wasn't the answer. Did it all come over by boat?

'There must be an access road in here,' said Noble Brian.

I sort of wished there wasn't. I wanted to think of it as an isolated island in the middle of the river. But there had to be something.

Noble Brian's head was swimming with the logistics of it all, of getting anything over here. 'Irrigation pipes, bunker sand, fertilisers ... bloody hell ... seeding, turf, diesel machines ... It's a unique appointment for a greenkeeper. You can't take it for granted, transporting goods. Can't have ten-ton trucks coming over delivering sand. A lot of bunkers here to fill with sand ... '

It was a mystery that needed solving.

Noble Brian and I had a pint and a sandwich in the club-house, looking out on the course. A deer crossed the 18th fairway. Five minutes later, a couple crossed the 18th green with a child in a buggy, the woman pushing the buggy, the man carrying a bunch of flowers. It was a more startling sight than the deer. A few of the members got up to look. The natural order of the golf club had been disrupted. No one was upset though. This was a relaxed golf club. The members shrugged and smiled at what was just an odd sight. I figured that if you didn't play golf you might not think twice about walking across a green with a buggy, if that was the direction you were heading in.

A group of older men who'd completed their round sat in the corner chatting about golf and whatever else came to mind. They reminded me of the One o'Clock Gang. I think most golf clubs must have a One o'Clock Gang.

'Rules are there to be broken,' I heard one man say.

'But if you break the rules in golf, you're a cheat,' countered another man.

'Well, as my father said on his deathbed, "if at first you don't succeed, cheat!"'

Noble Brian and I spoke to Marion and Mark who ran the bar and the catering at the club. They actually lived on the island. I asked them about access to the island, other than the railway bridge. It turned out that there was a causeway that could be crossed at low tide. So that was how everything was transported. 'We've got three mules,' joked Mark.

Marion explained that Wednesday was delivery day. 'The greenkeepers go across with tractors and trailers, collect all the stock and come back. Everything comes in that way. All the deliveries have to be co-ordinated with the tide. If we say ten o'clock, the suppliers have to be there for ten. They can't make it 11 or later. They all turn up at the same time.'

'Sounds like a bit of a military operation,' said Noble Brian.

'You've really got to think everything through first before you do anything,' said Marion. 'You've got to time it.'

I said it must be interesting living on the island.

Marion smiled. 'Sometimes, if I run out of something, I get the backpack on and go over the bridge into town, get what I'm needing and come back again. One time it flooded and we were actually stranded for four days. We phoned the police and said, "By the way, we're stranded. Just letting you know we're here." And they asked, "Can you get off on your own steam?" We said, "We're in the middle of the River Tay!"'

As Noble Brian and I left the clubhouse, we bumped into Bill, a past captain of the club.

'It's been a super day so far,' said Bill. 'You enjoyed it?' We said we had.

'That's the main thing. It's always good to get a good report on the course. Trains go over the bridge and folk never think this is here. It's quite unique in that respect.'

On our way back over the bridge we were passed by the postman carrying a golf club shaped parcel. A delivery to the club shop.

Having successfully negotiated the bridge for a second time, Noble Brian and I were almost knocked down at the Pelican crossing by an old woman who drove straight through it, showing no regard for a pair of golfers. I don't think she saw us. We recovered with a pint of the local Inveralmond ale in Greyfriars, a tiny city centre pub. The brewer happened to be in the bar. I told him I liked his beer. Noble Brian and I reflected on a good day's golf. It hadn't been the most arduous of trips, but it had been a unique experience, the river island setting and the railway bridge.

On the train back to Glasgow, I sat next to a businesswoman tapping away on her laptop. I couldn't help glancing at her screen. She was composing an e-mail.

RE: Rebate Scheme/Pricing and Communications Revenue.

I was glad to have been able to spend the day playing golf.

The following day I phoned the King James VI club manager Martin Butler. He had been planning to meet us during our visit but had been called away from the course at the last moment. I asked him about running a golf club on a river island.

'It's all got to get across,' said Martin. 'It's a constant logistical war. But it's worth putting up with the headaches for the superb setting. When the water's too high, it can be a bit frustrating. No other club in the world has to think about these things. An essential piece of my equipment is the tide book.

'The walk over the bridge separates it from the rest of the world. I came to Perth 20 years ago and took up this cursed game. I looked around for a golf course and settled on this one, a decision I never came near to regretting. It's a damn test as well, there are 75 bunkers out there.'

I think I'd found most of them.

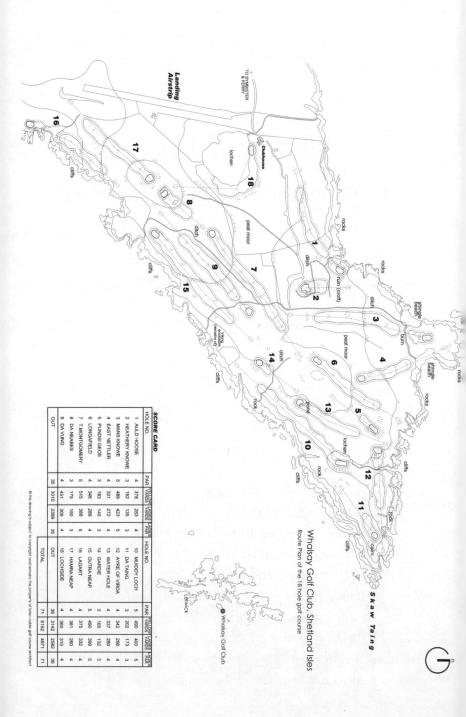

Whalsay Golf Club, Shetland Isles
Route Plan of the 18 hole golf course

Landing Airstrip

TO SYMBISTER & FERRY

Clubhouse

lochan

peat moor

ditch

runn (croft)

cliffs

rocks

rocks

shingle beach

burn

shingle beach

rocks

rock

calm

Skaw Taing

peat moor

pond

lochan'

rock

cliffs

Viking enclosure (remains of)

Lerwick

● Whalsay Golf Club

SCORE CARD

HOLE NO.		PAR	YELLOW YARDS	LADIES YARDS	PAR
1	AULD HOOSE	4	378	283	4
2	HEATHERY KNOWE	3	152	135	3
3	MANS KNOWE	5	489	423	5
4	EAST NETTLER	4	321	272	4
5	PUNDSI GEOS	4	183	140	4
6	LONGAFIELD	4	346	289	4
7	T.MONTGOMERY	5	515	388	5
8	DA NEABES	3	175	150	3
9	DA VUNG	4	451	309	4
OUT		36	3010	2389	36

HOLE NO.		PAR	YELLOW YARDS	LADIES YARDS	PAR
10	MUDDY LOCH	5	490	400	5
11	DA TAING	3	202	173	3
12	AYRE OF VIRDA	4	342	296	4
13	WATER HOLE	4	337	280	3
14	GARDIE	3	165	132	3
15	OUTRA NEAP	5	490	399	5
16	LAGART	4	375	332	4
17	HAMRA NEAP	4	381	280	4
18	LOCHSIDE	4	360	310	4
OUT		36	3142	2582	36
TOTAL		71	6152	4971	71

Chapter 14

The Northernmost Toppermost – Whalsay

Base camp: the Prince of Wales pub, Aberdeen. Sitting comfortable with a pint, and his clubs at his feet, was my brother Stewart. I went and got myself a pint of Atlas Wayfarer (the golf adventurer's beer) and joined him. Minutes later, Noble Brian arrived on the scene, clubs in one hand, pint of Guinness in the other. I introduced Noble Brian and my brother to each other.

'Brian, Stewart; Stewart, Brian.'

'You picked the easiest trip, didn't you?' said Noble Brian to my brother.

Stewart laughed. We were taking the boat to Shetland.

Noble Brian turned to me. 'Have you *seen* the forecast?'

'Aye,' I said. 'It's going to be bonnie tomorrow.'

'Aye, but the day after we're going to be blitzed! I saw the TV weather report and it's just a blue rain pattern all over Scotland.'

'It's best not to believe the weather forecast.'

Noble Brian gave me a look that suggested he believed more in the weather forecast than in anything I said.

I looked to my brother for backing.

'We'll be fine,' said Stewart. 'Maybe.' He took a sip of his pint.

We managed to get another round in. And we would have got another round in after that had we not a ferry to catch. We dragged ourselves from the comfort of the Prince of Wales and made our way down to the harbour.

It had been a while since I'd last been in Aberdeen, the city where I went to university and met my future wife. Aberdeen brought back memories of my dad. Him being there on my graduation day. Marischal College quadrangle in the rain following the ceremony, and drinks on the lawn at King's College once it had cleared up.

Another time. A Donovan concert at the Music Hall. My dad loved Donovan and I managed to get some front row tickets. Donovan completed his set and my dad got up to shake his hand. Donovan just sort of looked at him as the audience applauded. Afterwards, Donovan was signing autographs. 'I've got all your records,' dad said to him. 'So have I,' replied Donovan. We moved on to the Wild Boar for drinks and my friend Grant laughed so hard at one of my dad's jokes that he fell off his seat.

Another night. Wintertime. Walking up Union Street with my dad. The pavement was icy and my dad's shoes had little grip. He was slipping all over the place and having to hold on to me. He was doing a fine impersonation of a drunk and we hadn't even reached the pub yet.

Another time. Now. Walking down to the harbour with my dad's putter in my bag. Remembering going down to the harbour to meet my dad when his boat came in, after his month at sea supporting the oil rigs. That boat still comes in. It's just not captained by my dad. And I think how much I love my daughter and I'm missing her with all these golf trips. And I think how much my dad must have loved his children and missed us when he was away at sea. And I only really understand that now he's gone for good and I'm a dad.

Having reached the harbour, Noble Brian, my brother and I boarded the ferry. We dumped our bags in our cabin and made for the bar. As we sat with our pints of Orkney Dark Island – OK, so we were heading to Shetland – I looked out to the harbour and saw the granite buildings of Aberdeen from a new perspective, seeing the city more through my dad's eyes.

We had taken sickness tablets in preparation for this 12-hour overnight voyage in the North Sea. Noble Brian wondered if Stewart and I were better prepared for this journey, seeing as we were the sons of a sea captain.

'You've been on smaller boats than this,' said Noble Brian.

We had been, but not often.

'Did you take tablets on your dad's boat?' asked Noble Brian. 'Ach, he probably just waved a haddock in front of ye. "Here lads, smell this!"'

We sat with our drinks staring out at a shrinking coastline lit by the low sun. It was beautiful. How many times had dad seen that coastline? It must have been a welcome sight for him after a month at sea in all kinds of weather. We always asked him when he got home, 'How was your trip?' We never asked him what he saw.

Soon the coastline had disappeared. Scotland had vanished. Now it was just us and the North Sea.

'There's a bit of a roll now,' said my brother.

'Dad would dispute that,' I said. 'He'd call this flat calm.'

I once asked my dad if he'd seen the film *The Perfect Storm*.

'What would I want to watch that for?' replied the man who'd seen 40 years' worth of waves.

The hours after dad got home were always the same. The bedroom in darkness in daytime. Dad sleeping, recuperating, readjusting to life back on land. And then he was ready for a month of family and golf. Until the month was over and he would be standing in the lobby looking smart in his captain's uniform, ready to go again.

After some more pints of Dark Island, we thought it would be a good idea to go out on the top deck and practise our putting. A number of passengers were out there, watching the sunset. My dad often took pictures of sunsets at sea. He saw hundreds of them on the boat. Now I saw what he saw. As well as the sun, the flame of an oil rig burned in the distance and I felt my dad's presence now more than ever on this journey round the islands.

I had gone back to the cabin to fetch my dad's putter and a few golf balls. Our improvised hole out on deck was a yellow circle with the words WINCH ONLY next to it. It was a big target but we were putting on the top of a rolling ferry. My brother had a go first, but the ball kept rolling away before he could putt. So I lay flat out with a finger on the ball, like a rugby player holding the ball in place for his team-mate. I removed my finger from the ball as my brother swung dad's putter.

We all had a go at putting, much to the bemusement

of our fellow passengers. I was doing pretty badly at ferry golf and Noble Brian decided to give me a lesson. He started with the ball, the object I was meant to hit. He held it up and pointed at it. I said I knew what a ball was. He told me to shut up and listen. By the end of Noble Brian's ferry golf lesson I had a single figure handicap. I didn't even have to pay for the lesson either. Eventually the novelty of putting on the top deck of a ferry wore off. We were getting blown about by the wind. We saw sense and went indoors for a late meal. I believe I had some roast lamb.

After a good night's sleep – in all honesty, it was a mercifully calm crossing – we woke up with the ferry nearing Lerwick. Dad would often end up in Lerwick when the weather was really bad. 'Your dad's in Lerwick,' mam would say to us, having come off the phone to him.

My brother and I told Noble Brian about the time dad had arrived in Lerwick with the television cameras waiting for him. He'd been out on the stand-by boat and was in his cabin getting some sleep when he was thrown out of bed and crashed through a partition. That woke him up. He knew something was wrong. He went to climb the steps to the wheelhouse. Water was rushing down on him. A wave had smashed through one of the wheelhouse windows. Captain James feared the worst but when he got to the wheelhouse he found that the men on watch were OK. One of them had seen the wave coming and had hauled his crew-mate to the ground just in time. The immediate challenge now was getting ashore. Dad had to steer the boat into Lerwick in a storm with a missing wheelhouse window. He ended up on *North Tonight*. We sat in the living room in Hopeman watching him being interviewed. Your heroes grow bigger when they're gone. Dads are no different. It's no wonder he'd never seen *The Perfect Storm*.

I'd been to Lerwick once before, though I'd flown to Shetland. It was in the middle of winter. I'd gone to witness Up-Helly-Aa, the annual Viking festival. I watched the spectacular torchlight procession and saw the Vikings burn their longship. I stayed up all night drinking and dancing at one of the hall parties. Shetland's different. For many centuries it was under Norse rule. You can't come this far north and not think you've left Scotland. And in some ways you have. You've arrived in Shetland.

After getting off the ferry, Noble Brian, Stewart and I waited with our clubs at the bus stop for the No. 19 to Laxo. From there we were making the short ferry crossing to Whalsay for the first of our two rounds of island golf in Shetland. Whalsay is a little island off the east coast of Mainland Shetland. It happens to be the heart of Shetland's fishing industry. I looked at my watch. Half-seven in the morning.

'Just dump your bags there, lads,' said the driver as we boarded the bus.

I noted how modern and spotless the bus was compared to the buses in Glasgow. I'd once shown some French friends of mine round Glasgow. We'd jumped on a bus and climbed the stairs to the top deck to find half the seats missing. Only the bare frames were left. 'Um, let's sit here,' I'd said, indicating seats we could actually sit on, albeit seats that were torn and covered in fag burns. An extreme example of a Glasgow bus perhaps, but it made quite an impression on my foreign guests.

Back on the nice Shetland bus, we journeyed north and before long arrived at the pier for the ferry to Whalsay. The small ferry turned out to be as immaculate as the bus. In fact it seemed brand new. It was a short but unforgettable crossing with the ferry gliding across the water. I'd never seen a sea look so still and the sky was blue and cloudless. It all boded well for our first round of golf in Shetland.

The conductor came along and sold us tickets. Seeing our golf clubs, he told us a story about a fisherman whose boat had broken down off the coast of Whalsay, near the golf course. The fisherman had waved to a group of golfers to indicate that he was having some trouble. The golfers had waved back, no doubt thinking him to be a friendly fisherman. The fisherman, who eventually got ashore, wasn't much of a golf fan. 'Mention golfers to him,' said the conductor, 'and he just curses them … "fucking shower of stupid bastards".'

The conductor moved on and an advert on the wall caught my eye. It was a picture of some attractive coloured timber-frame homes and the message, 'If you want to live on Whalsay, call … ' On a day like this, I thought, I could seriously consider it.

We arrived at Symbister harbour and Harry, the Whalsay Golf Club secretary, was waiting for us. We put our clubs in the boot of his shiny 4x4 and Noble Brian and Stewart got in the back of the car. I sat up front with Harry as we set off for the golf course. Harry was a big, friendly man. At first I struggled with his thick accent. Gradually it became clearer. It was like tuning in to a different radio station.

'Do you like fish?' Harry was asking us.

All three of us said that we did.

'Well,' said Harry, 'one of our women players, Mary, asked if anybody was makkin' you anything to eat. Her son caught the fish. I'll just nip in and tell her.'

Harry got out of the car and popped in to Mary's to confirm that we were OK with fish for lunch in the clubhouse.

'Right,' said Harry, getting back in his seat. 'She's all ready! I'll just gie her a ring on the phone when we're nearly done with the golf.'

Off we went again. Harry, in the tradition of Whalsay men, was a fisherman. He worked on one of the pelagic trawlers, huge vessels built for deep-sea fishing. 'How's the fishing at the moment?' I asked him.

'Pretty good,' said Harry. 'Can't complain. Getting a good price for the herring and mackerel. We just maybe fish a couple of months and lie ashore most of the year. Usually fish January, February and March for mackerel. Going back to sea on Monday though. Got a few herring to catch. But it's mainly mackerel.'

I told Harry that my dad had been a fisherman. 'Skipper of the *Adonis*. Fished out of Peterhead.' Harry had heard of the *Adonis*.

'When he was home,' I continued, 'we had lemon sole for supper every other night, and me and my brother would say, "Oh no, not fish again."'

'Aye,' said Harry, 'when you're getting it like that, you're taking it for granted. Lemon sole, a grand fish like that. You pay for that in a restaurant.'

As Harry drove along the coast towards the northeast tip of the island, where the golf course was, he pointed out some other islands in the glass-like sea.

'That's the Out Skerries you're looking at. And see the point there? That's Fetlar. Unst is the next one. It's a very peaceful place up here, right at the end of the island.'

Whalsay is the northernmost golf course in Britain. There had been, for a time, a course further north on Unst. I had made enquiries about it; phoned a few numbers on the island and everyone I'd spoken to had told me the course no longer existed. Harry confirmed it. 'We're the northernmost.' He had actually played the course on Unst, when it had existed. 'Me and the skipper of another boat played nine holes.'

We came to the golf course, next to the island's airstrip. Standing outside the clubhouse was Harry's friend Stewart, one of the members. Harry introduced us and we all went inside. The lobby was full of pictures of Scottish golf courses. There was one of the final hole on the Old Course at Moray Golf Club in Lossiemouth, surely one of the finest closing holes in the country. Harry and Stewart had once played there. They remembered well the large bunker by the 18th green.

My brother pulled from his bag a copy of Hopeman Golf Club's centenary brochure and gave it to Harry. It was a nice touch. We all signed the club's guest book.

Some people had come a long way to play Whalsay, us included.

'We get quite a few visitors,' said Harry.

'What size of membership do you have?' asked Noble Brian.

'We have 95 men, 30 ladies, 40 juniors. A good number. There's only a thousand people on this island.'

'How much is full membership?'

'£130 a year. We have country members too. There's a guy from Glasgow who's a country member.'

'How much does he pay a year?' I asked.

'£80.'

I guessed there was the small matter of getting here.

We entered the nice lounge with its bar and dance floor. I imagined they had some good nights here, knowing from my experience of Up-Helly-Aa how much they like a party in Shetland.

Harry showed us a display of trophies, including one with a mounted golf ball. The golf ball had belonged to Ronan Rafferty. The Irishman had played Whalsay a few years ago.

'But he'd have done it the easy way,' said Noble Brian. 'He'd have flown in.'

'Small aeroplane,' said Harry. 'Getting his clubs out, like the boot of a car. He just had enough fuel to get him back to Wick. He's played the most northerly, southerly, easterly and westerly.

'He lost his ball at one of our par fives. The week after, I came down to see if I could find it and get it mounted. Put my finger in a rabbit hole and there it was.'

It was time to get out on this most northerly golf course on this beautiful day. Harry was playing with us. His friend Stewart, on account of a sore knee, wasn't able to join us. Stewart wished us a good round and said we would enjoy playing the 16th. 'A bonnie hole,' he smiled. We would see him later for lunch. I was very much looking forward to Mary's fish. We were being very well looked after on Whalsay.

I stood on the first tee by the sea, put on my dad's hat and pulled out my driver. A flash of sadness, maybe more regret. He'd have liked playing a round here with Harry. The pair of them would have had plenty to talk about, as men of the sea who liked their golf.

Harry gave us the rundown on the course. 'It's long; 6,200 yards. My brother Graeme pretty much designed the course. It's preferred lies. The Golf Union came up and reviewed the course. In a couple of years we hope to get preferred lies lifted.'

So I was allowed to improve the lie of my ball on the fairways. If only I could improve as a golfer.

As for the opening tee shot. 'Don't go left,' said Harry. There was only sea to the left. 'See those two sheep?' he said, pointing down the fairway. 'That's your line.'

It was a stunning opening hole, enhanced by the sea and the islands in the distance. A pair of seals watched us, their heads above the flat calm water. Behind the green was a ruined croft. 'Two crofts of land were bought for the golf course,' explained Harry.

We quickly settled into the round. The drive at the fourth involved hitting over a shingle beach. Noble Brian likened it to Pebble Beach. I wondered if Pebble Beach could possibly be as beautiful as this.

Harry pointed out the Out Skerries again and said there was a school with just a few pupils. He indicated another tiny island nearby that could be reached at low tide. 'There's a chapel from centuries ago.' And then he pointed in another direction to the biggest hill in Shetland. 'Lots of lochs up there.' Harry liked his fishing, as well as his golf.

It was a fair climb to the fourth green, the steep fairway full of sheep. At the top of the hill we were met with more stupendous sea views. Everywhere you looked there was water. This was the most island golf course yet, in the sense that from every angle you were reminded you were on an island. It was as if the golf course was the island and that was it. I spotted a tiny fishing boat and was reminded of the man who had broken down and waved to those golfers for assistance. Maybe it was him.

I chipped onto the most immaculate of greens and rolled in a long putt for my par. The greens at Whalsay were incredible. They were in amazingly good condition. I'd have said that they were the best yet. 'This far north, you wouldna think it possible to have greens,' said Harry. 'We've two full-time greenkeepers over the summer, both local boys. It was all just free labour at first. Now we get a lot of grants from Shetland Islands Council. Helps our running costs.'

Blue sky and not a breath of wind. This wasn't how I imagined golf in Shetland to be, but it's how I found it. I understood that it couldn't always be so benign and that we'd caught Whalsay on a good day. A really good day. It was actually getting pretty warm. There was no shade on the course. There are very few trees in Shetland. But I had my dad's hat on. I could cope with the Shetland heat.

Harry told us that in wintertime they had to go out in the morning because it got dark in the afternoon. Shetland gets as little as six hours of daylight in the winter. In the summer you could easily play golf on Whalsay until 11 o'clock at night. In fact, the club champion had recently played ten rounds in the space of 24 hours for charity. He'd scored respectably too, said Harry. My arms would have been falling off after ten rounds. Long before the end, I'd have wanted to be carried around the course.

We'd had it easy so far on Whalsay, but on the seventh hole the course bared its teeth as the wind picked up. 'You get weather oot here, right at the northern end of the island on the hills, it's really tough,' said Harry. 'The southeast gales in the winter time.'

The hole was a monster par five and, added to the wind, the deterioration in my driving wasn't helping matters. I topped my tee shot. If I wasn't topping the ball I was thinning it, hooking it, doing anything but getting it right. I needed to get my act together. The only saving grace was that I was recovering well, playing some decent shots off the fairway with my trusty five iron. I held on to that. It hadn't let me down, though every other aspect of my game had. My driving had deserted me and my pitching was pathetic.

I tried not to get too down about it. And I couldn't get too down about it. Not in a place as beautiful as this. I turned to my brother at one point and, in spite my ugly golf, said, 'This round is passing too quickly.'

The tenth hole was one of Harry's favourites. He'd fished hundreds of balls from that lochan in front of the green. I put another one in for him to find later, ruining my prospects of a good showing at the hole with some hesitant pitching. It was a pleasure being here on Whalsay, but my game wasn't giving me much joy.

I'd recently read an interview with some golf guru in a newspaper. He'd said, 'There are two things you need to control: the ball and yourself.' And I'd wondered if flying instructors offered the same advice to trainee pilots. 'There are two things you need to control: the plane and yourself.'

In reaching the 12th, we arrived at a moment of great significance. This was the northernmost hole on the northernmost golf course in Britain. Seals floated in the sea behind us as my brother hit a wonderful drive. 'Aye, you're on the island,' said Harry. 'As long as you're not off it.'

Stewart then found the green with his second, before stunning us all by ramming home a 40-foot putt. He'd only gone and birdied the most northerly golf hole in Britain, in spectacular style. I wouldn't have enjoyed it much more had I pulled off the magnificent feat myself. He was some golfer, my wee brother.

When we got to the 16th, I saw that Harry's friend Stewart had not been guilty of talking it up. What a stupendous hole, a real cliffhanger. Down the hill we were invited to hit, the fairway abruptly ending to the left with the cliff edge. Harry said that, from here, you could sometimes see killer whales off the coast. That would make the 16th at Whalsay a candidate for the best golf hole in the world.

The key thing was to not hook your tee shot. And what did I do but hook my tee shot, my ball stopping maybe two club lengths from the edge of the cliff. I stood over my second shot, then walked away from the edge. I couldn't play it. It was too close. Not the kind of shot for someone who suffers slight vertigo. I picked up my ball and moved it to a less nerve jangling spot, from where there was nothing for me to concern myself with besides trying to reach the green.

Having moved away from the edge of the cliff, I listened to Harry's story about the runaway golf trolley. A golfer had once gone to play their shot and their trolley had taken off. They'd run after it, but couldn't catch up with it before it toppled over the cliff. The clubs were actually salvaged, but the trolley was mangled beyond repair.

After we'd putted out at the 16th, Harry gave Mary a phone to let her know where we were and that she could get the lunch on soon. Fish and tatties would be served in the clubhouse upon our return. This was the life.

Having got to the bottom of the hill at the 16th, we now had to go all the way back up again with the 17th. It was one heck of a climb. Harry said that when the wind got up it was a 'murderous' hole. It was still murder climbing it on a warm day like this. I imagined golfers coming to grief here, perishing on the slopes of the 17th at Whalsay. Somehow we made it to the top.

From the summit we stared down on the most unbelievable finishing hole. What an inviting, yet at the same time daunting, tee shot. Dominating the entire hole was a lochan. You could play safe, treat the hole as a dogleg and go right of the lochan. Or you could go for broke and try and drive over the water to the green.

I was never going to manage that, but Noble Brian felt he could. As he got ready to give it his all, I saw a couple of cars leaving the clubhouse car park. They must have noticed Noble Brian teeing up and decided they didn't want their car windows smashed. In the event, there was no cause for concern.

Noble Brian topped his tee shot in the most comical fashion. It was almost a fresh air. His ball went all of five yards. It was by far the ugliest and funniest shot I'd ever seen him hit. I couldn't help but laugh. Neither could my brother and Harry. Noble Brian even came up with an excuse. 'My tee broke.'

I went next, wiping tears from my eyes. I tried to play it safe, not that it worked. It might have been my intention to aim right of the lochan but my ball still caught the edge of the water. It wasn't my day. But what a day.

'I'll put the treasurer's trolley back,' said Harry, coming off the 18th green. 'He'll be relieved it's in one piece.'

In the clubhouse, Harry went behind the bar to pour some pints, but couldn't get the taps working. He fiddled about and we told him cans of beer would do, but we'd asked for pints and Harry knew a man who lived just down the road who could probably fix it. He phoned him, but he wasn't in. Harry's friend Stewart, who had joined us again, tried to see if he could get the beer flowing. He took a pair of glasses from a pouch behind the bar and put them on. They were the 'clubhouse glasses' for anyone who needed them, for situations like this. Stewart didn't have any joy with the taps either, so we ended up with cans of beer.

We sat round the table and Mary served us the fish caught by her son. It was simply fried and accompanied by peas and tatties from Mary and her husband's croft. After polishing that lot off – we had several pieces of fish each – Mary brought out a massive bowl of her home-made crunchy strawberry pudding. The bowl took up most of the table. We got through half of it and thought we'd leave it at that, but Harry urged us to carry on. 'Are you going to finish it off, boys?' We went back to the bowl, helping ourselves to the rest, and I knew I wasn't going to eat now for a week.

Everyone thanked Mary for a magnificent meal and we chatted about golf for a bit, mentioning different courses we'd played. Mary recommended the Stromness course in Orkney. It was on my list. Noble Brian and I would be going there in a week or two.

With our ferry not due to go for a while yet, Harry took us on a tour of the island. He pointed out a large house on a hill overlooking the harbour. The local school, it had once been the home of the laird who had had his own little golf course in the grounds. 'Just a few holes,' said Harry. 'There's an account of which clubs he used and how many shots he took.' Harry then pointed out another house. 'The woman that lives there, it was her birthday yesterday. She's 101 years old.'

Harry drove us past lochs and peat bogs and remarked

that the heather on the hills was more purple than normal due to the good summer they'd been having. We were slowed down by a farmer on a tractor. He was pulling a trailer full of barrels but the barrels kept spilling onto the road and rolling into the fields, the farmer being oblivious to it all. Harry swerved to avoid a couple of the barrels – I say swerved, we were only going at about two miles an hour – then managed to drive up alongside the farmer and inform him of his lost cargo.

Having toured the island (it didn't take long) and with it still not time yet for our ferry, Harry invited us back to his house for a coffee. The coffee turned out to be a large dram of Highland Park and a can of Tennent's lager chaser. We sat with it in Harry's living room, enjoying Whalsay hospitality and a nice view of the harbour.

The phone rang and Harry answered. It was his wife. She must have asked about us. 'Aye,' said Harry. 'They're sitting in oor hoose drinking all oor drink.'

When we left the house, Harry pointed at a pair of boots sitting on his front wall. He was going fishing at the lochs tomorrow. 'Put me trootin' hat on,' he said. On the way to the harbour, Harry's fishing pal drove past us and Harry gave him a wave.

Before we boarded the ferry, Harry showed us the boat he worked on. You couldn't miss it. These pelagic trawlers were huge. It was much bigger than my dad's old fishing boat. Harry had his own cabin with an en suite bathroom. Even from the pier the boat looked luxurious.

We thanked Harry for a wonderful day on Whalsay and got the ferry and then the connecting bus back to Lerwick.

When 'New York, New York' came on the bus radio we sang along, changing the words to 'Whalsay, Whalsay'. It must have been the size of the dram Harry had poured us. Or maybe we were just drunk on Whalsay.

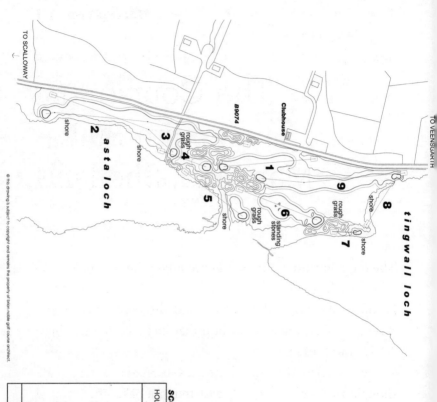

TO VEENSGARTH

TO SCALLOWAY

shore

2 asta loch

shore

3
4 rough grass

5 shore

1

Clubhouse

B9074

9 shore

8 shore

6 rough grass
standing stones

7 shore

tingwall loch

© this drawing is subject to copyright and remains the property of brian noble golf course architect.

Asta Golf Club, Shetland Isles
Route Plan of the 9 hole golf course

Asta Golf Club
Lerwick

SCORE CARD

HOLE NO.		PAR	YARDS
1	STANDING STONE	3	214
2	ASTA POINT	5	480
3	KNOKHA	4	317
4	PEERIE TATTIE	3	115
5	FOY	3	170
6	STENCHWALL	3	197
7	DA NEUK	3	58
8	WATER TRAA	3	132
9	HOMEWARD BOUND	4	340
TOTAL		31	2023

Chapter 15

The Course that Jim Built – Mainland, Shetland

The morning after Whalsay. Three men roaming the streets of Lerwick looking for breakfast, nowhere appearing to be open. We stopped a woman and she pointed us in the direction of sustenance: a shop that had a coffee machine AND sold butteries.

I was surprised to find butteries in Shetland. I'd always thought of them as a north-east thing, a baked delicacy of Moray and Aberdeenshire (though in Aberdeenshire they're known as rowies). I pretty much grew up on butteries – the king of morning rolls! The Scottish croissant! – and often bemoaned the fact that I couldn't get them in Glasgow. Whenever any of my family were visiting, I always asked them to bring down some butteries.

Noble Brian, Stewart and I picked up three coffees and a bag of butteries from the shop. That should see us through the morning.

We'd had a good night's sleep at Lerwick's fabulous hostel and now, chewing on our butteries, we were off to catch the next bus heading to Scalloway, Shetland's ancient capital. We left Lerwick and soon the bus was tackling a hairpin bend on a hill and descending towards Scalloway. The driver stopped at the bottom of the hill and let us off at the turn off for Tingwall. Waiting for us in her car was Winnie, as she'd said she would be.

She'd been sitting waiting for us and watching the Shetland ponies in the field. 'Excuse me if the car is smelling of onions and garlic,' said Winnie. 'I'm preparing my Sunday dinner. I prepare it on Saturday morning with church early on Sunday.'

Winnie drove us a short distance through the valley to Asta golf course, which she lived beside. Winnie's husband Jim had conceived and built the nine-hole course a number of years ago. 'He passed the farm over to our five daughters and two sons,' explained Winnie, 'but he wanted to keep these three fields to make this little golf course as his retirement thing. So he started it and it's done quite well.

'Unfortunately Jim's in care now. He's in his mid-80s. We'd kept the course going and this year we've gone down the road of forming a golf club. Not Jim's private golf club, but a public golf club. Vivienne – that's the eldest daughter – got advice from the local council, and one of my other daughters, Anne, she's done clubs before. So we got the committee set up and the constitution written and we've taken it from there. It was nice this year when all the memberships came in.

'Jim used to do all the grass cutting, but once he's not able for it, then, well, you've got to pay for it. We employ a man called Charlie to cut the greens. He's retired, Charlie, so he's quite happy to cut them. He's a bit fed up with the rabbit holes. I know they're everywhere at the moment. Vivienne cuts the fairways. She usually does them on a Friday, but was very busy yesterday. She and her husband have the farm next door and I noticed she wasn't out and was still taking in silage at ten o'clock at night.'

We'd come to the small clubhouse, Winnie parking in front of it. 'We have a music night in here on a Thursday,' she said. 'The family's into music. We get a good turnout. Anybody that plays or sings can join in. The whole thing is very informal.'

The golf course was across the road. A hill towered above the course and I could see that some of the holes were next to a loch. 'Good for losing balls in!' said Winnie. She pointed to the hill. 'See that ruin up there? That was once a dwelling house. It was always called the Cobbler's House, so it must have been a cobbler who lived up there, away from everything and no real road to it. It seems a strange place for somebody to build a house. Perfect isolation. An escape hatch.'

I mentioned the last part of our bus journey, coming down the steep hill towards Scalloway. Winnie laughed. 'I remember my mother – she was born at Scalloway – she said the first time she was ever in a car coming out from Lerwick and down to Scalloway she screamed the whole way from the top to the bottom, because there was no horse in front to slow down this thing she was sitting in.'

As well as living next to the golf course, Winnie was surrounded by family, with several of her children living nearby. 'I can see five of them out the kitchen window! They're all grannies and grandads now. At the moment we've 13 great grandchildren. Waiting for the next one. It's good; we're fortunate. It's fine to have them all around.

'It's unfortunate Jim being in care, but he's very contented where he is. Extremely contented. And that's the biggest blessing you could ever ask for.'

I wondered if Jim ever asked about his golf course.

'On a good day, when he can remember about it, yes he does. We tell him what's happening, but whether he remembers it the next day it's difficult to tell. No, he was very proud of his golf course. He was quite into golf. And it is a fine setting.

'As long as everyone wants to keep the course going, that's fine. It's nice to have it in the family – but also nice to pass it on. It was either that or close it down, and so many people get a lot of enjoyment out of it, so we didn't want to do that. It's been going 17 years. We hope it keeps going. I see no reason why not.'

Winnie left us to our round, having kindly offered to give us a lift into Scalloway once we were done. We were hoping to have lunch there, before getting the bus back to Lerwick. Noble Brian, Stewart and I got ready to play, leaving our few other things in the clubhouse, then crossed the road to the golf course. The mist clinging to the top of the hill thinned a little, revealing a couple of wind turbines. They disappeared again and when they reappeared there seemed to be more of them, as if they'd just been thrown up.

It was a dreich, breezy day. Scottish weather – you could

patent it. Not that we'd had much Scottish weather recently, not with all that sunshine. I was glad that it had turned wet and dull. This was the first time I'd had cause to wear the pair of waterproof trousers I'd invested in, several islands ago.

Asta opened with an unfussy par three. Noble Brian fired his ball into the rough, my brother found the green (he's good that way) and I fell short (typical) but at least I was on the fairway. The fairway was very soft and made for pleasing iron shots, provided you got them right. Noble Brian went looking for his ball in the rough and emerged with a handful of them.

I thought about Winnie's husband and his golf course. How many times had he cut the grass, walked the course, played it? It must be something to build your own golf course and see people come and play it.

I'd run out of tees so I borrowed one from Noble Brian. I promptly lost it on my next drive and had to ask for another one. Noble Brian sighed. 'I think we should invent a tee on a leash for you.'

At the fourth hole, I pitched to four feet. A par on the cards. Though the cup didn't look too inviting. It was full to the brim with brown water. I'm sure it was just rain-water, but I still didn't fancy putting my hand in there. It was an incentive not to putt.

'Go on,' urged Noble Brian. 'Putt it into the septic tank.'

I knocked the ball into the hole and stepped forward to retrieve it.

'Watch out for the leeches!' said Noble Brian.

I ignored him. Sometimes it's the best way. Instead of

getting my hand dirty, I used my dad's putter to scoop the ball from the murky depths.

We came to the fifth tee where a sign in the shape of an arrow pointed towards the water. Either the arrow was pointing the wrong way or this was the first ever hole for amphibious golfers. We decided to ignore the arrow and faced the fairway instead, all three of us hitting good drives. My brother was playing exceptionally well. He's usually good, Stewart, but he really was on top form, making the game look very easy. 'I'm hitting the ball better than I have in ages,' he said. I said something about the change of scenery perhaps doing him some good, but really he was just good. He had the ability in the first place to have days like this.

We were taking on a run of holes by the water, which was great except that the midges also liked it by the loch. The result was three men flapping their arms about in between golf shots. Midges aside, I felt very comfortable on this golf course, in the rain, in my waterproofs. It was really refreshing. Judging by the contented looks on their faces, Noble Brian and Stewart were enjoying Asta too. In fact this was going to be over far too quickly.

As we left the sixth green, one of the only other golfers out on the course came over and asked if we'd played here before. 'Because if you haven't,' he said, 'you're not going to find the seventh hole. Hard to believe there's one down there.' He was looking towards the loch. We weren't really having to go underwater were we? 'See the mound there?' said the man. Yes, we saw the mound. 'Well, there's a wee path and there's a tee box right there. The hole's 58 yards.' I thought he said 58 yards. 'I would send one of you ahead to the green. You need a spotter or you're going to lose your golf balls.' What on earth lay in store for us? We thanked the man for pointing us in the right direction and went off to find this mysterious hidden golf hole.

We edged closer to the loch and it seemed that pretty soon we'd be in it. There couldn't possibly be a golf hole down here. But there was. Noble Brian and I stood on the tee as my brother fought his way through the long grass. 'Found it!' he said. He'd found the green. He was standing only 50 yards away from us. This was the shortest golf hole in existence, and I still couldn't see the green. It really was quite remarkable.

A puzzled Noble Brian went first, my brother up ahead, acting as the spotter. Noble Brian gamely took a half-swing with his pitching wedge and plunged his ball into the long grass that accounted for all of the hole apart from the green, which my brother swore was there, and we'd taken his word for it. Noble Brian had another go but ended up with the same result; a more than likely lost golf ball. He put away his pitching wedge and pulled out his putter. Now this was going to be interesting. Noble Brian took a half swing with his putter and, not surprisingly, didn't make the green with that one either.

'It's a cracker of a hole,' he said, 'apart from the fact it's cost me three golf balls.'

I had sympathy for the loss of the first two, but that third one served him right.

Stewart came back and had a go, Noble Brian swapping

places to act as spotter. My brother knocked his ball into
the long grass too. He decided not to have another attempt,
which I thought was very wise of him. He trudged through
the thick rough to join Noble Brian.

I stepped up for my shot at it. The least likely candidate, I actually succeeded. With a delicate half swing of
my pitching wedge, I punched my ball into the air and it
came down to shouts of approval from Noble Brian and
Stewart who were both giving me the thumbs up. Somehow,
I'd found the front edge of the small sloping green. I even
got my par. Trust me to deal with the strangest golf hole
in Scotland.

'So,' I asked the golf architect. 'Does it fly in the face
of course design, this hole?'

'Aye,' said Noble Brian. 'It's exactly what not to do with
a par three. Blind tee shot over the rough and some mad
postage stamp green.' But I could tell that he loved it.

The eighth hole was a beauty in a slightly more conventional manner. You had the choice of playing safe by going
left, or going for it by hitting across the water to the green.
Choices, choices. After my miraculous display at the last
hole, I decided to be bold and went for it. I was very
nearly rewarded too. My primary concern had been
clearing the water, but I managed that easily, my ball
bouncing through the green and over the fence. I played
my next shot from the side of the road. This was my take
on the Road Hole.

Before playing the final hole, we turned round and
smacked a few tattie balls we weren't going to miss into
the loch. We then tackled one last par four and shook

hands on the green, our two rounds on Shetland completed. Rain-drenched Asta had been very different from sun-kissed Whalsay. Besides the difference in the weather, the Asta course hadn't been nearly as epic, but then not many courses were as epic as Whalsay. All in all, Asta had offered a nice contrast. We'd encountered a 58-yard par three that we weren't going to forget in a hurry, and the story of the course was a wonderful one.

We got changed out of our wet weather gear and relaxed for a bit in the clubhouse. Looking around the room in more detail there was much evidence of the live music nights Winnie had mentioned. As well as there being both an organ and a piano in the room, there was a sign above the door – incorporating a treble clef, some quavers and a flag (golf and music) – with the words 'there are no strangers here – only friends who have not met yet'. A call for a celebration if ever there was one.

The walls displayed snippets of golfing wisdom. 'A bad day's golfing beats a good day's working.' And a photo collage of some of the great nights had here – pictures of people playing accordions, banjos, fiddles, everyone smiling. 'Asta Music Nights and the people who make them special,' was the heading on the collage.

'They look like right hoolies,' said Noble Brian.

There was a golf map of Britain that seemed to miss out Shetland. I wondered if that was the reason it was pinned up. It wasn't like my golf map of Scotland, which highlighted both Asta and Whalsay.

We looked at photos of Asta's opening day – 18 July 1992. I especially liked the picture of a long-haired youth wearing a leather jacket and high top trainers and teeing off with a fag in his mouth. He looked quite the dude.

Then we spotted on the wall the clubhouse rules:

Asta Social Behaviour Orders (ASBOs)
- The bar staff are all extremely respected members of the community who the management have trained to a very high standard. We should be treated with respect, courtesy and dignity at all times.
- Bar staff must not be heckled or traumatised in any way, shape or form.
- All criticism directed at bar staff shall incur a written warning.
- We retain the right to separate any undesirable elements lingering in the corners up to no good.
- Proof of age is essential. Decrepit old relics shall not be served.
- Rejoicing is forbidden on any occasion where one or more of the bar staff is absent.
- Rangers tunes shall not be tolerated.
- Mental and physical bullying and teabag throwing shall not be tolerated.
- Musicians shall play in the same key as the bar staff.
- Bar staff shall have the final say in everything.
- Complaints against the bar staff shall be ignored and shredded and the complainer shall be escorted from the building and banned for 20 years.

Having digested all of the rules, we read a poem entitled 'Da Clubhouse'. It began:

Jeemie Leask fae Tingwall hed a lifelong dream
To own a peerie golf coorse wi lovely velvet greens
And a classy clubhouse whar fock could hae a bledder
To sit oot ta git things goin and it son cam together

But alas da clubhouse wisna joost da Ritz
You hed ta gae outside ta pee wi toorie, scarf and mitts
Noo Jim is determined ta keep da clubhouse clean
He runs wi mops and dusters da lick im never seen

The poem concluded:

So if you hae a lifelong dream
Dinna gie a skit
Be inspired by Jeemie Leask
An joost gae efter it

If you have a dream, just go after it. I could think of no
better sentiment.

We got our bags together and walked up to Winnie's
house. She was out the front with another woman who
said hello and asked us, 'So do you think you'll be back?
Pass it on to folk that you ken that's coming up here.
Membership is £65.'

There. I've passed it on.

'This is Hazel,' smiled Winnie. 'One of my troublesome
daughters. She stays in the house that's got the grass on
the roof, Norwegian style.' Winnie pointed up the hill to
a house with a grass roof. 'Her husband's Norwegian. I'll
forgive him for that.'

I asked Hazel if she played golf.

'I can try and hit a ba, but I don't really,' she said. 'Family games for a laugh, when naebody really cares far it goes.'

Hazel told us that halfway through the month the layout of the course changed.

'The flags that are oot jist noo are the first nine and fae the 16th then they change. They go the ither way. A' different holes. So if you're back efter the 16th it'll be the other way roon!'

Hazel spoke about the recent bigger changes and future plans.

'Mam and dad ran it basically themselves until this year and me and three of my sisters and various club members taen it oor from them. So we're hoping to have different things now in the winter, like quiz nights. Something that can draw in a peerie bit o money. You get different groups in Shetland that want the golf course and the clubhouse with the bar, so the mair folk we can encourage to do that the better for us really.

'And hopefully we can keep it going. Because dad used to just go and cut everything, do the whole thing himself, because it was his dream to build a nine-hole golf course. And basically that's what he's done.'

Mother and daughter then filled us in on some of the colourful local history.

'See the standing stone just inside the gate there,' said Hazel pointing over to the course. 'It was you,' she turned to her mother, 'who decided it was actually called the "Murder Stone". The frustrations of playing golf!'

'There's actually what looks like the marks of a chain

aroon that stone,' said Winnie, 'and folk were chained there for some reason.'

'Nice community!' laughed Hazel.

'There's a story of two brothers who had a fight there,' her mother continued. 'I don't know if it was a fight till the death or not, but when we moved here somebody said, "You'd better watch, because the ghosts of those that were killed there are probably walking up and down the hill." But so far we havna seen them!'

'And the Gallows Hill!' said Hazel. 'I mean a lot of folk think that's where they used to burn witches, up above Scalloway, but actually the highest point up around here is called the Gallows Hill. So this is a great place!'

'If you see a lot of smoke,' said Winnie, looking at her daughter, 'it'll be you lot burning me on the hill.'

'Surely not!' said Hazel. 'But apart fae ghosts and folk chained up and fighting, I mean, it's a nice place.'

'There's also the story,' said Winnie, 'that they used to carry the coffins past here because the churchyard for Scalloway is up at the Tingwall church there. And they'd have the half bottle in their pocket. So they laid the coffin doon here at the standing stone and had a few drams before they moved away. And when they were almost at the church-yard they remembered they'd left the coffin here. Before my day … '

'So,' said Hazel. 'We'll see you after the 16th!'

'Yes,' I said. 'We'll just need to book the ferry back up.'

'Did you enjoy your game then?' asked Winnie.

'We did,' I said. 'We really enjoyed that eighth hole, hitting across the water.'

'Did you lose many balls?'

'I lost three on that really short one,' said Noble Brian.

'He was trying to be clever,' I said.

'Was he?' said Winnie.

'He was punished,' I said.

Stromness Golf Club, Orkney Islands
Route Plan of the 18 hole golf course

Hoy Sound

Stromness harbour

TO STROMNESS
TOWN CENTRE

Clubhouse

rocks

© this drawing is subject to copyright and remains the property of brian pickle golf course architect.

Stromness Golf Club

Kirkwall

SCORE CARD				
HOLE NO.	PAR	YELLOW YARDS	RED YARDS	PAR
1 LOOKOUT	4	335	335	4
2 GREENWALL	3	206	206	4
3 NESS BRECK	3	219	219	4
4 BLEACHGREEN	4	403	403	5
5 BRAE	4	365	365	4
6 READYPENNY	3	186	186	3
7 DOGS LEG	4	402	402	4
8 BOWL	3	105	105	3
9 BUNGALOW	3	263	263	4
OUT	32	2474	2444	36
10 BATTERY	3	163	163	3
11 DOCTOR	3	142	142	3
12 FLAGSTAFF	4	279	279	4
13 SKYLINE	4	266	266	4
14 LIFEBOAT	4	376	346	4
15 MAESHOWE	3	221	221	4
16 POINT	3	251	251	4
17 MEADOW	4	333	303	4
18 HOME	4	299	299	4
IN	33	2330	2270	34
TOTAL	65	4804	4714	69

Chapter 16

Storm-tossed Stromness – Orkney

Orkney is nearer the mainland than Shetland, but we still had to get there. We might have swung by on the way back from Lerwick had the ferry timetables been more suitable. Instead, Noble Brian and I found ourselves heading to Orkney the week after we'd come back from Shetland.

My brother, having bagged two island courses in one trip AND birdied the most northerly golf hole in Britain, was happy to sit this one out. He wasn't too bothered about racking up more courses. He'd had a fantastic time of it in Shetland. My mam was up for a wee jaunt to Orkney, as was my sister, which was great. Better still, Julieann volunteered to drive us up to the top of the mainland to Scrabster for the ferry to Stromness, which was exactly where this next golf course was.

My sister loves driving. When Julieann lived in London she thought nothing of driving the length of Britain overnight to reach Hopeman. By comparison, Hopeman to Scrabster was a breeze, even with her being seven months pregnant. She had actually gone and played 18 holes at Hopeman the other day. Julieann wasn't planning on playing

in Orkney, and neither was my mam for that matter. They
just fancied the break and I was delighted that they'd joined
us.

The biggest difficulty my sister had regarding the drive
to Scrabster – and this went for my mam too – was having
to cope with being cooped up in a car for four hours with
Noble Brian and myself and having to put up with the
quality of our chat. My mam and sister were used to me
talking rubbish but when you added Noble Brian's ques-
tionable banter to the equation, well, it must be said they
dealt admirably in the circumstances. They just didn't take
anything we said seriously, which was the most sensible
approach they could have taken.

Having left Hopeman very early, we made it to
Scrabster by mid-morning, parked the car and boarded
the ferry. It was this ferry portion of the journey that
got to my sister in the end. It wasn't a long crossing
but it wasn't the smoothest either. Due to poor weather,
the ferry took the more sheltered passage through Scapa
Flow, rather than the regular, more exposed route round
the cliffs of Hoy. But it was still bumpy enough for my
heavily pregnant sister to spend most of the voyage in
the bathroom. Poor Julieann. I felt terrible that she felt
terrible. I imagined she was regretting the trip already
and I wanted us on dry land as swiftly as possible for
her sake.

In the ferry bar, a group of around a dozen guys in golf
gear were getting stuck in to the pints. I imagined they
were playing Stromness too. I wondered what time they
were teeing off. Then wondered if, given the rate at which

they were drinking, they would be capable of teeing off. Oh well. They seemed to be having a good time.

My poor sister though. My mam came back from checking on her to give us an update. 'She's feeling a wee bit better.' There we go. Julieann was on the mend! She's made of strong stuff, my little sister.

And here was Stromness, greeting us now, its centuries old stone houses huddled by the water. It's a beautiful town, Stromness, with its narrow cobbled streets and alley-ways. Not that my sister was appreciating much of that beauty as we stepped off the ferry into the wind and rain.

Fortunately our guest house was nearby. We checked in and Julieann went for a lie down. The plan was for Noble Brian and I to go and play our round of golf, while my mam and sister would have a wander about town. It wasn't really the weather for wandering. They decided to relax in their room for a bit and venture out later, when hope-fully the rain would have stopped and the wind died down a little.

Noble Brian and I had no choice but to head out now. We'd a game of golf to play. We carried our clubs to the edge of town, to the golf course at the Point of Ness with its views over the water to the tiny island of Graemsay and the larger island of Hoy.

Waiting for us in the clubhouse was Glen, the club captain, and his friend Kenny, the handicap secretary. Glen and Kenny were young men, around our age. Pretty young then. The course was quiet today, partly because of the weather but also because there was a competition on in Kirkwall. There was no sign yet of the gang of golfers from the ferry. They'd probably hit the pub as soon as we'd landed.

We got ready in the locker room – I put my cagoule on straight away – and stepped outside. 'Kenny will show you the way!' said Glen. The first hole was an uphill dogleg – the whole course sat on open hillside – and I found it pretty demanding, what with the wind and all. Kenny was a big hitter and Glen could fairly whack the ball too. Of course, Noble Brian was no slouch either in the distance department. I did my best to keep up with the three of them.

The second hole, a longish par three, looked even longer with the pond before the green. Building the pond had been a big job. 'We were down here at nights working on it,' said Glen. 'One of the members is a contractor so we got the diggers in and altered the course a couple of years ago.' I aimed my tee shot for the pin but my ball caught the far edge of the pond. Kenny fished it out for me with his club.

Glen asked me where I was from. Whenever I say I'm from Hopeman, people's response is usually either, 'Where?' or 'Oban?' So I said to Glen, 'Hopeman, it's near Elgin.' But Hopeman was enough for Glen. 'Hopeman? My uncle Kenny was the headmaster of Hopeman Primary School.'

What a funny coincidence. Glen's uncle had been the headmaster at Hopeman when my sister was a pupil there. 'How is he?' I asked Glen. 'Oh, he's fine,' said Glen. 'He's spending his retirement surfing.' I would have to tell my sister that one.

Glen had been to Hopeman himself and played my home golf course. Well, most of it. He'd been forced to come in at the 15th having run out of golf balls. All that broom and gorse you see. At least he'd managed to play the Prieshach.

The weather was getting worse. At the fourth tee, we took Glen and Kenny's lead and hid under a dyke from approaching black clouds. When you grew up here, you could spot a storm brewing, and I could see the point of these dry stone dykes. They helped keep you dry. 'Only good thing about the wind,' yelled Glen, 'is that a storm passes over quickly'.

Over on the other side of the dyke were the wartime gun emplacements of Ness Battery, built to defend Hoy Sound against the German naval threat. Of course it is Scapa Flow that is famous for the scuttling of the German fleet during the First World War. Glen and Kenny had spent a good deal of their childhood scrambling around Ness Battery, exploring the bunkers and tunnels.

We capitalised on the calm after the storm and made our way down the fourth fairway. Glen told me that as well as being into his golf he was a bit of a rugby man. He had the build. He described a typical away match on the mainland. 'Sleeping on the way down from Kirkwall to Aberdeen, everyone drinking on the way back up.'

As we neared the fourth green, a truck sped along the road with its horn beeping. On the back of the truck was a bunch of people making one hell of a racket and one of them in a hell of mess, covered from head to toe in flour, feathers, treacle and other stuff that's difficult to get off.

It was a blackening. It's traditional before you get married.
They have them in Hopeman too.

Kenny said that he'd managed to avoid being blackened
by getting married in Inverness. I'd been able to escape
one too, telling my brother that it was one of his main
tasks as my best man to ensure that I didn't get blackened.
I trusted him and he came through. Though looking back
now, I perhaps should have been blackened. You grow up
in Hopeman, you get blackened. I'd either been too serious
about the whole thing or not serious enough.

Glen, on the other hand, had been blackened twice!
Once by his rugby team-mates and once by his mates in
Stromness.

As we were about to putt out on the fourth green, the
heavens opened and we huddled next to a dyke. All these
dykes were coming in handy, though we were still getting
soaked. The rain was torrential and Glen took an execu-
tive decision. He halted the round, suggesting we head
inside for a pint and continue our round once the rain had
stopped. Drink and shelter. It sounded good. Kenny picked
up all the balls from the green and we ran to the clubhouse for cover.

They brew good beer in Orkney. After one sip of my
Raven Ale, I really wasn't missing the golf all that much.
Glen gave us a tour of the clubhouse, pointing out a picture
of a man on the wall. 'Ronald Wilson,' said Glen. 'He only
missed four days that year. He was Stromness Golf Club.
He died a couple of years ago.'

Glen showed us a glass cabinet full of trophies and told
us about some of the competitions they held at Stromness.

The serious ones and the not so serious ones. He mentioned the Mutton Cup (at least I think he did) and Da Low Breeks trophy. 'Whoever shows the most arse crack wins,' explained Glen.

And then there was the Final Fling on the last Saturday in September. 'The north side of the toon against the south side of the toon. It's just a piss up really. There's a great song and dance made about it. It's a good laugh.' Glen had taken part in the Final Fling for the first time last year. For once, it hadn't clashed with his rugby. The Final Fling seemed to be as much about eating and drinking your way round the golf course as playing your way round it. 'Soup, starters, main course, pudding,' said Glen, 'cheese and biscuits and port ... drink a few drams at the seventh ... the ninth ... the 11th ... '

'The vodka was cracked opened on the 15th tee and finished by the 18th green,' said Kenny.

'And did you hit the bar when you came in?' I asked.

'Aye,' said Kenny.

'I can't remember doing the presentation,' said Glen.

Meanwhile the rain had stopped. This was our chance. While we'd been in the bar, the gang of guys from the ferry had somehow turned up and teed off. It was one thing being held up by the weather, but another being held up by under-the-weather golfers. Glen and Kenny, however, had it all worked out. We'd restart our round on the 16th hole, beside the clubhouse, play the final three holes, then do five to 15. That way, we had a better chance of enjoying a clear run at it, provided the extremely changeable weather didn't scupper everything.

Kenny hooked his tee shot at the 16th over the dyke and into the neighbouring campsite. He went off in search of his ball and found it next to a tent. Thankfully, there wasn't a camper lying unconscious next to the tent as well.

The 17th played along the shore and into the wind. As I walked the fairway, I realised I had a big grin on my face. I think I was having fun. In order to get to the green, you had to hit over a dyke and a road. Next to the road was a ruined building. Two teenage boys were capering about, trying to climb it. Glen told them to get lost and they did. If you tried that in Glasgow, you'd end up with your club wrapped round your neck. Mind you, Glen was a rugby man. His shoulders spelt trouble.

I had a bit of trouble with a pot bunker, in that it took me five shots to get out of it. As I emerged, I somehow struck myself on the chin with my sand wedge. It kind of hurt. Minutes later, after playing another shot and putting my bag back over my shoulder, I collided with Noble Brian.

'What are you doing?' he asked.

'Don't know.' My co-ordination had completely gone to pot.

A while later we reached the Halfway House, a smart little building between the ninth green and the tenth tee. The Halfway House became a well-stocked bar on big occasions and, by the sounds of it, a restaurant during the Final Fling. I stood next to the Halfway House on the tenth tee, facing the choppy sea and the hills of Hoy. The hole itself was a beauty, a downhill par three that required us to hit over an old wartime gun emplacement. The hole itself was called Battery.

A couple of holes later, we encountered some of the guys from the ferry playing a parallel hole. Or at least trying to. Glen pointed out to them that they were hitting towards the wrong green. 'It's confusing!' cried one of them, stumbling about. I supposed it would be confusing if you'd drunk that much.

By the time we reached the 15th hole – in our case, the final hole – the weather had taken another turn for the worse. At least we had another dyke to sit under. The brollies went up and the Highland Park came out. Glen had thoughtfully brought some whisky miniatures out with him and kindly handed us one each. The warmth from the whisky made the rain and wind seem less relevant. After some minutes, the weather calmed down again and we stood up to play the very peculiar 15th hole.

'We all have our opinions on this hole,' said Glen. 'The bane of the Stromness golfer … '

I'd been staring at it since we'd sat down and was still having trouble taking it in. The bare facts were that it was a par three of 221 yards. Then there were the extra little details. First we had to hit over the dyke and the road we'd encountered earlier in the round. If all that lay beyond the road was the green, then it would have been an unusual short hole and no more. But there was more. The green was surrounded by a moat. Tailing off steeply to all sides, this green really should have had a castle on top of it instead of a flag pin.

I was confronting this bizarre golf hole for the first time and it had me flummoxed. This was downright lunacy. Glen and Kenny had faced the hole on many occasions, which only made it worse for them. They knew the score, and it wasn't good.

'What are we going to hit, other than the water?' asked Kenny, with a sense of hopelessness. Glen said that he'd only been able to par the hole once this year.

'How often do you play?' I asked.

'Twice a week.'

Noble Brian asked me if he could borrow a ball, as he was clean out of them. I was tempted not to give him one because of his refusal to loan me his sand wedge back on Skye. A long time ago, yes, though it still rankled. I decided that I would give him a ball and for some reason the ball I handed him had the word 'hope' printed on it. Looking down towards the dyke and the road and the green and the moat, Noble Brian said that all of our golf balls should have the word 'hope' printed on them. What on earth was this golf hole all about?

My colleague went for the green but it all went wrong. His ball – or rather my ball – cleared the road but missed the green, plopping into the water. We now had one golf ball between us. Noble Brian was done and it was now my turn. I too failed to reach the green, but at least I missed the moat. I came nowhere near it because I didn't even reach the road. Basically I shanked my tee shot, my ball stopping just short of the dyke. I faced a tricky second shot, but at least I had a shot.

Neither Glen nor Kenny had found the green with their drives. I doubted anyone ever had. I stood over my ball next to the dyke and tried to figure out what to do. The lie wasn't great, the whole situation wasn't great. I needed to get the ball up and over that dyke and hopefully clear the moat and hopefully keep it on the green. This was all very hopeful. I'm a Hopeman man. I had a stab at it with my pitching wedge and the ball flew high into the air. It was flying a little bit left, but the wind was strong and in my favour and brought the ball round. It came down on the green and stopped five feet from the pin.

Glen and Kenny reacted as though it was the greatest golf shot ever. Perhaps it was the greatest golf shot ever. I got the sense that if I was to hole this putt for my par I'd be the talk of Stromness for a long time to come. Hardly anyone managed to par this fiendishly difficult hole and certainly not in the manner I was threatening to. Shank, hack, putt. The only problem was the putt.

And what did I do? I missed it. There were groans from the gallery. Well, from Glen, Kenny and Noble Brian. I'd crumbled under the pressure. There had simply been too much riding on that putt. Golfing immortality, that sort of thing. I'd gone from man of the hour to not worth mentioning. Oh well, by the time I had another sip of Raven Ale I'd be over the disappointment.

As we chatted in the clubhouse bar, Whalsay cropped up in the conversation. Glen and Kenny had been asking about the other island courses we'd played. I mentioned Harry's story of the golf trolley falling over the cliff. Glen knew the story well. In fact, he knew more of it too.

'Seemingly after the guy's trolley went over the cliff he went back to the clubhouse and got the greenkeeper's buggy. He drove out and parked it, tied a rope to it and himself, and off he went doon the cliffs and got his bag.

'I thought the story was a load of rubbish. But when we were up there at Whalsay someone hit their tee shot over the cliff. They were standing there thinking they'd lost their ball and a boy came over and said "I'll have a look" and off he went over the side. And he worked his way doon and came up five minutes later with six or seven balls in his hand and held them oot and said, "Is one of them yours?" And it was.

'They built the course so they widna be on the piss. That's why they did it. They're at sea three months o' the year max – and in the winter months too. One of our pals up there has eight weeks a year fishing. They can go oot and get their entire herring quota in one day basically if they get a big haul and catch it right. It's unbelievable.'

Only a week ago we'd been in Whalsay and here we were in Stromness. I liked golf in the north. Hopeman's fairly north, but this was proper north. Maybe, I thought, I should check out golf in the Faroe Islands sometime.

A man came over and informed Glen that a cruise ship was stopping at Stromness tomorrow and that a dozen Germans were coming off the boat to play golf. 'I'll go down and meet them,' said the man.

'If they want trolleys,' said Glen, 'there's only nine.'

I liked that. The idea of German tourists asking if there were trolleys and some Orcadian saying, 'Nine'.

'We get dozens of liners into Orkney throughout the year,' said Glen. 'They come for the historical sites and some of the passengers fancy a game of golf. These boats have driving ranges on top of them.'

Our ferry to Shetland had had a putting green on top of it.

It was time for Noble Brian and me to head back and see how my mam and sister were doing. I hoped that they hadn't strayed too far from the guest house, given what an atrocious afternoon it had been weather-wise. Hopefully we could all go out for a nice evening meal.

Glen offered us a lift into town. He and Kenny had been wonderful hosts. We'd had a stormy introduction to golf on Orkney, but the warmth of the welcome had meant everything. Conditions had been dreadful, the company terrific. They knew how to have fun up here.

Golf's just a game when it comes down to it. It should be fun.

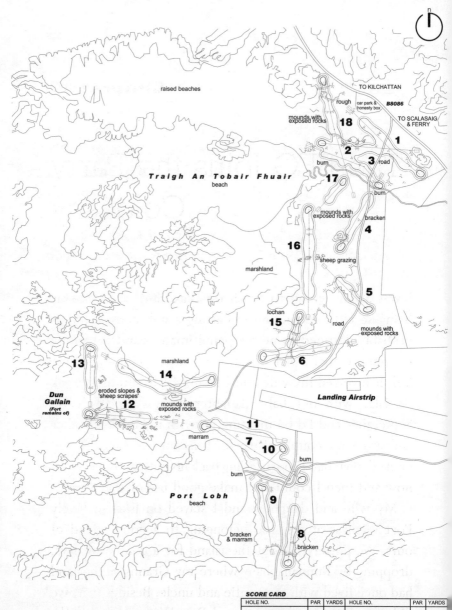

Isle of Colonsay Golf Club
Route Plan of the 18 hole golf course

SCORE CARD

HOLE NO.		PAR	YARDS	HOLE NO.		PAR	YARDS
1	ROAD HOLE	4	312	10	PORT LOBH	3	136
2	WESTWARD HO!	4	317	11	SAND DUNES	4	260
3	THE BURN	4	271	12	DUBH HEARTACH	4	324
4	MOOR & FEN	4	265	13	DUN GALLAIN	3	161
5	MACHRINS	3	199	14	THE RUSHES	5	376
6	VIKINGS GRAVE	4	301	15	ADHARCAN	3	160
7	THE FANK	5	391	16	MUCKLE CARRY	5	341
8	ARDSKENISH	4	238	17	AIR ADHART	3	124
9	REEKIN KELP	3	206	18	KILCHATTAN	5	370
OUT		35	2500	IN		35	2252
				TOTAL		70	4752

COLONSAY

Scalasaig

Isle of Colonsay Golf Club

Chapter 17

The BFG Joins the Party
– Colonsay

I was always going to finish on Islay. So with Colonsay being so close by and also boasting a golf course, it was probably destined to be my penultimate island.

I put together a plan of action for my concluding double bill. It involved my wife and I taking a late summer break on Islay with our baby daughter. It was already early September and I'd be meeting up with my mam, brother and sister in a couple of weeks' time for our game of golf on dad's birthday. I'd be handing back his putter, but between now and then I could still make good use of it.

My wife and daughter and I stayed on Islay in lovely Port Wemyss at a house belonging to a good friend of ours. We pottered about the island for a couple of days, dropping by Bunnahabhain where my Granny Sutherland had once lived with my auntie and uncle. Besides that, we did very little but hang around Port Wemyss and neighbouring Portnahaven, watching the seals during the daytime and relaxing by the fireside at night with the flashing lighthouse framed by the living-room window.

Of course, there was the golf angle too and, in the

middle of our break, Noble Brian pitched up on Islay with our good friend the BFG (big Fraser guy). Like Noble Brian, the BFG was an architect living in Edinburgh (though he didn't dabble in golf course design). But the thing about the BFG was that he was absolutely huge. How huge? Twice the size of Ernie Els. And therefore 23 times the size of Noble Brian. The BFG made me look tiny. He made most people look tiny. And he had ginger hair. He was a true Scottish giant, and friendly with it too. In fact, the BFG was nothing but a big softy. I was glad to have him on board and just hoped the ferry would stay afloat when he set foot on it. I supposed he had made it to Islay, so we'd probably be OK for Colonsay.

The three of us (Little & Large & Somewhere in the Middle) boarded the morning ferry at Port Askaig. The idea was to play a round of golf on Colonsay and return on the evening ferry. Then tomorrow we'd play the Machrie, on Islay, the final course. My islands golf adventure was nearing its end.

Since Stromness, Noble Brian had taken a day-trip to Bute with Abbi and played Port Bannatyne. He described the round as 'a damp squib'. I believe that the course had been like a waterslide. Waterslides are fun, but perhaps not when you're trying to hit golf shots. Anyway, having made the effort to go to Port Bannatyne, Noble Brian was now level with me. Colonsay would be his 17th course too, and Islay his 18th. Everything was pointing towards a tidy finish.

We'd been on the ferry five minutes and it was still floating. It seemed that it had been built to handle the BFG and other giants of this world. I had my half-set of clubs with me, Noble Brian had his half-set in his pencil bag, while the BFG had brought along a full set of clubs. I really couldn't have imagined him with a half-set.

Soon we were sailing past Bunnahabhain distillery and the house my granny had once lived in. She used to look out the living-room window through binoculars at the passing boats and to the majestic Paps of Jura. This setting was so familiar to me.

I was taken back 20 years, to when I was a student in Aberdeen, to the day I woke up and decided I was going to visit my granny on Islay. And I jumped on the bus to Glasgow and caught another one to Kennacraig and took the ferry to Islay, landing at Port Askaig. I knew that I was still several miles from Bunnahabhain and I knew that I was going to walk it. I set off across the hills and it started to rain and soon I was soaked to the skin but I didn't mind one bit. It was just me, the road and the sheep and I was walking to Bunnahabhain to see my granny and I couldn't wait to see the look on her face. I was enjoying the fresh air, the freedom, the spontaneity of it all. Looking back now, I was enjoying my youth.

I'd walked maybe three miles when a car splashed past. It stopped and reversed. The driver of the car was my uncle and with him were my auntie and my granny. When my uncle had driven past, my granny had said from the back of the car, 'That's oor Gary.'

Twenty years on, I'm glad I went to visit my granny on Islay that time.

My thoughts were interrupted by a man who had seen

us board the ferry with our golf clubs and wanted to talk golf. He told Noble Brian, the BFG and myself that he'd played the Machrie just the other day. 'Lightning greens,' he said. 'So you're off to play Colonsay then? It isn't a championship course.' We weren't really expecting a championship course. In fact, what we sought was the exact opposite.

The man proceeded to give us a blow-by-blow account of a round at the Machrie, describing every single shot, omitting nothing. We got the names of the holes, how long they were, where best to place our drives. After a while, I realised he was still only on the third hole and it dawned on me that he wasn't going to stop. There'd be no skipping a hole or two. No, he was going to keep going until he reached the 18th green. We were getting the complete, comprehensive, unabridged guide to playing the Machrie.

Or at least I was. Noble Brian and the BFG had disappeared to the other end of the deck and were pointing at some scenery. To be fair, Jura was a splendid sight, but it wasn't helping me any. I was an audience of one. There was nothing I could do but hang in there. He was a nice man, a friendly man, an incredibly chatty man who loved his golf, but what detail he went into. By the time he finished, I felt like I'd played my round at the Machrie and thought about making Colonsay my final course.

As the ferry approached Colonsay, a big black cloud hung over the island. By the time we stepped ashore, the cloud had moved on, leaving nothing but clear blue sky. It was going to be another one of those days. Noble Brian and I had been fortunate to have had so many of them. Mind you, Stromness hadn't fallen into that category.

When I'd made enquiries about golfing on Colonsay, I'd spoken on the phone to a man called Angus. He'd asked which ferry we were getting and said that we should look out for his Land Rover when we arrived on the pier. I spotted a Land Rover so we went over with our clubs and stood next to it. A few minutes later, Angus appeared. He told us to get in and he'd drive us to the golf course.

The BFG squeezed into the back of the Land Rover with Noble Brian and I sat up front with Angus. As he drove away from the pier, it became evident that he didn't have much patience with pedestrians or cyclists. They just got in the way of his Land Rover.

'That's right, walk on baith sides of the road! Bikes an a'. Hope they fall in the ditch.'

On the way to the golf course, Angus pointed to a hill and a house with a red, white and blue fence round it. 'That's my hoose.' Angus was a Rangers fan. 'Only two teams in Scotland: Rangers and Rangers reserves. If any of youse is a left footer, you can get oot and walk.'

I got right in there and told Angus I was a Rangers fan.

He looked at his other two passengers in the rear-view mirror.

The BFG owned up to being an Airdrie fan.

'Airdrie?' said Angus. 'Nothing that one.'

Noble Brian wasn't saying anything. He was conspicuous by his silence.

'I thought so,' said Angus. 'He's got that look aboot him.

Notice you kept that quiet when you got in the Land
Rover. You can all walk back.'

I got the impression that he wasn't joking. Oh well. At
least he still appeared to be driving us to the golf course
and hadn't slammed on the brakes and chucked us out.

I thought I'd kick the conversation away from football
so I asked Angus if there were any sheep on the golf course.

'Sheep on the golf course ... goats on the golf course
... cow shite on the greens.'

That kind of golf course then.

'Don't play yellow balls by the way,' warned Angus.

'Why's that then?'

'The ravens will take them away. And keep it low. Wind
picks up and your ball's 100 yards behind you. There's also
an airport right in the middle of the golf course ... now
the rule is that the cyclists stop and get off the bikes!'

A family of cyclists in coloured cagoules was pedalling
towards us, making it difficult for Angus to get past them
on the narrow road. I sensed they were about to get an
earful from Angus. I was right. He stopped, leaned out
the window and laid down the law of the road on Colonsay.

The man, who had a child on the back of his bike, didn't
seem to understand. He may have been foreign. In any
case, shaking his head was probably the wrong thing to do
when Angus was talking to him.

'Don't shake your head! That's the rule! The law is you
get off the bike and let the vehicles past ye. Read it! The
police printed it!'

With that, Angus pulled back into the Land Rover and
drove on. 'Shake his heid! I could have been nicer, but I

didn't feel like it. They call me Angry Angus for some strange reason. I never knew he had a kid on the back there. I widnave shouted at him like that.'

We reached the golf course. 'There you go,' said Angus. 'Right on the tee!'

It was in fact the green, so Angus drove up the fairway to the tee.

'Watch oot for the rabbit holes by the way. Enjoy your day boys. Hope you have got hiking boots, wellies ...'

And with that, he was off. I was pretty sure he wasn't coming back for us.

We put our money in the honesty box and got ready to tee off. There was a woman sitting on a bench and a dog running about. Then I noticed a man over in the long grass having a pee. When he turned round, I saw it was the chatty man from the ferry. Having answered the call of nature, he came over for a chat.

I braced myself for a blow-by-blow account of a round on Colonsay but he didn't provide it. Instead he was concerned on our behalf. He couldn't figure out where the 18th green was. Normally on a golf course the 18th green was never far from the first tee, but we were standing on the first tee and there was no sign of an 18th green. We looked around and I noticed the top of a flag on higher ground surrounded by rocks.

'That must be it,' I said. The chatty man dismissed my suggestion. That couldn't possibly be the 18th green up there. It must be a putting green or something. I still felt that it was the 18th green, however unlikely the pin position, but I didn't want to enter a big debate about it. We would deal with the final hole when it came to it. The chatty man sat down next to his wife to watch us teeing off.

I went first and duffed it completely. A truly woeful drive. The BFG made a mess of his too. Noble Brian showed us how it was done, hitting a typically super tee shot.

'You're going to do all right,' the chatty man said to Noble Brian, 'but the other two are struggling. I think you're part-time golfers.'

'Hopefully it'll get better,' I said.

'You can always resort to irons off the tee,' said the chatty man. I wondered if he'd still be sitting there when we came in.

We set off down the fairway and understood why Angus had mentioned rabbit holes. There were so many of them. I figured that we might be losing a good few golf balls before this round was over. 'It's a treacherous golf course,' said Noble Brian as we stumbled across what was essentially grazing land. 'It's just that you canna see fuck all.' We spent a good deal of time on that first hole trying to spot our golf balls, even though we'd all kept to the fairway, such as it was. Thankfully, our ability to see what we were doing would improve as the round went on. Otherwise we'd have been there all day.

I decided to take my eyes off the ground and take in the entire golf course. It spread across the undulating machair, reaching not one but two gorgeous bays. Also there was the airstrip that Angus had spoken about. From here, it was hard to see how the course fitted around it. And then, of course, there were the sheep. I couldn't see any cows and didn't want to see any. Take away the runway and the Colonsay course had a similar feel to Iona. And like Iona, I liked it. It was rough and ready, yet ravishing all the same. How could you not be inspired by such a beautiful place?

The BFG admitted to me that he was feeling a wee bit nervous. He had been keen to join us on this Colonsay and Islay expedition, but he didn't play much golf and he hadn't played with Noble Brian or myself before. I said I'd felt the same way, back on Skye, teeing off with Noble Brian for the first time. Better to relax and anyway it was a game among friends. If the BFG was nervous, he was also making the sheep nervous. He thinned an iron shot, missing a sheep's arse by about an inch. I think I saw the sheep flinch.

A car drove across the golf course. I'd no idea where it was heading, perhaps to one of the beaches. It slowed down and one of the vehicle's passengers leaned out of the window to take a photograph of the three of us, golfing among the sheep. We posed for the camera. Now there was a holiday snap for them to take home and show their friends. 'This is what they do for fun in Scotland.'

Having putted out on the sixth green, we had some difficulty tracking down the seventh tee. We were at the airport perimeter fence. Surely we weren't required to hit over the runway. We walked along by the fence, getting bogged down in the mud, and finally saw a green.

With still no sign of the tee, we chose to improvise, dropping balls and treating the hole as a par three. I hit a nice seven iron to within a few feet of the pin. The BFG went just as close with his fine effort, except that his path to the hole was now blocked by a huge cowpat. All I was thinking was cows, cows, cows, where are they? Perhaps one had just passed by, taken a big dump on the green and moved on to pastures new.

The BFG moved his ball to a spot where he had a shot at the hole. He was learning about the hazards of island golf. Golf on the rocks could get very dirty, very quickly. The BFG lipped out with his putt, missing out on his birdie. I made mine, even though we'd just made up the hole.

We were nearly halfway round, and despite the torn up terrain and the hundreds of rabbit holes, I hadn't even lost a ball yet. In fact, I was a few up, having found several, including a yellow ball a raven must have dropped.

The 12th hole at Colonsay is spectacular. A high tee on a rocky outcrop, a rolling fairway by the shore and the most inviting green on a ridge in the distance. A simple golf hole that made the most of the landscape, the most natural and wonderful golf hole you could hope to play. Noble Brian raved about it. Sheep ran from the green as we approached. They'd caught sight of the BFG.

We enjoyed a good run of holes, loving every minute of it in the sunshine. The 16th fairway – though the fairways on Colonsay weren't always easy to identify – seemed overly generous. It appeared to cover half the island. 'Between the beach and the road and you're in play,' said the BFG.

After dealing with the short 17th, we moved on to the final hole and agreed that the flag I'd pointed out at the start of our round was indeed the one we were aiming for. There was no fairway to speak of. It was just one stark and never-ending hill that we were required to climb in order to reach a hidden green guarded by rocks. As final holes go, it was a formidable one.

The BFG went first, slicing his drive big time, his ball nearly ending up on Islay. Noble Brian stepped out of character and hooked his tee shot. While I played mine straight up the middle. Not very far up the middle, but straight up the middle. With his next shot, from the other end of the island, the BFG definitely hit a sheep. I'd never seen a sheep jump so high. I'd never seen a sheep jump. Another sheep walked over to the stricken sheep, seeming to check that it was all right. It looked all right. It wasn't lying on its back with its legs in the air or anything.

The view from the final green, when we eventually got up there, was astonishing. We were able to look back on the whole course and the sea and say that it had been fun. We all shook hands, smiling and then readied ourselves for the hike back across the island to the pier. We thought it was a couple of miles at most, but that in this heat – it had really warmed up over the past hour – it might end up feeling like more.

Along the road we walked with our bags, the sun beating down on us. The BFG, who wasn't wearing a hat, was turning redder by the second. Of course, he was also nearer the sun than the rest of us. He stopped to pick and eat wild berries from the bushes. The BFG was foraging. Noble Brian and I were near perspiring in the heat.

We got plenty of waves from passing cars, but no one

stopped. A wave wasn't the same as a lift. Then one car did stop. It was the chatty man. He wound down his window and advised us that if we stuck our thumbs out, someone would probably stop and give us a lift. Having given us this advice, he promptly drove off, leaving us wondering why he hadn't offered us a lift.

Our great effort at walking those miles in the heat was rewarded when we reached the lovely Colonsay Hotel and each got our hands on a pint of the excellent Colonsay IPA. We sat down in a corner of the bar to recover from our exertions and to reflect on our round of golf.

Noble Brian felt that the Colonsay course had pretty much offered everything. Every type of golf shot, all kinds of scenery. 'It's a microcosm of all the island golf courses,' he said as he brought his pint to his mouth. So there you go. If you fancy a quick island golf fix, head to Colonsay. And make sure you try the IPA.

Between the hotel and the pier we discovered the brewery that brewed this fine beer and the BFG bought a mini-keg of the stuff. The mini-keg looked more like a mini-mini-keg in the BFG's hands, and when he handed it to Noble Brian it became a full-sized keg. The woman at the brewery asked how we'd got on at the golf. 'Pity about all the animals,' she said. We said that we'd seen the funny side of it and that we'd had a great time.

We carried on down to the pier to board the ferry back to Islay. Noble Brian had his pencil bag over one shoulder and was carrying the mini-keg. 'They're taking the 19th hole with them!' cried one of the ferrymen.

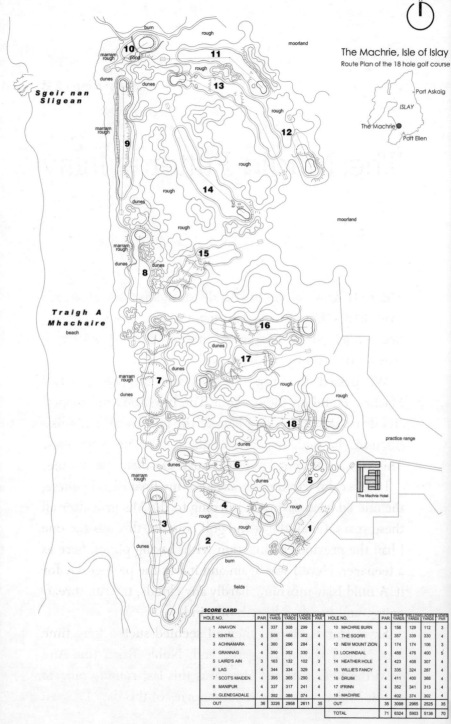

n

The Machrie, Isle of Islay
Route Plan of the 18 hole golf course

Port Askaig
ISLAY
The Machrie
Port Ellen

burn
rough
moorland
marram rough
pond
dunes
dunes
rough

Sgeir nan Sligean

marram rough

rough

rough

moorland

rough

rough

Traigh A Mhachaire
beach

marram rough

dunes

dunes

dunes

dunes

practice range

marram rough

dunes

dunes

marram rough

The Machrie Hotel

rough

rough

rough

rough

burn

fields

SCORE CARD

HOLE NO.		PAR	WHITE YARDS	YELLOW YARDS	LADIES YARDS	LADIES PAR	HOLE NO.		PAR	WHITE YARDS	YELLOW YARDS	LADIES YARDS	LADIES PAR
1	ANAVON	4	337	308	299	4	10	MACHRIE BURN	3	156	129	112	3
2	KINTRA	5	508	466	362	4	11	THE SGORR	4	357	339	330	4
3	ACHNAMARA	4	360	296	284	4	12	NEW MOUNT ZION	3	174	174	106	3
4	GRANNAG	4	390	352	330	4	13	LOCHINDAAL	5	488	476	400	5
5	LAIRD'S AIN	3	163	132	102	3	14	HEATHER HOLE	4	423	408	307	4
6	LAG	4	344	334	329	4	15	WILLIE'S FANCY	4	335	324	287	4
7	SCOT'S MAIDEN	4	395	365	290	4	16	DRUIM	4	411	400	368	4
8	MANIPUR	4	337	317	241	4	17	IFRINN	4	352	341	313	4
9	GLENEGADALE	4	392	388	374	4	18	MACHRIE	4	402	374	302	4
OUT		36	3226	2958	2611	35	OUT		35	3098	2965	2525	35
							TOTAL		71	6324	5903	5136	70

Chapter 18

The Magic Putter – Islay

The BFG drove along Scotland's straightest and strangest road, Islay's 'Low Road'. Through the peat moors, blasting Bruce Springsteen on the car stereo. 'Glory Days. Well, they'll pass you by. Glory Days.'

We passed the airport, then saw the whitewashed Machrie Hotel on the horizon. The BFG took the turnoff and drove down the long lane to the golf course. 'It's like Augusta,' he said. Except that there were no magnolias. This was a different kind of beauty. Desolate, yet divine.

I felt a calm excitement ahead of my final island course, the one I'd been saving. Returning to the Machrie after all these years. Of all the island golf courses, this was the one I had the previous connection with, having played here as a teenager. Here I was again and it was the perfect day for it. A mild Islay morning, hardly any clouds, the sun threatening, and barely a breath of wind.

Skye, Harris, Arran, they all seemed such a long time ago. Now I was nearing the end. Noble Brian too. And we'd the BFG with us! How was this last round going to unfold? What would be my memories of this day? I'd even

dressed for the occasion, smartening up in a T-shirt with
a collar, and a pair of trousers instead of a pair of jeans. I
had to look the part in order to play the part.

The BFG parked the car and we scrunched across the
gravel driveway to the hotel entrance. I noticed the cobwebs
above the door. The hotel was pretty tired looking. There
was an air of neglect about the place. But we weren't here
for the hotel. We were here to play a classic golf course.

We wandered about inside until someone pointed us
down a gloomy corridor to a shop where we paid our
green fees. It was costing three times as much as anywhere
else we'd played, but that was fair enough. This was the
Machrie.

Back in 1901, the course hosted a famous match between
the Great Triumvirate of James Braid, Harry Vardon and
John Henry Taylor, the three competing for the princely
sum of £100, reputed to be the largest prize of its kind
at the time. The Machrie has history and it crops up today
in those lists of memorable golf courses. Now it was playing
host to the Unlikely Triumvirate of Noble Brian, the BFG
and me.

'This looks like a golf course!' said the BFG, standing
on the first tee. 'A really good golf course.' It had that
look about it. Linkstastic and more luxurious than anything
else Noble Brian and I had encountered in our exploration
of the islands. It was the sort of golf course that made you
stand up straight. I had my game face on, whatever that
was. It meant looking like I meant business, being kind of
serious, within reason. I got off to the perfect start, sending
an immaculate drive over the hill.

The fairway felt wonderful underfoot and the undulating landscape by the sea had me in a trance. The first green was delightful, a pleasure to putt on. This was a place to play golf. I wanted to make sure that I measured up to my surroundings. I wasn't going to fall to pieces on a pedigree golf course on my last island. I was intent on doing myself proud. When my wife and daughter met me on the final green, I wanted to be able to say that I'd played well here today.

The second hole was a dogleg left, a dark peaty burn running down the left side of the fairway, to the left of the burn a field of cows. I refused to toy with the idea of cutting the corner. I wasn't going to hit over that field. Instead I took the safe line, aiming straight ahead. I was rewarded for my caution, my ball resting in the middle of the fairway. I could have made the hole shorter, but I might have come a cropper. Like Noble Brian, who gambled, trying to eliminate the field and ending up in the rough. The BFG was brave too, with a similarly disappointing result. He ploughed his ball into the field. Not content with alarming sheep, he was now terrifying cows.

From my good spot on the fairway, I struck a lovely five iron. I was revelling in this setting. The Machrie carried the drama of Askernish but it was more pristine. It had been around much longer. Or at least it had been maintained much longer. It was like I was spoiling myself. The Machrie was the dessert to all the other courses I'd feasted on.

The greens were fast, though not lightning fast as the chatty man on the ferry had reported. I knocked in a six-foot putt for a bogey, my second bogey. By my modest standards, on a course as good as this, I was not doing badly.

Everywhere you looked on the Machrie there were red and white poles, an indication not of the number of barbershops on the course but the number of blind shots. Two qualities you needed on this island course – besides golfing ability – were a sense of humour and a sense of adventure. Every now and again, then again and again, you were required to hit over the dunes. The drama quickly increased on this bewitching and, it had to be said, eccentric golf course.

At more than 6,000 yards in length, the Machrie was a marathon compared to most of the island courses. So many of them had been nine-hole affairs. But I was prepared for this. I wasn't going to fall short. I had struggled here as a teenager. I remembered being overwhelmed by it all. But not this time, definitely not this time.

The BFG was splashing on the sun lotion, seeming to use up the best part of a bottle for his arms and neck. He'd fair caught the sun on Colonsay and was being a little more careful today.

Facing a blind approach to a green, I punched a seven iron over the hill. My ball landed in a hollow at the front of the green, leaving me with a difficult uphill putt. But I judged it well and tapped in for my par. That I was keeping my score was an indication of how well I was playing. I was placing pressure on myself to keep it up. I knew that it wouldn't last, but I hoped to maintain this run for as long as possible.

Then we came to the seventh tee. A giant wall rose in front of us, a massive grassy dune with a pole at the top that seemed to say 'aye, just follow me'. This was Scot's Maiden, the Machrie's signature hole, its outstanding demand being the mother of blind drives. You really needed to gain some height on your tee shot to clear the top and goodness knew what lay on the other side. Hopefully a fairway.

We were all standing about staring at the impossible wall, this monstrous tangled mound. I decided to grab the bull by the horns and took my driver from my bag. You could not afford to be cautious here, you just had to go for it. Block out that dune, I told myself. It's only there to put you off. Pretend it isn't there and if you think it is, you're a goner. To be quite honest, I was shitting myself. I'd coped well so far, but one wrong move here and all my good work would be ruined.

'This hole could be the card wrecker,' said Noble Brian.

'Thanks Brian,' I said.

In the end, my nerve failed me. On my backswing, I was thinking that I was never going to make it, and I was never going to make it thinking like that. So much of the game is played out in the mind. I skied my hesitant tee shot into the dune.

'Have another go,' said Noble Brian, trying to soften the blow.

Should I? And risk further humiliation? Or walk on, chastened by my failure. I decided that I would have another go. Of course, this time I played it to perfection. As soon as the ball left the clubface I knew it was clearing that

dune. It's what I should have done in the first place. What
had I done differently? The difference was that the pressure was off.

Somehow, I escaped Scot's Maiden with a six, parring
this skyscraper of a golf hole with my second ball, getting
up and down with a good chip and a great putt. Perhaps
I should still be keeping my score, I thought.

Then, at the next hole, I cleared the dune with my drive
but couldn't find my ball on the other side. It was my first
lost ball of the trip. I hadn't lost any on Colonsay. I hadn't
bothered hitting a provisional at this hole, because I hadn't
expected to have to look for my ball. And I wasn't about
to head back over the dune to hit another tee shot either.
I decided to stop counting my score. From here on in, I
was just going to enjoy myself. I wasn't good enough to
keep such close tabs on my performance.

At the tenth hole, a par three called Machrie Burn, I
had the feeling of déjà vu. It was a quirky little hole with
a pond and not the kind of hole you expected to find on
this course, given what had gone before. And this probably was the reason that I remembered it from 20 years
ago. My memories of the Machrie were vague. All I could
recall were those massive dunes towering above me as I
struggled to cope with them. But this tenth hole, I recognised it, because it was different from the others. It might
have belonged to another course, but it was nice all the
same. The BFG hit a brilliant tee shot and should have
birdied Machrie Burn. He didn't. Still ... nice work big
man.

The course was turning away from the sea. Now we

were winding our way back towards the hotel, in a fairly pedestrian fashion. We'd caught up with the group ahead of us, a foursome in bright jumpers. These men had been way ahead of us but now we were having to wait on them, especially when they were putting out.

Noble Brian called them TV golfers, types who see the pros take all the time in the world and then decide to emulate them, even though they aren't playing for the trophies or the prize money. Green tortoises.

I made the effort to put my frustration to one side. It's not like we were in a hurry or anything. We were pretty much on the home stretch. It would all be over too soon, so why get annoyed? Gents! Sometime today?! I turned my back on them and appreciated the beauty of Islay. That did the trick.

I managed to par the 13th, no mean feat for me since it was a par five. A chip and a putt got me there. 'Up and down,' said Noble Brian. Yes, up and down. I'd done that a couple of times during this round. Given the number of blind approaches and the trickiness of the greens, I was excelling in my short game.

The 16th was my finest moment yet. Another hill stood between me and the green. I picked out my nine iron and made my pitch. The BFG, who had walked on ahead, gave me the thumbs up to indicate that my ball was sitting pretty. I got to the green and saw that my ball was about 12 feet from the hole. I promptly sank the putt.

'That's delightful,' said the BFG. 'You should get that putter insured.'

I'd single putted quite a few greens today. For the first

time in a while I thought about my dad's putter. I'd been so many places with it, putted with it on so many greens (and from off the greens) that it had become almost, but not quite, just another club in my bag. During the course of my travels, I'd worried about losing it, been concerned that someone might pinch my golf clubs along the way, on the ferry or wherever (as if that would happen). But when I'd been putting recently, I'd not been thinking so much that it was my dad's putter. Now, with all these putts I seemed to be holing, I couldn't help thinking about it. My raised performance on the greens was beginning to draw attention to it. My playing partners were commenting on it.

The 17th hole at the Machrie is called Ifrinn. That's Gaelic for Hell. The chatty man on the ferry had told me. Though, for the life of me, I couldn't remember how he'd told me to play the hole. Oh, to hell with it. Nothing could harm me now. I'd walked on 18 islands and I could handle whatever this Ifrinn threw at me. And if this was Hell, it was beautiful.

After a good drive and an average iron, I found myself in the kingdom of the blind shots again. My task, in a way, was straightforward. Get the ball over the hill and onto the green. I opted for my nine iron and chipped the ball over. I could tell it was good. I marched forward and found my ball 15 feet from the pin.

Here we go again. I stood over my ball, without really lining up the putt properly. And I pulled back my dad's putter and I set the ball rolling and I wasn't in the least surprised when it dropped into the hole. It felt more like it was happening to me than me making it happen. I'd never been this way on a golf course. 'I'm not even thinking about it,' I said aloud.

'Well, don't think about it,' said Noble Brian.

'I've never putted like this in my life.'

Noble Brian shook his head. 'There's something afoot here. You're using up all your credits. You need to save one for the last, for a grandstand finish!'

'I think that's pretty unlikely now,' I said.

'Are you kidding?' said the BFG. 'The way you're putting?'

It was something, this hot streak on the greens. My dad's putter had given me so much pleasure these past few holes and now I really didn't want to part with it. And it occurred to me that of all the island courses, this was the one dad had played. I hadn't thought about it until now. I'd been too wrapped up in my own memories of the Machrie, but my dad had played this course too during some of his visits to Islay to see his mam. He'd been here. Not with this putter, but he'd been here.

Coming off the 17th green, I rang the bell. There was no one behind us. I just wanted to ring it anyway. For the glory of the day, this golden day. For the golf we'd feasted on, for the friendships, for the fine weather and for the unbeatable setting.

How the sun was shining also now as we embarked on the final hole. My final tee shot turned out to be my best of the day, my ball landing on the right side of the fairway. The BFG, who was struggling and reminding me of me at Askernish, topped his tee shot left. Noble Brian got rid of another good drive and walked with the BFG, as I set off down the fairway to my ball.

I accepted now that it was all drawing to a close. My 18 islands adventure. Bute, Skye, Harris, North Uist (still counting it), Benbecula, South Uist, Barra, Arran, Tiree, Iona, Mull, Seil, Moncreiffe Island, Whalsay, Mainland Shetland, Orkney and Colonsay. And Islay.

They were the islands, but the islanders make the islands.

I pictured Captain Hugh diving behind his golf bag to shelter from the hailstones, Donald rolling his cigarette and Bill laughing. Colin Bannatyne walking briskly up into the Crow's Nest. Glen and Kenny sitting under the dyke in the wind and rain and cracking open the Highland Park. Sandy the shepherd back on Bute. Robert Ross giving us a lift on Barra when we most needed it. Colin and his dad both offering us a lift on South Uist. Alisdair driving us to Askernish after Morag's cooked breakfast. Julia showing us the salvaged whisky on Eriskay. Mary and Jim keeping busy with both the B&B and the golf course on Mull. Harry, Stewart and Mary making us feel welcome on Whalsay (so long and thanks for all the fish!). Winnie and Hazel and the rest of the family ensuring the future of Jim's golf course at Asta.

And I thought about other travellers we'd bumped into, like Ali the PE teacher and David and Jules the honeymooning couple in their campervan. And my companions on this golfing journey. Noble Brian and the BFG. At the very beginning, Riley. My mam, brother and sister joining me too. And all of this accomplished in the space of a few months. What on earth was I going to do once this was all over?

I caught sight of the roof of the Machrie Hotel under a blue sky. The final green lay over the hill (of course it did, there was always a hill). My wife and daughter would be waiting for me and I couldn't wait to see them.

Looking back down the fairway, I saw the BFG preparing to play a shot and Noble Brian appearing to be offering him advice. It didn't work. The BFG knocked his ball a few yards into the rough. I turned away and carried on walking, unaware that the BFG had dropped another ball and was about to play it.

The first thing I knew was the shout. I spun round and saw a yellow ball – thank goodness it was a yellow ball – rocketing towards me. The BFG had managed an incredible shank and I was about to get it. I ducked for cover, the ball shooting over my shoulder. My heart was racing. That had been very close. Noble Brian was in hysterics. The BFG was aghast at having almost clocked me on the final hole. He came over and apologised and we all had a good laugh about me nearly being felled by a stray golf ball at the very end.

Once I'd composed myself, I settled down for my second shot. I wasn't expecting to reach the green. I just wanted to get close enough so that I had a shot at a decent finish. I wasn't for mucking it up at this late stage. I played a reasonable five iron, it was straight at least, and my ball even sneaked over the hill. This was looking OK.

It got even better when I came over the hill and saw my wife sitting off to the side in the long grass with my daughter. Of all the sights I'd seen on 18 islands, this was the best one. I went over to them and we hugged as a family, a Machrie moment to treasure. Clare asked how I was getting on and I was able to say that I'd played well here. I then tried to focus on what I had to do next.

My ball was lying in a hollow. It was a tricky shot for someone of my calibre and I felt my goal was simply to get that ball on the green and deal with it from there. I caught it a little thin with my pitching wedge, my ball shooting through the back of the green. At least, I thought, I'd be able to putt from the short grass. I'd have my putt for par, even if it was from 40 feet.

I took my daughter and carried her with me to the back of the green. Noble Brian meanwhile had chipped onto the green, while the BFG had given up and had his camera out now. He was taking lots of snaps, including plenty of me and Isabella. I stood her up in a comical pose, making it look as if she was holding my dad's putter and was judging the putt. I asked her the line and she smiled. She was 16 months old. She hadn't quite learned to walk yet, so I sat her down on the grass and took a quick look at the putt myself. Ten feet to the green and another 30 feet after that. Slightly downhill with a couple of breaks along the way. I'd been holing everything this past hour and couldn't explain it. But this was asking an awful lot. The BFG held the pin and even he looked far away.

Isabella started shuffling towards me and I had to pick her up and move her to the side again. She was still smiling. I had to putt now, before she got on the move again. If I could get down in two from here, I'd settle for that. I

didn't want to three-putt the final green on the final course
on the final island. Even though technically I wasn't on
the green yet.

I sensed Isabella shifting again so I just played the putt,
quicker than I would have liked, and I also struck it harder
than I would have liked. That ball was travelling at a fair
pace. I certainly wasn't going to be short. Oh, it was going
much too fast. I might be leaving myself with another long
putt back across the green. At least it was heading in the
right direction. If it would just slow down a bit.

The closer it got to the hole, the more I realised it was
going to be close. It looked to me like it was heading
straight for the pin. Now I felt nervous. This was getting
all too serious. This was no joke. I had a chance. This was
ridiculous. A hundred thoughts went through my mind and
then just the one. You have to go in. Suddenly I'd never
wanted anything so much in my life, which was silly really.
But I wanted it, I really did. How about the perfect ending?
I hadn't asked for it, but now I was. Everything was riding
on this putt, it quite simply had to go in or frankly I was
going to be gutted. Please go in, please. Don't let this end
in disappointment! The ball struck the pin and dropped
into the hole.

I didn't jump. I didn't shout. Noble Brian shouted. I put
my hand over my mouth, as if I'd done something wrong.
Then I paced back and fore for a bit. The truth was I was
struggling to take it all in. I think we all were. The BFG,
still at the flag, was shaking his head in disbelief. Noble
Brian was shouting something else. Clare was laughing.
She'd never seen her husband play golf before and now

she'd witnessed this. I lay down for a moment and looked up at the sky. Not a single cloud. Isabella shuffled up next to me. I picked her up and walked on over to my wife. How lucky could a man be?

Certainly I hadn't dreamt it. That would have been an absurd dream to have. No it had most definitely happened. I had too many witnesses.

I bent down to pick my ball out of the hole. We took pictures of everyone next to the flag, my dad's putter featuring prominently in the pictures. I was still thinking about that putt. We all were. Nobody was really saying anything. We were just standing about, laughing. I shook hands with the BFG and thanked him for joining us. He thanked us. And I shook Noble Brian's hand. 'Well done,' he said. 'Well done, yourself,' I said back. Then I kissed my wife and daughter again.

The five of us left the green, Isabella smiling, and the rest of us still laughing. The sense I had was one of complete and utter contentment. And total exhilaration. Life didn't get better than this.

I looked up and smiled. Why was that? I guessed I'd always looked up to my dad. And his putter had just delivered the perfect ending.